W9-BNO-185

The Heart of Grief

Death and the Search for Lasting Love

THOMAS ATTIG

OXFORD UNIVERSITY PRESS

New York • *Oxford*

2000

OXFORD

UNIVERSITY PRESS

Oxford   New York
Athens   Auckland   Bangkok   Bogotá   Buenos Aires   Calcutta
Cape Town   Chennai   Dar es Salaam   Delhi   Florence   Hong Kong   Istanbul
Karachi   Kuala Lumpur   Madrid   Melbourne   Mexico City   Mumbai
Nairobi   Paris   São Paulo   Singapore   Taipei   Tokyo   Toronto   Warsaw

and associated companies in
Berlin   Ibadan

Copyright © 2000 by Oxford University Press, Inc.

Published by Oxford University Press, Inc.
198 Madison Avenue, New York, NY 10016
http://www.oup-usa.org

Oxford is a registered trademark of Oxford University Press

All rights reserved. No part of this publication may be reproduced,
stored in a retrieval system, or transmitted in any form or by any
means, electronic, mechanical, photocopying, recording,
or otherwise, without prior permission of
Oxford University Press.

Library of Congress Cataloguing-in-Publication Data
Attig, Thomas. 1945–
The heart of grief: death and the search for lasting love / Thomas Attig.
p. cm.
ISBN 0-19-511873-1
1. Bereavement—Psychological aspects.   2. Bereavement—Psychological aspects—
Case studies.   3. Grief.   4. Grief—Case studies.   5. Death—Psychological as-
pects.   6. Loss (Psychology)   I. Title.

BF575.G7 A788 2000
155.9'37—dc21   99-049842

A Grief Observed, by C. S. Lewis, Faber and Faber Ltd.
"Old Friends," words and music by Mary McCaslin, copyright © 1977, Folklore
Music (ASCAP).
"Old Friends." Copyright © 1968 by Paul Simon. Used by permission of the pub-
lisher: Paul Simon Music.

1 3 5 7 9 8 6 4 2

Printed in the United States of America
on acid free paper

In loving memory of my father, Clare Attig,
and my grandmother, Mary Nagel,
and in gratitude for all they have given and
continue to give.

Contents

III. MEMORIES

IV. PRACTICAL LIFE

V. LIFE OF THE SOUL:
RETURNING HOME

VI. LIFE OF THE SPIRIT:
REVIVING HOPE

Preface

Death ends a life, not a relationship.

—Morrie Schwartz

As a teacher, speaker, and author I've listened to count-less grieving persons in the last twenty-five years. Most of what I know about grieving I've learned from their stories. I've never spoken to anyone who mourns for someone they love who does not want to continue loving them in some way. Not knowing how to continue to love brings great pain and anguish.

Recently a man came up to me at a conference to say, "I want you to know how much I hated you years ago." I'd never been approached quite like that before by someone with such gentle eyes. He seemed as eager to explain as I was to hear what he had to say.

He said he was in an audience seven years earlier when I spoke about what it is like after someone we love dies. He said it was as if I was looking directly into his raw grief over his daughter. He remembered my talking of how we naturally want someone we love to be with us. How we fear that if we stop wanting their return when they die, we will stop loving them. Then he said, "There I was wanting my daughter back more than anything. And you put your finger on my deepest fear."

He recalled how I said that the worst agony of intense grief comes when we realize that the return we want more than anything is the one thing we cannot have. "I was in the darkest place I'd ever been in my life. And you told me that the only light I could imagine was one I could never see. I felt so desperate I wanted to scream and rush you at the front of the room."

I asked him why he hadn't. He began, "Deep down, I realized you were right. I hurt so terribly because I wanted what could not be. But I still wanted it. Your words brought me face-to-face with the futility of staying where I was in my grief. Thank God you didn't stop talking."

He recalled other things I said: Grieving persons who want their loved ones back need to look for some other way to love them while they are apart. Desperate longing prevents their finding that different way of loving. Letting go of having them with us in the flesh is painful and necessary. But it is not the same as completely letting go. We still hold the gifts they gave us, the values and meanings we found in their lives. We can love them as we cherish their memories and treasure their legacies in our practical lives, souls, and spirits. He said, "Through my hurt and anger I began to see how I would always be different because I had those precious years with my daughter."

I thanked him for approaching me and asked how he was doing currently. He said, "Things are going well with my wife and son. I'm afraid I got lost in my grief for a while, and I'm glad they waited for me. I still miss my daughter, and I always will. But I miss her in a different way. It's not the gut-wrenching longing it was. I've found other ways to keep her in my life. It's not like I lost all of her. Still, every once in a while, like right now, I wish I could just see or hold her again." He did not elaborate about how he keeps her in his life. But I could see the gratitude and love in his peaceful eyes.

At another recent conference, I spoke to a large audience about how lasting love for those who die is both possible and desirable. A woman caught my arm as we were all leaving the session. "I want you to know that I never allowed myself to grieve my mother's death. I didn't want to let go. Now I'm going to let myself grieve." Before I could respond, she withdrew into the crowd.

Behind her tears I saw relief and gratitude in her face. She seemed released from a painful refusal to grieve. It was as if she had believed that if she grieved, she would have to let go of her mother, to stop loving her. That was the last thing she wanted to do. Her tears expressed the agony of a paralyzing refusal, relief from that agony, and the beginning of grieving itself.

It didn't matter whether she was brought to believe that grieving requires complete letting go by a counselor or therapist, through her own professional training, or by well-meaning family or friends. The belief is widely held. I have always thought it is profoundly mistaken. What mattered was that she now saw how the belief had misled her and cost her dearly. She broke free from it. And she seemed grateful to realize that grieving can lead instead to lasting love.

The next day she approached me again in a crowd, "I don't think I made myself clear yesterday. My mother died twelve years ago." She checked my eyes to see if her words registered. She managed a reassured smile through more tears and disappeared again.

Her words helped me see more clearly the extent of her hurt. She had chosen to dwell for years in the pain of missing her mother rather than to endure the unacceptable pain of completely letting go. Her refusal to grieve her mother's death had kept her distant from the lasting love she might have found in those dark years. She seemed eager to open her heart again to her mother's goodness. She saw room in it to carry both the pain of missing her mother and continuing love for her.

I couldn't help wondering what life had been like for her and those who loved her through those twelve years as she stifled her grief. Did she have a husband and family? Had she been distant and withdrawn from them? How might her agony have affected her own children? I shuddered at the thought of the possible costs of her belief about grieving and letting go.

I shuddered, too, when I thought that hers is only one story among thousands, perhaps millions, of those whose lives have been changed for the worse by the belief that grieving requires that we let go of those we love. Some, like her, swallow their grief, linger in the pain of missing those they love, and never experience the consoling benefits of lasting love. Equally tragically, many others struggle to sever, forget, or ignore meaningful ties to those they love for the sake of grieving "properly" as they believe they must. Still others feel uneasy or become secretive about enduring connections they still maintain with those who have died. Some actually feel shame about lasting love.

Such stories are among the saddest that grieving persons tell me. They are stories of missed opportunities and deep anguish. Whenever I hear them, I respond with assurance that loving need not stop with separation in death. We can find lasting love for our children, parents, spouses and companions, siblings, other family members, and friends. This assurance most always brings comfort. The capacity to find, acknowledge, appreciate, and cultivate enduring connections with those we love is unbounded. It is never too late to revive love deeply felt. Much of the damage caused by the belief that grieving requires complete letting go can be reversed.

I offer such reassurance because I have seen life-affirming and life-enhancing lasting love in the eyes of so many other grieving persons and heard it in the stories they have told me. Love that was real does not die when those we love die. Many have told me of places in their hearts where they hold and love those who have died. I have learned how cherishing memories and continuing to care about some of what they cared about has enriched survivors' practical, soulful, and spiritual lives. What I have learned has enabled me to recognize such love and its benefits in my own heart, in members of my family, among my friends, and in the culture around me. And I have witnessed how the hope for lasting love can motivate us to grieve in ways that bring consolation and restore our wholeness.

This book is primarily for those of us who are grieving. To them it offers encouragement and guidance in seeking and finding lasting love. And this book is for those who care for and about us as we grieve, including our family and friends as well as caregiving professionals and volunteers. To them it offers understanding of why finding lasting love matters so much to us. The ideas it contains can help them to encourage and support us as we do what we most want to do when someone we love dies.

My instinct has always told me that wanting to continue loving after death is fully natural and appropriate. My teaching and contributions to professional dialogue have consistently run counter to the predominant and powerful stream of thinking that as we grieve we must let go completely. As an applied philosopher, I have not been captive to the prevalent theories, training, approaches, and vocabularies that encourage complete letting go. I have long tried to prod theorists to reconsider their ideas about grieving and letting go.

Over the years, I have found and developed vocabulary that fits comfortably with and reflects the richness and depth of what I have heard and learned about such lasting love. I've ventured into new territory in articulating what most professional literature on grieving neglects and what most of us find difficult to put into words in everyday life. I have found apt and effective ways to speak and write about love in terms of heart, soul, and spirit. Real-life stories and accounts of personal experiences make the possibility and desirability of lasting love transparent and concrete. I have used detailed stories and accounts to ground these matters of the heart. Audiences of grieving persons and professionals have responded with similar enthusiasm to these fruits of years of listening and reflection and encouraged me to bring my thinking to you.

No doubt we do need to let go of what stalls our grieving, hinders our ability to thrive, or blocks our returning to the fullness of life. Sometimes we are gripped by deep and often unconscious desires to avoid the pain of grieving, deny the finality of death or the reality of separation, dismiss ambivalence or serious difficulties in our relationships, or delay moving into a daunting future. Sometimes we are held by destructive aspects of our relationships, including dependence, possessiveness, abuse, or control and manipulation. Sometimes our holding on to the past or those who have died is obsessive, preoccupying, or excessive. And no doubt therapists, counselors, and writers about grief have served us well in identifying such hazards in grieving and developing strategies to help us avoid them.

But there is nothing in all of this that implies that we must let go completely. There is no reason to let go of the good with the bad. The great majority of our closest relationships with family and friends have good in them. Those we mourn lived lives filled with value and meaning. What we have shared with them in the past powerfully influences who we are and become. Death does not erase our past with those we want to continue loving. We can constructively hold on to the good in lives now ended and sustain rewarding connection to the past.

Of course, stories of grieving are not simply stories of life-affirmation, hope, and an easy transition to lasting love and the consolation it brings. We will experience pain and anguish. We will meet daunting challenges. The stories I include here reveal the shattering effects of losing those we love: the anguish of longing for an impossible return. Broken hearts, homesick souls, and grounded spirits. Encounters with worlds transformed by loss. Wrestling with the great mysteries of life, death, and suffering. Learning to carry pain. Finding the courage to go on living without those who have died by our sides. Struggling to feel at home again in our physical surroundings, with fellow survivors, and in the greater scheme of things. Reshaping our daily lives. Redirecting our life stories. Changing ourselves. Reviving our souls and spirits.

Stories show us how different we are in our grieving. Each of us experiences loss, even of the same person, uniquely. No two hearts ache the same way. We each face distinctive challenges in our own corners of the worlds we inhabit. No one can respond to loss and challenge for us. We alone can change our lives and our selves. We play our own parts in reshaping and redirecting life in our families and communities.

Love is the heart of these stories of grieving. Love is the bond that connects family and friends. So it's not surprising that everything within us is poised to keep love alive. Our feelings and desires for them do not change the moment they die. Neither do our motivations, habits, dispositions, expectations, and hopes. We fear that if we change these things, we may forget or stop loving them. Nearly all of us want to keep our love alive. But we are at a loss as to how to do it.

Most of us want to continue loving because we have had the good fortune to love and be loved in return by those closest to us. This is not to say that many, or any, relationships or persons we love are perfect or ideal. They are all human: at once wonderful and flawed. We are ambivalent about most of our loving relationships. The familiar John Denver song "Perhaps Love" captures their sometimes placid, sometimes stormy, sometimes joyful, sometimes painful, sometimes enriching, and sometimes challenging character. His lyrics reflect what we all know: that loving relationships can be both powerfully constructive and often troubling forces in our lives. Typically, we continue to love others while they live because what we love about them or about sharing life with them matters more to us than what disappoints or bothers us. We struggle to hold on to and cultivate the good and to let go of the rest. We continue this struggle when they die.

Sadly, some of us survive relationships that were deeply troubled and even profoundly destructive in which there is little love to continue. Your story of grieving may be dominated by tales of such troubles and your struggles to break free of their lingering effects. If so, I am sorry to say, this book is not likely for you. At least not at this time. It may become useful for you later, if and when you reach a point of wanting to find a saving grace within your dark tales.

Grieving is a journey that teaches us how to love in a new way now that our loved one is no longer with us. This journey from loving in presence to loving in separation is possible because the lives of those who have died remain real in the lives of those of us who knew and loved them. The times we spent together are not erased from history. We retain our unique acquaintance with those we love. We still hold memories that we can review privately or share with one another. We still feel the imprints of their lives on us where we hold their practical, soulful, and spiritual legacies.

If our journeys in grief are to lead us to lasting love, we must reshape our feelings, desires, motivations, habits, dispositions, expectations, and hopes. Hopeful paths beyond the worst of our suffering lead through often painful transformations.

The paths on this journey are both arduous and hopeful. Walking them requires that we mount the courage to move through our hurt. And that we open ourselves up to receive what those we love still have to give. The paths lead through heartache, soulful pain, and spiritual pain unlike any other suffering we know. Staying the course on the grieving journey requires that we believe that lasting love can penetrate our worst suffering and move us beyond it. It calls for steady resolve to move toward treasuring what we retain from knowing and loving those who have died. And it requires trust that when we work through the worst of our hurt, what we have not lost will return to us.

In the most intense agonies of grieving, it is tempting, *very* tempting, to believe that "All is lost." In the midst of the worst of our pain and anguish, it can seem as if we are losing again. Fear that hurt will overwhelm us keeps us from confronting painful reminders of the life now ended. This retreat adds distance not only from what triggers pain but also from what rouses cherished memories and feelings of connection. Our tears cloud our memories. The past recedes painfully behind our desperation for its return. If only they could be here once more for a brief while. We could then experience their sharp reality in person. But, alas, we cannot. It can seem as if those we love are leaving us a second time.

But if we can let go of our anxiety grounded in the belief that all is lost, we will find there is little basis for either the anxiety or the belief. When we hurt least, we remember best. Our memories become vivid and detailed again. When we long least for its return, we recover access to the past we shared with those who have died. The good that is in that past can still touch and move us. And we can discover and make our own the practical, soulful, and spiritual legacies it contains. Our journey in grief can bring us to lasting love that honors those who have died, enriches our lives in survival, and takes a place alongside our other relationships with fellow survivors and new people who enter our lives.

We have no choice about whether we will grieve. The world changes irretrievably when those we love die. Respond we must. We only have a choice about what paths we walk in response. We will suffer, no matter which paths we choose. When we walk paths toward lasting love and find it, its many rewards make the journey worthwhile.

Stories of personal journeys toward lasting love are the heart of what I offer in the pages that follow. Stories that show how to find and embrace life-affirming and life-enhancing legacies. Stories that show how to avoid the hazards of obsession, preoccupation, and excess. Stories of holding on to the good and letting go of the rest. Some are stories people have shared with me. Some come from my own experiences. None of us walk identical paths on such journeys. Still, we can learn a great deal from such stories. I know I have. So, too, have others with whom I have shared many of these tales in my years of teaching, speaking, and writing about grief and loss. It is a privilege to know these stories and share them here with you.

We can identify with the longing for lasting love in these stories. With the suffering that bereavement brings. With the anxiety about whether we can find lasting love for ourselves.

With the anguish that accompanies the reshaping and redirecting of our lives in the process. We can know that others have walked similar difficult paths and met similar challenges.

We can also resonate with the hope that pervades these stories. With the promise they offer. We can take heart from others' finding consolation and reward on such journeys. We can find inspiration.

We can also imagine and begin to find ways to help others. Others who survive with us. Family, companions, friends, or others we know who are grieving losses that do not affect us as directly or as powerfully. Or those whom we serve as volunteers or professionals.

It is hard writing a book when you really wish you could sit down to have a conversation with each and every reader. I hope you can take away from your reading something of what good conversation offers. Look in these pages for encouragement, suggestions, and hope. Go at your own pace. Enter the conversation wherever it looks most promising or helpful to you. Pick it up at other points where it appeals to you. Or follow it through from beginning to end. I hope you will find it a good companion on your journey.

November 1999   T. A.

I

Places in the Heart

Where Are They Now?

But where is the part of Papa that loves me and you and Daddy?

—Laura, age five

When her grandfather had a fatal heart attack, it was the first time anyone close to five-year-old Laura had died. How strange to see her father, Frank, cry openly and shake so hard. And to see her mother, Joanne, comforting him as she, too, wept. Laura sensed a big change in her world, and it frightened her. Joanne glimpsed Laura's distress while she consoled Frank. Laura appeared as much confused as upset. Joanne reached out her hand for Laura and held her close as she kept her other arm around Frank. She explained that Daddy had to leave very soon and promised her full attention then. Frank left in half an hour to make funeral arrangements with his mother, brother, and sisters.

Joanne then took Laura onto her lap. As she held her, she did her best to comfort her. Stroking her daughter's hair, she explained that Daddy was crying because he loved Papa very much and missed him. She said he would probably be sad for a long time. She explained that she was crying both because of how it hurt to see Daddy and because she would also miss Papa. Laura began crying, and they held each other for several minutes. Joanne told her that it

· 3 ·

was okay to cry when someone you love dies because it is a sad time.

When she stopped sobbing, Laura turned her face up to Joanne's and asked, "What happened when Papa died?" Joanne explained that Papa died when his heart stopped working. "When your heart stops and the doctors can't start it again," she said, "the rest of your body stops working, too." She went on to explain very gently that Papa wouldn't be coming for visits or playing with Laura again.

After sobbing again for several minutes, Laura asked, "Mommy, will I ever see Papa again?" Joanne explained that she would never see her grandfather alive again on this earth. She would never again be able to sit in his lap. She went on, however, to ask Laura to close her eyes. When Laura did, Joanne said, "Try to think of Papa. Can you see his face? Can you see him coming through the door with a big smile? Can you see him laughing and playing with you?" Laura smiled, and she said with some enthusiasm, "Yes, I can see Papa, Mommy." Joanne then reassured Laura that she could see her Papa in that way any time she wanted. This was a great comfort to Laura. She sat with her eyes closed for several minutes.

Laura then opened her eyes and again turned to look into Joanne's. She asked, "Where is Papa now, Mommy?" The question took Joanne's breath for a moment. Then she responded, "That's a hard question, Laura!" "Why, Mommy?" Laura came back immediately. Joanne paused. Then she said, thoughtfully, "Because Papa's body is at the funeral home. But the part of him that loved and cared for us isn't there anymore."

Joanne went on to explain about funerals and burial. She told Laura about what people do at calling hours and funerals. She told her what she would see and hear if she chose to be part of events before Papa was buried. She said Laura was welcome to be with her and Daddy if she wanted to be. She explained that she could see Papa's body if she wished. Laura said immediately that she wanted to see him and be with Mommy and Daddy as much as possible.

Joanne barely relaxed when Laura asked a bit impatiently, "But where is the part of Papa that loves me and you and Daddy?" Again,

Joanne paused before responding. "That part," she said at last, "is in our hearts as long as we remember Papa." She went on to reassure Laura that she and Daddy would always remember Papa and that they would help Laura to remember. Joanne then added, "Daddy and I will always love Papa, and I believe he still loves us. I'm sure he still loves you." Laura, smiling through tears, said, "I'll always love Papa."

This simple story stays with me and I tell it often. Joanne responds so wonderfully to Laura. She sees Laura's hurt and reaches out to her. She comforts simply through touch and sharing her own hurt. She tunes in to how her child's world, too, has changed. Patiently, she answers Laura's questions in words that a five-year-old can understand. She explains directly how Papa died and in enough detail so as not to mislead. She recognizes that young children think very concretely. So, she carefully explains in terms of what Laura may see, hear, feel, and experience firsthand. She also gives Laura choices about the kinds of experiences she would like to have in the days immediately ahead.

Joanne teaches Laura about remembering Papa and holding him in her heart. Like Laura, we can all "close our eyes" and remember those who have died whenever we want. We cannot literally see, hear, or touch them again. And, yes, we will miss them, as Joanne wisely notes. But our memories can be vivid and richly varied and textured. Through them we can still connect with those we love and the lives they lived. We can still cherish them and treasure their lives and what we have shared with them. Like Laura, we can have and hold the part of them that loves us "in our hearts." We can give places in our hearts to those who have died. As we do, we experience lasting love. We continue to love them. We sense that they still love us.

Joanne's simple words about holding Papa in her heart comfort Laura. Children like Laura readily associate the heart with love. Joanne's gentle figure of speech also responds to Laura's curiosity.

As with most figures of speech, her words are abstract and tinged with vagueness. But for five-year-old Laura, they say enough. Joanne lays the ground beautifully for later explanations when Laura's thinking matures and she raises new questions. Joanne may then offer more precise and elaborate accounts of love and what it is to be human, our place in the greater scheme of things, and what happens when we die. She may or may not explain what it means to hold another "in your heart" in the terms of great religious traditions. It would be best for Joanne to introduce such complex ideas when Laura is ready for them.

Joanne's words may comfort you, as they did Laura. You, too, likely associate the heart with love. But you are not five years old. In effect, Joanne simply affirms that Laura can continue to love Papa even though he has died. That's what holding him in her heart means. Joanne's affirmation is welcome, but how can she be right? You may have a sense of how you can hold someone in your heart while they live. Yet, you may wonder, "What does it, or can it, mean to hold another in your heart after he or she dies?" In other words, "How is lasting love possible?"

I agree with Joanne's gentle affirmation that it *is* possible. I want to show you what it means for us to hold someone in our hearts by describing ways in which loving give-and-take can and does continue after another dies. Those who have died give us the legacies of their lives. We, in turn, give them places in our hearts, places at the vital centers of our lives alongside everyone and everything else we hold there.

Implicit in Joanne's words is an added belief that holding Papa in her heart is a good thing for Laura to do. She is saying not only that Laura need not stop loving Papa when he dies but that it is better if she doesn't. Like Laura, and as Joanne recommends, you may want to continue loving. But you may still wonder, "Is lasting love really a good thing?" In other words, "What is the good that can come from holding those who have died in our hearts?"

I believe in Joanne's implicit endorsement of lasting love. I also want to show you how holding someone in our hearts after death is good for us, our fellow survivors, and those who have died. Our lasting love affirms the enduring meanings of their lives, meanings not canceled by death. Lasting love consoles us and moderates our suffering as their legacies enrich our lives.

Living with Sadness

*Life is like an onion. You peel off one layer at a time,
and sometimes you weep.*

—Carl Sandburg

C. S. Lewis *kept a journal following the death of his wife
Joy that he first published under the name N. W. Clerk as* A Grief
Observed *in 1961. One of the richest and most profound personal
accounts of grieving ever written, the slim volume has since been
reprinted continuously. Lewis's writing is at once remarkably eloquent
and powerfully affecting. (Because it was first released under a pseu-
donym, Lewis refers to Joy as 'H' throughout.) In an early entry he
tells us how disconcerting and awful it is to be the same within himself
as he was before Joy died and to confront a world where being that
way no longer makes sense:*

> *Thought after thought, feeling after feeling, action after action, had
> H. for their object. Now their target is gone. I keep on through habit
> fitting an arrow to the string; then I remember and have to lay the
> bow down.*

*Lewis records observations of what the world is like when we walk
it in sorrow and separation:*

Grief is like a long valley, a winding valley where any bend may reveal a totally new landscape. As I've already noted, not every bend does. Sometimes the surprise is the opposite one; you are presented with exactly the same sort of country you thought you had left behind miles ago. That is when you wonder whether the valley isn't a circular trench. But it isn't. There are partial recurrences, but the sequence doesn't repeat.

The walk in grief is long. Different life settings arouse different responses. Challenging surprises abound. We never go back to the beginning—we do progress.

He writes compellingly of marriage as if it were a dance and suggests that separation is not an end of the dance but rather a new phase of relationship. Separation is in itself painful. But there is more to the continuing relationship than that pain. Though he refers to "marriage," what he says applies not only to dances in separation between spouses but also dances with life's companions, parents and children, siblings, other family pairings, and friends:

We shall still ache. But we are not at all—if we understand ourselves—seeking the aches for their own sake. The less of them the better, so long as the marriage is preserved. And the more joy there can be in the marriage between dead and living, the better.

Finally, Lewis comes to a profound insight about how our most intense grief and longing actually block our paths to lasting love:

Passionate grief does not link us with the dead but cuts us off from them. This becomes clearer and clearer. It is just at those moments when I feel least sorrow . . . that H. rushes upon my mind in her full reality, her otherness. Not, as in my worst moments, all foreshortened and patheticized and solemnized by my miseries, but as she is in her own right.

We will always ache for those who have died. But when the ache no longer dominates our experience, they come into view again. We can embrace them still even while we are apart.

Our hearts ache when, like Lewis, Joanne, Frank, and Laura, we experience the death of someone we love. Our feelings, desires, motivations, habits, dispositions, expectations, and hopes aim in their direction as before. It is as if our love for them is suspended in midair with no place to land. Their absence frustrates us constantly. We have lived as if they would always be with us. Our pain and anguish derive in part from reminders of how we took their presence for granted in the intimate corners and public places where we knew them; they also derive from our sense that even the small part of the world that we know best is not ours to control.

We realize helplessly that our daily lives can never be as they were. We will no longer see and be seen, hear and be heard, touch or be touched, or hold or be held by them. Nor will we share a room or a view, converse or wrangle, laugh or cry, break bread, walk or dance, hope or plan with them. We will not know them as they grow older, and they will not know us. We will no longer be party to their joys and sorrows, their successes or failures. Nor will they be party to ours. Central characters in our life dramas and comedies no longer share the stage with us. Our biographies veer from their expected courses. We are powerless to connect with those we love in the usual ways. We are repeatedly caught up short by reality transformed by loss. When we lose those closest to us, their absence spreads like dense clouds over our lives. We are easily tempted to conclude that our pain and anguish will never relent and that all is lost.

Our stories of loss differ in every detail from one another. Yet we know we are vulnerable to comparable pain and anguish. We recognize the shapes of the challenges others face. As we grieve, we struggle in the same human condition. There is some comfort in these family resemblances among our loss experiences: Many know the bitterness of deprivation. We are not alone in our sadness, loneliness, longing, frustration, disorientation and confusion, anger, guilt, anxiety, fear, and helplessness. Others, too, are daunted by challenges to reshape their daily lives and recast the next chapters of their life stories. In this shared plight, others know us as fellow travelers who struggle to find our way again in worlds transformed by loss.

However, we never meet loss in the abstract. We never grieve generically. No particular loss replicates any other. Each of us shares life with those we love uniquely. No parents, grandparents, siblings, children, grandchildren, spouses or life's companions, friends, acquaintances, or colleagues touch our lives identically. We lose this dear person but once. We then dwell day-to-day in the residue of what someone special leaves behind, in the details that make all the difference. We find a different comfort when others appreciate how our losses are without precedent for us.

When someone we love dies, we lose their physical presence and all that it means to us. We lose the fulfillment of many desires, expectations, and hopes centered on them that we still carry within us. We lose our abilities to interact daily and to continue into the future with them as our habits, dispositions, and motivations still incline us. We begin the rest of our lives without them ready to go on as if they were still here. But we cannot, try as we might. In losing them, we have lost the possibility of going on as we would have had they lived. A possibility is intangible. Yet, we feel the reality of that loss in the deepest recesses of our being.

We should never allow ourselves or others to underestimate, or dismiss the significance of, the loss of another's presence. Presence is one of the most precious things we can give one another. We sometimes learn most poignantly just how precious presence is when we lose someone. We simply cannot have things as they were before death intervened. Momentous change alters permanently the worlds we experience. Our familiar life patterns are irretrievable. Whatever story captures the unfolding of the days to come, it cannot be a story of a return to life just as it was. Our hearts ache with a kind of homesickness.

Some among us believe that reunion will come in another life. Some do not. For both groups this is certain: In this, the only life we know, separation is tangible and will last as long as we survive. When we first lose someone, we are acutely aware that we are suddenly in a strange place that is far from what brings value, meaning, and hope in our lives, distant from consolation and comfort.

When someone we love dies, the pain of separation is often excruciating. One of the worst aspects of any experience of pain is the fear of what we do not know. The unknown compounds panic and terror. There are no road maps that will guide you on ideal paths beyond suffering. No detailed weather forecast is possible. Each of us walks a unique path through the hills and valleys of our pain and anguish. But we can anticipate some common features of such journeys. The most reliable sources of this learning are our own memories of past loss experiences and the testimony of those who, like Lewis, have walked similar paths. These sources assure us that, difficult though it will be, we can bear our pain.

Any story of our journey through suffering will be one of our emerging from chaos where hurt prevails to finding new order in life where it does not. We will search for new patterns of living and a course into the future without the presence of those who have left us. We will seek ways to let go of the intensity of our longing for that presence. We will seek ways to recover what is still viable in our ways of living. And we will seek ways to transform our lives and ourselves.

Early in the journey, pain and anguish are our constant companions. Hurt permeates every waking moment and casts the world around us in darkness. Virtually all of our physical and social surroundings and daily routines arouse pain and anguish when we meet them for the first time after a loss. First encounters are among our most difficult experiences—they cluster and fill the early days of our grieving. Pain and anguish hold center stage, no matter where we turn. We often feel desperate and tortured by the least little thing. Sometimes our early agony is so great, our pain and anguish so preoccupying, that it seems we are nothing but the hurt we feel. No wonder we fear there will be no end to it.

Fortunately, we have first encounters only once. They never cluster again as they do at the beginning of our journey when our entire world is new. Our hurt moderates with time. As we encounter them repeatedly, our life circumstances and living patterns become familiar again. We grow accustomed to the light and shadow that our loss casts upon them. Later, some of their Technicolor aspects return and new ones appear. Over time, moments, then hours, even days of relative happiness penetrate the pervasive darkness. A balance between sorrow and joy begins to emerge in our lives. Even these most familiar parts of our worlds may at times still arouse pain and anguish as fresh memories and associations surface. But the intensity is rarely as great or longlasting. We can and do relearn how to be and act at home and at ease, in ways old and new, in the worlds we experience.

There can always be later, painful meetings with people, places, and things. The paths we walk following loss extend throughout our lifetimes. We do not one day revert to old paths where it is as if we never felt the pain of loss. We can expect episodes of missing those we love down the road: We visit places half-forgotten. We find ourselves in spots where we had expected or hoped to go with those who have died. We are surprised by objects that surface unexpectedly that remind us of our loved ones long lost. We hear music once shared, we see a painting, we hear a familiar story that transports us back in time. We meet or hear from those who knew those we have lost. Others tell us they wish they had known them. We recognize something of those who have died in another. We see something we had missed before that overwhelms us with memories. Or we see and appreciate what is familiar in the new light of later experience. Or we lose another, and our earlier loss surfaces again. Encounters like these can arouse fresh, and sometimes powerfully intense, pain and anguish.

But the specters of early, preoccupying intensity need not frighten us. They are precisely specters. The intensity is real, but it does not last. We are not again at the beginning of our journey through suffering. Instead, we have come a long way. We carry the possibility of hurt with us for the remainder of our lives, but it no longer permeates every aspect of our day. Our hurt becomes companion to whatever joy and happiness we find.

The paths we walk as we grieve will take us to terrain we have not seen before. No matter where they take us, there will always be a place of sadness in our hearts where we miss those who have died.

Carrying the Hurt

I will learn to carry this.
I will, please God,
Grow into it.

—*Gina Logan*

Harvey and his wife Maita were riveted to the television as news unfolded of the bombing in a public square in an eastern city where their son Seth attended university. The scene was horrible. At least a dozen were dead with many more seriously injured. Names of victims were being withheld until families could be notified. They were dismayed as they watched, but neither Harvey nor Maita expected the call that came all too soon. Seth had been in the square and killed instantly.

News spread quickly through their neighborhood. Friends drew close to Harvey and Maita and remained with them late into the night. One well-intentioned soul brought a case of whiskey, anticipating that many would be coming to visit and console Harvey and Maita in the days ahead. Harvey adored Seth. His agony was excruciating, and he began to drown his sorrows in the alcohol. The airwaves and newspapers were filled with news of the incident for several days after it happened. Maita and Harvey's friends and family did all they could to shield him from any of it. They recognized how much he was hurting and looked past his excessive indulgence in and growing dependence upon alcohol.

Seth was their only child and Harvey's pride. He couldn't bear the thought that he had died so senselessly. He couldn't stand the pain of missing him that returned whenever he approached sobriety. He had been an occasional drinker before Seth died. Now it was different. He drank to numb himself and blot out memories of the tragedy that killed his beloved son. Others feared the power of his rages whenever the numbing effects of the alcohol began to wear off. So they backed off and allowed his substance abuse to worsen and continue.

It was four years before Harvey broke free of his alcoholism and faced his demons. The years cost him several friends and nearly his marriage. And no cherished memories of Seth penetrated his self-induced numbness.

Harvey finally joined Alcoholics Anonymous when Maita threatened to leave him. When he achieved lasting sobriety, the pain of his loss returned in full force. Maita could only listen in small doses before her own pain became too much for her. But Harvey's rabbi proved immensely helpful as he patiently listened to and supported him. After several months, the rabbi steered Harvey toward a support group for bereaved parents. There Harvey found great sympathy and patient understanding of his suffering. Painful as it was, he was immensely relieved to unburden himself of what he had held so deeply within, what he feared would consume him if he ever faced it. And he began once again to speak not only of the tragedy of Seth's death but also of the love he still held within.

There is much that we can do about the pain and anguish of missing another. To begin, we must acknowledge the realities of separation and our hurt. Only then can we hope to come to terms with them and one day emerge from the chaos that death brings into our lives. Attempts to mask the reality of separation or to stifle our hurt, like Harvey's, prolong the agony. The world made different by our losses can and will wait us out. Reminders repeatedly penetrate any pretense that nothing has happened.

Swallowed hurt corrodes from within. When, eventually, we face the reality of separation, there is no way around, over, or under the pain and anguish. The only path to something beyond the worst of our pain and anguish is through it.

We can only bring order back into our lives by wrestling with, not ignoring, the chaos. We can only delay the match, not postpone it indefinitely. Perhaps worst are the fear and helplessness at the core of our suffering. When those closest to us die, we fear that our pain and anguish will be unending, our agony relentless. First death deprives us, then bereavement turns the screws. We may suspect that the intensity of early pain and anguish will wane. But we dread that our loss will permanently drain our lives of all vitality. We anticipate an empty future. Our hurt transfixes us. It is as if we lie immobile and exposed waiting for more dreadful things to happen. We must choose not to linger in the lethargy of bereavement. If we do, our fears will be realized and our helplessness perpetuated. Coming to terms with pain and anguish requires that we move, however small and halting our first steps may be.

Grieving is not something more that happens to us after someone dies but rather what we do in response to it. We are not helpless. We have many choices about first steps in grieving. We take some of the most important first steps when we acknowledge the reality of separation, admit to ourselves that it hurts, and find effective ways to come to terms with that hurt. It is simply not true that "Everyone needs to talk about their feelings." It matters less how we do these things than that we find ways that work for us and respect others who may do things differently. Our pain and anguish bear witness to the values and meanings of what we have lost. When we acknowledge our hurt to ourselves or others, we affirm those values and meanings.

Pete and his wife Dolly farmed on the Nebraska prairie for over forty years. Pete never retreated from emotional pain. But he never said much to anyone either. Instead, he had a way of working through his hurt by plunging into work on the farm. Physical labor provided great release for his anger. And solitary silence in the fields allowed him a chance to cry when no one was looking and to talk to himself in ways that helped him to think things through and find consolation.

It did not surprise Pete's children or neighbors to see him plowing fallow fields for hours alone and even long into the dark the month after Dolly died one fall. They knew it was his way of dealing with hurt, and they suspected he might be talking to her as he steered down the long empty rows.

Friends and admirers always said that Samantha had a magical way with pen and ink. A person of a few well-chosen words, she was far more comfortable expressing herself in her artwork. Samantha became a professional artist and gained considerable public notice for her fine portraits of the elderly, including her own grandparents. Her abilities to capture the depth and nuance of the feelings their faces revealed grew in years of encounters with them in their homes, retirement communities, and even in hospitals, nursing homes, and hospices. Her affection and love for them was readily apparent on the surfaces of her drawings.

When her grandmother Charlotte was diagnosed with terminal cancer, Samantha began a series of drawings that followed her through the nine months of her illness and eventually her dying days. Sittings with Charlotte provided time not only for sketching but also for visiting, reminiscing, exchanges of loving glances, and long shared silences. The finished drawings not only capture Charlotte's loving soul and unwavering spirit, but they reflect Samantha's acute sensitivity to what Charlotte was experiencing and her love for her grandmother. Refining the sketches from the last days of Charlotte's life into finished drawings enabled Samantha to acknowledge and express both the fullness of her anguish at losing her grandmother and her abiding affection for her.

Some of us, like Pete, Samantha, and C. S. Lewis, hold and carry our feelings within. If we are reticent to reach out to others, we can still do much to bring our hurt to the surface and give it a voice. We can burn emotional energy through vigorous physical activity. We can allow ourselves to weep privately rather than choke back the tears. We can sort our feelings in an internal dialogue in a quiet place or on a long walk. We can find a "screaming place." (Some tell me that screaming is best in the car with the windows rolled up.) We can record our pain and anguish in a journal or diary that can become a trusted and patient friend. We can make music, draw, paint, sculpt, or write poetry. When we produce something tangible, we can choose to share it with others or not. When we do, we express ourselves to them indirectly.

Will had been HIV positive for several years. Donnie's worst fears were realized when he learned that his partner of twelve years now had AIDS. Will lived three more years. At first the good moments outnumbered the bad, but eventually the illness took a terrible toll. Will's family persisted in their refusal to accept his homosexuality, and Donnie was left to care for him without their help. Will was grateful for Donnie's devotion and attentive care, but still devastated by his family's refusals to take his calls or respond to his letters even as he was dying.

Donnie by nature needed to talk to others to work through his feelings. Will was his best support as they talked endlessly about the challenges they were facing as Will's condition deteriorated. When Will died, Donnie could still talk to him at his gravesite and in prayer. But he also needed warm human contact and interaction. He couldn't talk with his own family about his grief because they, too, had shunned him when he came out to them. Though he maintained his religious belief, he found the priest he used to trust was now unapproachable and too judgmental.

The AIDS Center ran a support group for survivors, and Donnie joined eagerly. He found comfort and solace among others who had had similar experiences. No one quieted his tears. They heard him out patiently. They had lived through dying days that resembled his with Will. They knew about the heartache of abandonment and stigma. None judged his anger harshly or told him not to feel as he did. They had met similar challenges and recounted the ways they had tried to address them, sometimes with success and sometimes not. He appreciated the gentleness and sense of shared humanity he found among relative strangers.

We can tell our sorrows to intimates and friends in quiet conversation or correspondence. We can entrust our sorrows to counselors, secular or religious. Or, like Donnie and eventually Harvey, we can bring them to support groups where those who know suffering listen without judging us or our feelings. We can bring our sorrows to the deceased prior to burial, at the cemetery, or in prayer. We can bring them to higher powers through prayer, meditation, or ritual.

We can also share our hurt with others in ritual gatherings such as calling hours, funerals, and memorial services. It is surely appropriate to think of these as occasions to be sad and distressed together. Unfortunately, we often ignore the separation that has brought us all together and swallow our hurt there, seemingly out of some confused sense of propriety or decorum. We could all learn to be better at this.

Those who care help us most when they offer, without insisting, to hear about our hurt and our stories of loss. Their willingness to listen says that they want to understand us in our suffering. Their openness to us helps us to overcome fears of isolation and abandonment that add to our suffering. If we accept their invitation, it helps most when they listen sympathetically and without judging us. When they sympathize, they comfort us as they appreciate our hurt and the values and meanings it reflects. When they refrain from judging us, they calm our self-doubts about whether our feelings are normal or whether we are "going crazy." When they are willing simply to be with us during the chaos of our most intense mourning, they assure us that they value us. They show us that our suffering matters to them. They assure us that we do not walk alone. By being patient with our expressions of suffering, they encourage us to move through it.

When we come to terms with our feelings of hurt, we tame them somewhat; we loosen their grip on us and gain some control over them. Rarely do we make them go away entirely or render ourselves immune to them. As we learn to carry these feelings, we realize there is room in our hearts for more than the pain and anguish of separation. We find that we can open our hearts to other experiences.

Longing for Their Return

And suddenly at the very moment when, so far, I mourned
H. least, I remembered her best.

—*C. S. Lewis*

When those we love die, we remain poised to feel, act, think, expect, and hope as if they were still with us. We hurt as we meet their absence again and again in public places and in intimate corners of our lives. We long for the past or for their return so that our feelings, actions, thoughts, expectations, and hopes might again find their targets.

When their absence frustrates us, we can't help wishing things were different. The wishing comes over us spontaneously, almost as an extension of, or expression of, our frustration. We wish that they were alive at just this moment so that we could still share our days and face life together. Such wishing is harmless yet unwelcome. We wish the disparity between what was and what is were not so great. We feel deprived and resentful. Such wishing is part of the pain of missing those we love. We experience it less frequently or intensely as time goes on, as we relearn our worlds. But it can recur whenever we find ourselves missing our loved ones, even years later.

Sometimes we more deliberately take time out from present concerns and allow ourselves to wish we could go back to the way we were. We divert our attention from challenges we realize we must address and experience the bittersweetness of nostalgia, a kind of homesickness.

Nostalgia is bitter because, even as we wish, we are only too painfully aware that our wishes cannot literally come true. We cannot go to those who have died by retreating into the past. Nor can we return them to life in the present. There is no denying the reality of our separation. Nostalgia is sweet because we focus not on our deprivation but instead on how good it was when our loved one was alive. The nostalgia comforts us. But it is merely a temporary respite from present concerns.

There is no danger in momentary longings for a happy past. Spontaneous or nostalgic wishing are natural companions in our struggles to relearn our worlds. We remain firmly anchored in present reality. We long temporarily. Our wishing neither controls nor preoccupies us—we experience some pain but no harm. We have no real expectations that our wishes will come true.

If, by contrast, we fervently desire the return of those who die, we court extreme heartache and danger. We then wholeheartedly want the impossible.

I think of Sonya whose husband and "soulmate" died nearly a year before I first spoke with her. She was obviously mired in a very painful place. She sobbed all the while as she spoke. She told me, "In so many ways, my life stopped the day Heinz died." She went on to say how she was, and remains, overwhelmed by her sorrow: "I cry myself to sleep every night. I can't tell the difference between nightmares and the hurt when I am awake. I want him with me so badly."

She admitted that her longing distracted her from what the world seemed to expect of her. "I can't take my mind off of him. Nothing else seems to matter." Unable to return to work, she lost her job. She lost contact with some members of her family and several friends who grew impatient with her incessant talk of, and longing for, Heinz. She barely had the energy to care for her physical needs and next to none for keeping house and the like.

Sonya insisted, "I know he is dead," as if she were trying to convince herself it was true and me that she believed it. She followed immediately with, "But I can't help wanting him back with all my heart. I just can't see how I can go on without Heinz. I've got to have him back somehow."

Sonya's story shows how intense and fervent desire for the return of those who have died differs from wishful longing. Our desire is irrational precisely because it persists even while we recognize that those who have died are irretrievably absent. Separation is not merely painful, it is intolerable.

Unlike ordinary desires, our desire for the return of the one who died cannot move us to do anything. There simply are no ways to satisfy such desire. Our longing intensifies and persists. The more it preoccupies us, the more it frustrates, immobilizes, and, potentially, paralyzes us. Our pain and anguish grow excruciating because there is nothing we can say or do to bring back those we care about. We feel utterly helpless. And helplessness debilitates.

Sometimes when we linger in such fervent desire, we let the recognition of the death recede into the background of our lives. We slip into deep denial. We hold to our dispositions to feel, act, think, expect, and hope as if the dead were still alive. We begin to act as if a return were possible.

A widower may religiously walk familiar streets looking for his dead wife, hoping to catch a glimpse of her in the neighborhood or in a favorite coffeehouse. A friend may joyfully anticipate a reunion as if his dead friend had gone on a trip. An adult may repeatedly call a deceased parent at a nursing home and curse a receptionist who insists that "no one by that name" lives there. A parent may continue to purchase things to add to a dead child's favorite collection. A friend may select gifts for someone she can never see again. A younger brother or sister may believe he or she can patch things up after a fight when a deceased sibling returns from the hospital. A grandparent may continue to contribute to a dead child's college fund. A companion may still plan for a joint vacation or even a shared retirement. A parent may yet dream and hope for a grandchild when an only child has died.

These possibilities illustrate what can happen when we retreat into self-deception. We are not helpless and immobile. Instead, we are motivated to unrealistic action. Our efforts cannot succeed, and our hopes cannot be met. We attempt to hold what we do not, and cannot, have to hold.

Most of us avoid persistent and paralyzing longing for those who die or the deep denial it can entail. The spontaneous wishing that comes with frustration at their absence subsides over time as our new world becomes familiar. We occasionally indulge in moments of nostalgia, realizing full well that the times we recall are no more. We do these things even as we become accustomed to, and find our way in, the world transformed by their absence.

We see the futility of desiring what cannot be. We recognize that dwelling in such desire can only prolong and intensify our pain and anguish in their absence. No path can lead us to life as it was. Those who die can never hold the same places in our lives as when they were alive.

We can detect when we begin to cross the line from harmless wishing and nostalgia into fervent longing for those who have died, as Sonya did. We can tell when our longing intensifies, threatens to preoccupy us, undermines our ties to family and friends, and makes us feel increasingly frustrated, helpless, and desperate. We can even sense when we are deceiving ourselves and clinging to denial. We are, after all, the deceivers. And the absence all around us gives the lie to our denial at every turn.

Aversion to the excruciating pain of missing them as well as the growing inertia can, and typically does, move us. But once we have begun to cross the line, it usually takes more. Denial and futile longing have their attractions. Whenever we deny reality, we are most often unconsciously defending ourselves from something that horrifies us. In our self-deception, we choose the pain of pretending those we love still live, though we cannot find them. We prefer it to the anguish of accepting that they cannot be found. In our futile longing for their return, we tolerate the helplessness it entails. We prefer that to facing the seemingly intolerable permanence of their absence.

More intolerable than our pain, anguish, and helplessness is letting go of our love for those who have died. We may fear that if we stop longing for them, even to the point of denying they have died, we will stop loving them. Our desire to be with them is a central part of loving them while they live. If we allow our desire to wane when they live, we stop loving them. How can it be any different now? This deep desire to have them with us is the core of what motivates our intense longing or even denial. These can seem the only ways we can keep our love alive.

But intense longing and denial fill our hearts with the pain and anguish of missing those we love. We dwell in a shadowy love. We focus on their absence or escape into fantasy. We cannot find them or hold them in our stagnant present. We do not cherish them. We lose the momentum of our lives. We do not find new direction in our life histories with our fellow survivors. We find no hope in these shadows. We can only hope to satisfy our desire to continue loving them fully if we turn in a different direction. We need to see ways to sustain our love in separation.

We need to see a way back into our present reality that does not hurt worse than the safety we unconsciously find in futile longing or denial. Wanting to hold on to those who have died is not the problem. Instead, it is the way we try to do it. We hold to ways of loving those who have died that require their presence. Simply wishing things were different prompts enough pain in missing them. Futile longing for what cannot be or persistent denial magnify and intensify that pain. We need to find a way out of these painful traps and dark shadows. We must find ways of holding them even though they are gone.

Consciously remembering those who have died is the key that opens our hearts, that allows us to love them in new ways. Remembering is not longing. When we remember, we bring those who have died to mind; we don't dwell on their absence. We may long for them while we remember. In nostalgia, we passively receive what memory offers, and we long simultaneously. But the more actively we engage with those we remember and what we remember about them, the more our longing recedes into the background. We are drawn to what we still hold of them as we begin to explore what we remember.

The more active our remembering, the more effectively we reconnect with the reality and meanings of their lives, which death cannot cancel. These things hold our attention, not our pain and anguish. As we remember what we love about those who have died, we welcome them back into our lives even though we are apart. We begin to learn how to love them in new ways. In memory we can cherish them. We can carry them with us into the future.

Believing They Live On

I am forever defined by my interactions within a web of beings that extends backward and forward in time into infinity.

—Sam Keen

When I joined my wife, Betty, in Vancouver a few years ago, she introduced me to the art of Roy Henry Vickers. His designs are contemporary, but they echo his North Coast Indian heritage. He believes that we have been overly self-indulgent for too long and that this threatens our families and communities as well as the environment.

We have one of his prints in our home called The Elders Are Watching. *It depicts the story of a young boy walking with his grandfather by the seashore beneath a clear red sky near sunset. As they walk, the grandfather tells tales of the Old Ones, the elders of the community, and of their wisdom. As the boy absorbs the stories and begins to make their wisdom his own, he begins to see them. In the print, the Elders are barely visible as shadowy images suspended within the bright colors of the sky. They are watching over the land and its inhabitants. Although their lips are still, their concerned faces seem to speak both to the boy and to those who view Vickers's work. It is as if they are saying, "We have left you to live on the good earth that supported us and our children. Do not forget what we and the earth can teach you." It represents compellingly the enduring connections between the living and their ancestors and between all of us and our natural surroundings.*

When I look at Vickers's work I am often reminded of another work based in native African tradition. It is a song that I first heard in a wonderful live concert by Sweet Honey in the Rock in the early 1980s. The song is based on, and has the same title as, a poem by Birago Diop entitled "Breaths." The African view of the world that is captured in the piece is remarkably like that of the North Coast Indians. The invisible spirit world, humankind, and the visible natural world are continuous and organically connected in one larger reality. So, too, are the past, present, and future.

In the verses of the song, we are first encouraged to listen for the breath (that is, the spirit) of the ancestors in the voices of fire and water. We are then told that those who have died "have never left" and that they are "not under the earth." Rather, they are in the rustling trees, the groaning woods, the crying grass, and the moaning rocks. They are also in the woman's breast, the wailing child, the home, and the crowd. The last line tells us, "The dead have a pact with the living." This work, too, powerfully captures belief in enduring connections.

Other, perhaps more familiar, traditional cultures, like these aboriginal cultures of North America and Africa, have long supported beliefs that the dead live on in some form. Death, then, is a door, not a wall. And survivors retain connection with those who have gone through it. Traditional cultures also insist that our connections with one another and to the world around us are vitally important to who we are and can become.

The story of Abraham is remarkable in this regard. Jews, Christians, and Muslims all trace their histories to him. All keep the memory of their common father Abraham alive, but each in a different way. Jews revere Abraham as the first to receive revelations from Yahweh, the God of ancient Israel. As long as they, his descendants, worship Yahweh, Abraham lives on through his people and the land where he died, Israel. Christians revere Abraham for his supreme faith in God. In particular, they view his near sacrifice of Isaac as a symbol of God's sacrifice of Jesus on the cross so that they may have eternal life. Muslims revere Abraham as the first prophet and as the father of their ancestor, Ishmael, who was born to Abraham and Hagar. They regard Abraham as the first Muslim because he practiced *Islam*— absolute obedience to the will of God.

In each of these great faith traditions, Abraham is a living presence. He is remembered, and the story of his life and deeds is retold and reexamined. He is a practical model of how to live the good life. His descendants identify themselves as his people and as members of the faith communities that he began. Adherents to these faiths draw inspiration from his faith and obedience to God. In these ways Abraham lives on in his descendants, and they in turn live as members of his family.

Judaism, Christianity, and Islam record and preserve tradition in sacred texts. They trace the lineages of prominent historical figures and record the stories of their lives. They preserve cultural memory in tangible form just as storytelling does in oral traditions. The availability of the stories allows those who read or hear them to connect with lives ended long ago. This enables them to reflect on, explore, and discuss their significance in their own lives.

Sacraments, rituals, and celebrations in each of these faith traditions give a central place to remembrance, the ability to identify with and draw inspiration from those whose lives on earth have ended. Jews celebrate Passover to commemorate Moses who led the ancient Israelites from slavery in Egypt to the promised land and to think of themselves as united with them as the surviving children of Abraham. Christians participate regularly in the sacrament of Holy Communion to celebrate the life and sacrifice of Jesus, obey his command to "Do so often in remembrance of me," and renew community ties among all adherents of the faith, both living and dead. Muslims turn daily in prayer toward Mecca and are charged to make a pilgrimage there once in their lifetime, to remember the birthplace of the Prophet Mohammed and to return in memory symbolically and literally to the origins of what unites them in Islamic faith and the Muslim way of life.

Jewish, Christian, and Muslim traditions go beyond encouraging enduring connection with central historical figures. Adherents of the faiths believe we survive death and find places in heaven, purgatories, or hell depending on our actions while alive. Many hope and pray for reunion at the time of resurrection of the dead. The faiths encourage lasting love and enduring connection with our own mothers and fathers, and other more immediate predecessors through prayers and rituals of remembrance. Some pray for the well-being of the dead in the afterlife, especially for release from the burden of their sins. Many offer prayers of praise or gratitude to those who have died for all that they have given and continue to give. Some believe the dead watch over them and pray for guidance in dealing with life's many challenges. Some pray that favors may be granted. Some traditions encourage regular ceremonies of remembrance: the Christian All Saints' Day and All Souls' Day, the Mexican Day of the Dead, and the Jewish *Kaddish* and memorial services for those who perished in the Holocaust. Such ceremonies revive both individual and collective memory of those who have died. In some instances, for example, the Day of the Dead, the living actually call the dead to return to commune with them.

There are many parallels in the traditions of China, Tibet, India, and Japan. Confucian, Taoist, Hindu, Buddhist, and Shinto traditions all promote enduring connection with ancestors. Some ritual practices promote the well-being of the dead through transitions: helping them to leave the body, supporting surviving consciousness as it gains liberation from the wheel of life, or supporting rebirth into a new incarnation. Popular religious practices in these traditions include rituals in the home, in temples, at sacred shrines, and during public celebrations to honor the dead, acknowledge their continuing presence, express indebtedness to them, show gratitude for their continuing benevolence, and ensure good fortune for the living and the dead.

Traditional cultures affirm that the meaning of a life transcends death. Those who have died not only live on literally in new forms or in later incarnations, they also live in the memories of survivors and their descendants and in valued practical influences, cherished legacies, and inspirations that shape individual, family, and community lives. They are woven into the fabrics of personal and collective histories that make us who we are and in part color and define our destinies.

Many of us still identify with these traditions. If you are one who does, you may be well acquainted with the desire to sustain a loving and enduring connection with those who have died. Or you may want to learn more about the traditional beliefs and practices within your family or community that sustain that desire.

We live in a time when many of us no longer identify with traditional beliefs or the cultures they shape. If you have lost touch with what is valuable in the traditions of your family or community, you may seek to renew your connections with them. You would not be alone since there is currently a large-scale spiritual revival under way. We yearn for the security, comfort, consolation, peace, hope, and meaning that so many find in traditional belief and practice.

Yet many of us find it impossible to revive the sustaining power of religious tradition in our lives, at least in orthodox ways. If you are one who cannot, you need not despair about finding lasting love and enduring connection. I will show you how you can discover them in remembrance and in cultivating a practical, soulful, and spiritual life. You may not identify with traditional cultures that endorse life beyond death—even believers struggle with this. Still, you can affirm that the meaning of life is not canceled by death.

Ghosts and Other Contacts

Spirits are everywhere, walking here with us.
—*Truly, Madly, Deeply*

Nina and Jamie are the central characters in the film Truly, Madly, Deeply. Jamie, Nina's true love, has died suddenly. Nina is distraught. Some time after Jamie's death, Nina still longs for him intensely and idealizes her memories of him and their relationship. She sits, sobs, and feels numb for hours. She has no motivation to do anything. Even going to bed makes no sense, because Jamie isn't there. Nina says that she "cannot forgive him for not being here." Friends and family, fellow workers, and even workmen who are repairing her flat express concern for her.

At first she senses Jamie's presence when she is lonely and hopeless. She feels looked after, watched over by him, and assured that he loves her. Yet her agony persists. Eventually, Jamie appears to her as a ghost, in the flesh she knows and loves. He had been watching her weeping and could stand it no longer. They have blissful moments together. In fact, Nina loses track of time for nearly a week. The renewed contact revitalizes her and brings assurance of how much Jamie still loves her.

As the film progresses, Jamie behaves in ways that are familiar but that had been obscured by Nina's idealizing memory. He brings his friends, also dead, into Nina's flat to watch videos and make music. He turns up the heat because he and they are cold. Nina remembers that she found things in a trunk that she had put aside because Jamie didn't like them. When she comes home one day and finds Jamie and his friends rearranging the flat and pulling up the carpet without consulting her, Nina protests, "I feel like I'm being burgled. This is my flat." When they begin to argue in front of the others and Jamie says he is embarrassed, Nina asserts, "I don't want to be in public in my own home." After Nina tells Jamie's friends to leave and he says that she humiliated him, she wonders out loud, "Was it like this before? Were we like this?" He asks whether she wants him to leave, and she says that she does not know what she wants.

Her understanding of what she wants emerges in several settings. Nina goes to be with a friend who is giving birth and is awed by the miracle of life. She is charmed by another man, Mark, and a new relationship begins. She and Jamie remember and tenderly cherish the beginning of their own relationship. Having tasted and been reminded of these beginnings, Nina concludes, "It's a life, a life I want." She is ready, albeit tentatively, to explore new possibilities in her life, including a relationship with Mark.

Nina meets Mark briefly and casually at first, but they finally spend an evening together. When Mark catches Nina crying, he senses that she is still living with someone else. He gently and patiently says, "If you're not free, I'm in trouble here." Nina responds, "I think I am free. I did love someone very much, but he died. I found it quite hard to get over it." Mark says Nina can tell him anything. They drive back to Mark's place, stopping for a toothbrush on the way, and their relationship begins to blossom. Nina returns to her flat and no longer finds Jamie there, only things that remind her of him. She begins to put life in order there. Some days later Mark comes to pick up Nina. As the two of them go to drive away, Jamie and his friends appear in the window of the flat once again. They look on approvingly as Nina and Mark kiss. Jamie smiles and cries. They wave good-bye.

Some of us, like Nina, have experiences after those we love die that powerfully suggest that they live on, not only in our hearts, but independently. Encounters so powerful that they are like meetings with ghosts are rare. But it is not only fictional characters like Nina who have them.

Typically, as in the film, the experiences are ambiguous. Such ghosts are substantial and compellingly real in the experience of those of us to whom they appear. And yet, unlike real people, they only appear to us selectively. Nina alone sees, hears, or touches Jamie.

Most commonly such experiences of ghosts occur when extreme and unrelenting longing for the return of those who have died grips us. Or our need for resolution of some lingering tension or unfinished business is so great that it threatens to paralyze us. The longing is often most intense when we idealize those who have died, believe that there is no point in living without them, or fear that we cannot contend alone with a world transformed by our loss.

Jamie appears to Nina out of love for her. He senses that only his appearance will help her to move beyond her longing. He reassures Nina that he will always love her. Revealing himself in his full humanity, flaws and all, allows her to let go of her fantasy of him and to remember realistically. Jamie's loving reappearance enables Nina to once again embrace the life she still has. Remembering Jamie will no doubt be a part of whatever life lies ahead for Nina, but only a part.

Far more common than ghostly appearances are encounters with those who have died that are not as direct, vividly embodied, or sustained as Nina's were with Jamie. A grieving mother's four-year-old son had died suddenly. While alive, she had taught her son about God and how God is good. During her son's funeral, she had a vision of her son sitting on God's lap in heaven. He turned to look into God's eyes and asked, "You're good, right?" And God drew him closer.

A grandmother saw the smiling and peaceful face of her grandson shimmering on the surface of the pond on the family farm where he had drowned. A young man heard the voice of his best friend assure him while he was weeping, "Don't cry for me. I'm in a happy place. You can make it." A daughter sensed that her dead mother came into her cold room one night, dried her tears, tucked her in, and whispered, "I'll always watch over you." A husband dreamed that his wife was happily reunited with her parents and brother who had died before her.

Still more common are events that we experience as indirect communications from those who have died or signs from higher powers about them. During a prayer at the outdoor funeral for a stillborn baby, there was a strong gust of wind. The child's mother feared that the solitary tea rose she had placed on the casket had been blown away. At the close of the prayer, she opened her eyes and saw several other flower arrangements in disarray. But the flower on the casket was still in place. She believed it was a sign that God was watching the service and that the baby was grateful for her love.

A child watched the first butterfly of summer, and her mother took the opportunity to explain her beliefs and answer the questions that troubled the child when her Grandpa died. A magnificent flock of geese soared into a sunset just when a grieving father, walking through a nature preserve, felt hopeless after his daughter's suicide. Because inclement weather canceled a man's business flight, he could be home with his wife when she had a major heart attack that afternoon, allowing him to speak to her of their love before she died that night in the hospital. A woman found a forgotten letter from her sister between the pages of a book when she was especially lonely for her company. A widow received some forgotten photographs from a friend just when she needed to recall her dead husband's zest for life.

Encounters with ghosts are at once the most dramatic and disconcerting of contacts with those who have died. But, as was true for Nina, ghosts of those we have loved and who have loved us are most often benevolent. They appear out of love. Still, such encounters can frighten us. They can even occur in the lives of those of us who "do not believe in such things" and deny that they have ever had such experiences. The incongruity with our deeply held convictions can shake us unless we know we are not alone in undergoing these experiences. We can calm ourselves as we recognize that the ghost does us no harm and then presume that he or she means well.

Often those of us who see those who have died, hear their voices, brush with them physically, or dream about them keep such fleeting experiences to ourselves. We may fear that others will not believe us or, worse, that we will be ridiculed. But few of us doubt the validity of these experiences. They tend to be powerfully compelling. We take comfort when we learn that others have had similar contacts with those who have died.

We may be secretive about indirect contacts or signs. But often we feel better when we tell others and point to how weird or uncanny we find the experiences. Many of us resist the idea that what we experienced are "simply coincidences." Instead, we insist that "there is a reason for everything."

Not all of us have such ghostly or other contacts with those who have died. We need not be troubled if we do or if we do not. When we do have such experiences, we can find a rich variety of meanings in them: Assurances that our loved one is in a good place. Hope that enables us to let go of unrelenting longing for their return. Help in finding and holding a balanced memory of them. Encouragement in facing the daunting challenges of living on this earth without them. Responses to practical needs for guidance. Support in embracing the love and good that life still offers us. And reassurance that they still love us.

Loving in Separation

Though lovers be lost love shall not.
—*Dylan Thomas*

We know a great deal about holding others in our hearts when they are alive, even when we are apart. In no way do we believe that our loving stops when we part, no matter the terms of our separation. We spend most of our waking lives apart from those we cherish most. Our daily routines take us in different directions. Often, our grandparents, parents, spouses, companions, children, and friends remain dear to us across great distances and times when we do not see, hear, or touch one another.

When we are apart, we give those we love places in our thoughts and prayers. We remember them. We speak of them with others. We shape our lives in terms of commitments and covenants with them. We share their interests and concerns. We model our actions and characters on theirs. We think of and appreciate how we and our lives are different for knowing them. They motivate and inspire us, even though they may be far away. We share their hopes and dreams. Sometimes they make us laugh; sometimes they make us cry. In these and so many other ways, their lives remain intimately linked and lovingly interwoven with ours. We often sense that they, too, hold us in their hearts at whatever distance or time separates us.

Loving in separation, then, is not foreign to our experience. We know these ways of the heart well. We could scarcely sustain a single relationship if we did not. Yes, there is the difference that, while we both live, we can come together again. We can renew and deepen our love face to face with those who share the earth with us. But we do not stop caring about and loving those from whom we are separated. Nor do we stop sensing their love in return. This is so even if we expect never to see them again. We may miss them terribly, but we do hold them in our hearts, at times tenaciously.

Loving in separation after death is not so very different. Missing those who have died once again gives them a place in our hearts. Beyond missing them, the give-and-take between us and those who have died assumes familiar shapes. We can still give our attention, interest, admiration, understanding, respect, acceptance, forgiveness, loyalty, affection, praise, and gratitude to them. And we can sense that they reciprocate or that what they have given is still with us.

We can also continue to receive and benefit from their material assistance, advice and counsel, instruction, intellectual stimulation, perspective, direction, honesty and candor, moral and spiritual guidance and support, modeling of how to be and act, encouragement, expressions of confidence, enthusiasm, a sense of belonging, and inspiration. We may believe that they literally watch over us or walk with us, sharing our joys and sorrows. Or we may sense that they are with us in spirit and remain our life's companions in our hearts.

Reciprocity in give-and-take does not stop when someone dies: It changes. We continue to give and receive. Those who have died give us their legacies, the fruits of their lives. Sadly, we cannot contribute directly to their lives any longer. We may, however, sense that they witness or support us as we, in turn, contribute to other lives. For our part, we sense that they are still with us in our hearts. We may sense that they hold us dear or that the love in their hearts is still with us.

Good and Troubled Loving

A friend is one to whom one may pour out all of the contents of one's heart, chaff and grain together, knowing that the gentlest of hands will take and sift it, keep what is worth keeping, and with a breath of kindness, blow the rest away.

—*Arabian proverb*

We care deeply about our relationships with our parents, spouses and companions, children, siblings, other family members, and friends when they are alive. Few things bring greater satisfaction and fulfillment when they are good. And few things distress us more when they are troubled.

We hold dear those in our families of origin, biological or adoptive, for many reasons. We owe our parents our very lives. We find many of our roots in life with our parents, siblings, grandparents, spouses, companions, and close friends and others. They typically introduce us to the give-and-take of everyday life: the dances of mutual respect, care, and love. They nurture our growth and development. They provide us with shared cultures and histories. We find rich and diverse identities through them.

We choose spouses or life companions, bring children into the world or adopt, or befriend others in the hope that we will love and be loved in return. We seek to bring something good into existence that would not otherwise exist. We hope to give to and receive from them some of the same good things we found in our families of origin or perhaps what we perceived as lacking in them. We want to become with them what we could not become alone.

When our loved ones are alive, we know a great deal about when loving is good and when it is not. We know loving is good when it is dynamic, vibrant, and motivating, and troubled when it is static, stagnant, and inhibiting. Good when it opens us to the fullness of life and troubled when it constricts us. Good when it nurtures and enlivens us and troubled when it smothers and deadens us. Good when it promotes our thriving and troubled when it hinders or undermines it. Good when it enables us to be and become all we can be and troubling when it limits or stifles us. Good when it brings out the best in us and troubled when it brings out the worst. Good when mutual respect, sensitivity, and reciprocity abound and troubled when such balance is lacking. Good when it allows us to find ourselves and troubled when we lose ourselves in it. Good when it opens us to others and promotes harmony and troubled when it closes us off from them or promotes discord. Good when it inspires us and troubled when it dispirits us.

We invite trouble into our loving relationships when we become too absorbed in one and neglect others. When we idealize one and fail to appreciate what others have given and continue to give. When we submerge our own identity in another's, replace our life agendas with theirs, and sacrifice our autonomy. When we become inflexible and fail to remain open to change, growth, and the ebb and flow of love and life. Or when we allow such things as dependence, control and manipulation, possessiveness, intense anger or guilt, and even abuse to infect and persist in them.

We know these ways of the heart well. Of course, we and our loved ones often fall short of the ideal in loving one another. We do not do as well as we would like in avoiding the paths that lead to trouble. Nor do we easily acknowledge, address, or overcome troubles when they arise. Such is loving in the human condition. Imperfect partners do not love perfectly or receive perfect love in return. We are in part fortunate when good loving comes into our lives. And we are in part responsible for it, as we and those we love do our best to make our loving ties as satisfying and constructive as they can be.

Good and troubled loving are not so very different after those we love die. Of course, loving them in separation cannot satisfy and fulfill us or trouble us in ways that require their physical presence. And the pain of missing them in separation for the rest of our earthly lives is a distinctive anguish not to be taken lightly. But loving them can enrich our lives in all the other ways it could when they were alive. And loving them can trouble us in all the same ways as when they lived.

We can find the best that lasting love has to offer by taking to heart lessons we have learned in all our relationships. We can seek to balance our devotion to those who have died by renewing our life with fellow survivors. We can seek to remember our loved ones realistically, flaws and all. We can work to complete unfinished business and let go of distressing negative ties with them. We can identify with them in ways that make us better for having known them, without compromising our own integrity. We can value their legacies while we value what others still offer us. We can give them places in our hearts while we open our hearts to those who still share life with us.

Receiving Their Legacies

Remember old friends we've met along the way.
The gifts they've given stay with us every day.

—*Mary McCaslin*

My dictionary defines a legacy as "something handed down from an ancestor or a predecessor or from the past." We receive legacies from those who have died whether they are our ancestors, family members, companions, or friends. Through their legacies, those who have died continue to make differences in, and enrich, our lives. They delight, touch, move, benefit, motivate, and inspire us. As we receive, use, and cultivate their legacies, we savor and cherish the fruits of their lives. The gifts they have given are with us every day.

Alex Haley's remarkable book Roots, *and the wonderful 1977 and 1979 mini-series that it inspired, recounts his recovery of the legacies of his family history. He traces his ancestry through seven generations to Kunta Kinte who was captured, uprooted from his African homeland of Gambia, and sold into slavery in America. As he unearths and retells the story of those generations, Haley finds much value and meaning in lives intimately linked through family ties. His appreciation and love for them deepen. His self-understanding grows.*

Although Haley's story is personal, it represents countless parallel stories of the experiences of black generations in America. Readers and viewers came to appreciate how they have much of what they have, and are in large measure who they are, because of often unacknowledged or unappreciated contributions of those who have gone before. It prompted many, no matter their racial heritage, to search their own family histories and recover the legacies within them.

Our own family legacies vary richly. We receive inheritances or shares of estates or businesses, grand and modest, accumulated over a lifetime. Wills specify that we shall be provided for in some ways or receive prized possessions: watches, jewelry, dishes, silver, glassware, linens, artwork, ornaments, books, collections, souvenirs from travels, furniture, equipment, even vehicles. Sometimes those who have died leave us things from their own hands: letters, diaries or journals, albums and scrapbooks, poems or other writings, drawings, cartoons, paintings, furniture, needlework, photographs, recipes, even homes and gardens. Often, we receive such things from friends who die "as if we were one of the family."

We also inherit physical and biological traits. We look for physical similarities to those who have died as we search through photo albums, home movies, and tapes. We scrutinize our fellow survivors and observe ourselves in the mirror. We note eyes, smiles, chins, noses, hair, skin, hands, feet, figures, postures, ways of moving, and the like to detect family resemblances and traces that link us with them. We even argue with one another, usually good-naturedly, about our readings of these legacies. We inherit the genes of our forebears, certainly including dispositions to health and disease, longevity, physical stature and constitution, and perhaps intelligence and talents. We also look for similarities in gestures, speech patterns, behaviors, habits, dispositions, and temperaments.

Our grandparents give us our parents, aunts, and uncles. Our parents give us our siblings, and sometimes members of our stepfamilies. Our aunts and uncles give us our cousins. Our spouses or companions give us our in-laws, children, or stepchildren. Our siblings give us our nephews and nieces. Our children give us our grandchildren. As challenging as some family relationships can be, these living legacies are surely among the most precious contributions others make to our lives.

Family members and friends, however, leave us much to treasure that is less tangible.

My children's grandfather on their mother's side, Bernie, was wise, kind-hearted, gentle, and a good storyteller. He delighted the kids and had a special affection for each. When my daughter Sheryl was little, he admired her gymnastic abilities, drew stick-figure cartoons of her, and called her "Rubber Legs." She loved his affection, attention, and praise, and giggled as he held and teased her. Bernie was also a prominent evangelical theologian with a doctorate in philosophy who taught in seminaries, spoke internationally, and authored over twenty books. When he died, Sheryl was an undergraduate in philosophy, with interests in religion and theology of her own.

In the summer before he died, Sheryl spent a month with Bernie in California reading and discussing theology and related subjects with him. Again, she loved his attention and affection, this time as a maturing young adult. She looked forward to spending more time with him. Unfortunately, that was not possible. When we attended his funeral, Sheryl's grandmother gave her a copy of each of the books he had written and several other items from his library that she will no doubt treasure for years.

Sheryl has now graduated with a master's degree in theological studies. She hopes eventually to teach and counsel, among other things, about spirituality. She both cherishes and embodies her grandfather's legacy.

Kenny's teen years were a trial. Communication with his parents, Brad and Janice, spiraled out of control. He asserted his independence aggressively. They read him as disrespectful rather than normally rebellious and came down hard. He began to disobey them and to disappear for long periods of time. He abused alcohol. He was in and out of trouble with the law.

Brad and Janice feared they might lose Kenny either to an accident while under the influence or even to a life of escalating crime. They agonized about what Kenny might learn or who he might meet in detention centers. They worried that those who ran the centers were more intent on keeping kids locked up than on helping them to turn corners in their lives. They felt that they had failed Kenny and hoped that somehow someone could reach him and draw out the good that they knew was in him.

Kenny did turn his life around, with the help of Marv, a social worker, who appealed to the inner strength and goodness he saw in Kenny. Marv helped Kenny to learn from his mistakes and resolve to make something of the shambles of his life. Kenny dried out. He began to take his schoolwork seriously, and he was good at it. With Marv's and his parents' support and encouragement, he set himself on going to college. Everyone celebrated when he was admitted to a nearby state university.

Kenny was remarkably successful in college. He decided to follow Marv and major in social work, hoping to reach out to troubled teens. He did well in his course work. He impressed his teachers with a winning combination of intellect, street savvy, engaging personality, and compassion.

Kenny also made significant breakthroughs with his parents. He apologized for having hurt them and let them know how much their faith and encouragement meant to him. Together they were able to see why communication between them had spiraled downward. He had needed patience, room to grow and make mistakes, evenhandedness, and constructive criticism more than insistence on obedience. They found new closeness, easy ways of talking, and deep respect and love for one another.

Everyone expected great things of Kenny as graduation approached. Brad and Janice were bursting with pride when Kenny's great day came. And Kenny was ready to make a difference in others' lives as Marv had in his. Tragically, all of their hopes were shattered when Kenny fell to his death from a rock ledge in the state park where his family and friends gathered for his graduation party.

Brad and Janice were devastated. They had come so far with Kenny, and then this terrible accident. They were determined to use what they had learned from Kenny's life to make life better for others. When they felt they had put the worst of their grief behind them, they approached Marv for ideas about what they could do. He connected them with a foster parents' program. And over the next ten years they welcomed three teenaged boys into their home during times of difficult transition in their lives. All three completed high school. Two went on to college and the third found a good job with a local business.

These stories illustrate some of what we find when we look deeper at the meaning of our inheritances. We inherit more than material, physical, or biological legacies. Death does not erase or cancel the meanings we shared with those who have died. In the time we have known them, they have touched our hearts, souls, and spirits. They have influenced the way we live, shaped our characters, and inspired us. They retain the power to do these things after they die. It remains only for us to acknowledge, accept gratefully, and cultivate what their lives still have to offer.

Giving Them Places
in Our Hearts

Anything good you've ever been given is yours forever.
—Rachel Naomi Remen

My Dad was older than most dads when I was born—nearly fifty. He worked hard as a cook in a restaurant that he and my uncle Ralph owned in the midwestern town where I was raised. Dad spent most of every day on his feet. The hard work and incredible six-day schedule, which featured alternating shifts, left him with little energy to spare. At home he was quiet and napped often. Though I have great affection for him still, I have little memory of his playing physically with me. None of our ever playing catch—I remember doing that with my older brother, John.

Yet I learned from Dad to love baseball, first while listening to radio broadcasts with him and later when watching the many daytime telecasts of White Sox and Cubs games. Dad's enthusiasm was infectious. When Ernie Banks said, "Let's play two," we said, "Let's watch two." Dad was somewhat of an historian of the game. He had listened to games from the beginning of broadcast radio, and he knew the exploits of many of the game's legends. He had even seen Shoeless Joe Jackson play before he and others were banned from baseball for throwing the 1919 World Series. Many think Shoeless Joe was perhaps the greatest natural hitter of all time, and Dad agreed. I followed baseball avidly long after my Dad died in 1969. Often I sensed that I kept that interest alive as a way to feel connected with him.

Years later, I went one night, alone, to see the movie Field of Dreams. I rarely miss a baseball movie, even though few seem any good. This one touched me so deeply that I decided to take my teenaged son Dan with me to see it a second time. Dan never met my father, and he didn't share my interest in baseball. I had never really told him much about my father.

The protagonist in the movie hears a mysterious voice in his field one night, urging him to build a baseball diamond in the middle of that field. "He will come," it promises. The young man had a father who was a baseball player. But he, too, had never played catch with his dad. The voice is compelling, and eventually the man does its bidding. Soon, the field is visited by the very real ghosts of long-dead baseball players, including Shoeless Joe Jackson. They emerge from the corn every night, play while the builder watches, and disappear when their game is done.

One night, the man's father appears in his catching gear. He asks his son to play catch, and of course the man does so eagerly. I expect you will have little difficulty imagining how this story resonates with my experience of my father. Dan and I had a terrific discussion when the movie was over. The film provided a perfect vehicle for introducing Dan to Dad and letting him see a side of me he did not know well.

In the spring of 1996, my mother visited my new home in Vancouver for the first time. Then eighty-one, she came with her sister, Gertie, who was seventy-seven. They and three other siblings survive of the original nine who reached adulthood. Their extended family remained close emotionally and geographically to my grandmother in the Chicago area. Some of my fondest childhood memories are of holiday and family celebrations with as many as thirty-five aunts, uncles, and cousins gathered around Grandma. There was always lively conversation and much laughter, and occasionally there was group singing.

My grandmother was a wonderful, old-fashioned woman who came with her first four children from "the old country," Germany, to join her husband just before World War I. Mom was the first to be born in America. My grandfather was a stern presence while the children were young. He died in the mid-1940s. Grandma devoted her life to her children and grandchildren. Her cooking, laughter, and broken English are unforgettable. She set a world standard for worry about things great and small (one of her legacies to my mother). Grandma died in the mid-1970s at age eighty-nine, still the center of her family's love and affection.

The week that my mother and Gertie were here was thoroughly delightful. Betty and I were struck by how often my grandmother entered the conversation as if she were a third guest. Mom and Gertie referred to her often. Memories were a dominant theme. They easily and comfortably recalled how "Ma" saw them through the hard times when they were growing up and how she gave them so much when the family had so little. At times it was as if the two of them became schoolgirls again or reverted to dinner table patterns from years before. They teased one another, giggled, and relived how it was when so many gathered around their mother's table.

Grandma's perspective on the world was second nature to Mom and Gertie. They often wondered aloud, "What would Ma think of this?" as they saw things in our home and the surrounding area or watched the film Grumpy Old Men *one night in our family room. More often than not they went on to answer their own question. Sometimes they agreed with "Ma," sometimes not. Sometimes "Ma's" views and ways amused and delighted them. Sometimes she instructed them. Sometimes they felt sad for her, the hardship in her life, what she had missed, and what she was missing now. Clearly, Grandma will be with them as long as they live. What a delightful presence she is! And how lovely they are when they are with her.*

All of these stories show us how we can find places in our hearts for the legacies of those who have died. When we love family members, companions, or friends, we care about what they care about. What matters to them matters to us *because* we see how much it matters to them. Sometimes we identify with them as we make their cares our own. We come to share some of their interests, concerns, values, hopes, and dreams.

We can continue to care about what family members, companions, friends, and public figures cared about after they die. As we thrive in activities, experiences, and ways of being ourselves that derive from having known and loved them, we continue loving them.

As we come to know and love others, we also come to know and value the stories of their lives. The stories prove endlessly fascinating. They often show us how to be and act in the face of life's greatest challenges. They move and inspire us. Sometimes they reveal their fallibility and disappoint us. Still, they teach us about life in the human condition.

Often, their stories are intimately interwoven with our own life stories. As we cherish the life stories of those who have died, we continue the interweaving process. Our love for them deepens as we allow the values and meanings in the stories to permeate our lives as survivors. When we share the stories with others, we enrich our family and community lives.

As we remember and cherish the stories of those who have died, we sustain our connection with them. We hold them dear as we welcome differences they still make in our lives. We retain and appreciate the gifts that were their lives. We give their legacies places in our hearts—and, in this way, we become their living legacies.

Lasting Love Is Good for Them

This is the thought that has always terrified me;
to live, to be so filled with ambition,
to suffer, to weep, to struggle,
and, at the end, oblivion!
As if I had never existed.

—*Nineteenth-century Russian woman's diary*

Jeremy knew that his cystic fibrosis would eventually end his life. He feared that his parents would remember only the suffering of their only child or the hardship he brought into their lives. They might even try to block out his memory altogether. But he loved his life: each breath more than most ever appreciated breathing itself. And he did all he could to fill his best moments with play and good cheer and to show others how much he loved life and them. He wanted to be remembered for these things, too.

When he died at eighteen, Jeremy's parents, Dale and Kay, joined a support group for grieving parents. In it they found others who willingly listened to their sorrows and to the story of Jeremy's life. Telling and retelling it enabled them to see through the suffering and hardship, and to reconnect with Jeremy's courageous, playful, and loving spirit. They participated in the annual holiday remembrance services and appreciated the opportunity to retell Jeremy's story on his birthday and the anniversary of his death.

They were eager participants in a group book-writing that collected the stories of their children who had died, which the parents circulated

*among themselves and published for other bereaved parents. They
included Jeremy's story in their first holiday letter after the book was
completed. They asked all who received a copy to share memories of
Jeremy with them and freely talk about him whenever the spirit moved
them. They didn't want him to disappear from their lives altogether.*

As strange as it may sound, our lasting love benefits those who
have died. Like Jeremy, they do not want to slip into oblivion
at the moment of death. They do not want the world, especially
those they love, to go on as if they had never lived. It is only
human for those who have died to want to make lasting im-
pressions on the world and those they leave behind. They want
to be remembered. They want to retain places in the lives of
those they have known and loved. In and through our memories,
we give our deceased family members and friends a symbolic
immortality, a continuity that transcends death.

*Sadie doted on Jeannie as a child and wryly joked that she was her
"favorite granddaughter," when in fact she was the only girl among
her four grandchildren. Late in life Sadie confided in Jeannie that she
sensed that others in the family were too busy to take her seriously
any longer. Sadie died at eighty-four when Jeannie was thirty-six.*

    *At Sadie's funeral Jeannie made sure that the service included
singing of her grandmother's favorite hymn, "Nearer My God to
Thee," along with others Jeannie's father and his sister chose. She
cherished the grandfather clock (made by Sadie's own grandfather a
hundred years earlier), letters and books, and the bracelet that Sadie
left her. She vowed to quit smoking as Sadie had so often begged her
to do. She decided that Sadie was right, she should work on becoming
closer with her older brother. She kept Sadie's confidences, but resolved
to take her own parents more seriously when they reached old age.*

We also benefit those who have died as we protect and further
their interests in the world even after death. Those who doubt

that they have such interests need only think of the power and authority of a last will and testament. We further their interests when we comply with wills, but not always lovingly.

We honor their love when we, like Janice, fulfill explicit promises and covenants we made to them or as we take their wishes seriously. We plan funerals and memorials with their preferences in mind. We keep their secrets and protect their privacy. We see a project through to completion. We care for things and places they leave behind. We look after their aging parents, their children, pets, or plants. We may even reconsider advice and counsel they offered during their lifetimes. And we may take better care of ourselves. We may break a nasty habit. We may consider a better life course. We may mend troubled relationships. We may renew a faith or keep a tradition.

Lucky and Jacques were best friends ever since their college days. Jacques introduced Lucky to his French-Canadian culture as Lucky did Jacques to his English-Canadian culture. Once agnostic, Lucky became a Roman Catholic because of Jacques, drawn first by the beauty of the services and later by the beliefs he came to call his own. They each settled in Montreal, served as the other's best man, and were godfathers to the other's children. They celebrated their birthdays together with their families. Jacques took up handball and recruited Lucky as his favorite playing partner.

At forty-three Jacques was killed in an auto accident. While devastated by the loss, Lucky is grateful to Jacques for the faith that helps him carry his pain. He remembers Jacques fondly whenever he savors French wine, pastry, music, or film. He encourages his English-Canadian friends to be sympathetic whenever they fail to appreciate how a French-Canadian heritage enriches all of Canada. He and his wife remain close to Jacques's widow and children, helping to raise them almost as if they were their own. And while the families continue to celebrate Jacques's birthday together, Lucky plays handball less frequently because no one brings the same delight and fire to the game that Jacques did.

We most clearly protect and further the interests of those who have died when we identify with them, when we make some of their interests our own. We allow them to color our characters and the ways we continue to live in a world transformed by their death.

We may follow their example in our practical lives. We may enjoy a similar hobby or pastime. We may even choose the same vocation.

We may feel drawn to aspects of traditions we shared with them. We may continue to care deeply about some of what they cared about. We may follow them in our spiritual lives, finding joy and celebrating life in similar ways. Consciously or not, we draw inspiration from them as we strive to better our life circumstances, become all we can be, or face life's challenges and adversity.

Ida often said that she lived too long. Her last years and months brought steady decline and debilitation. She couldn't enjoy even a moment, much less an hour or a day. She could see the terrible toll her suffering was taking on her dear, devoted husband, Willard. She finally came to a point where she could stand it no longer.

Ida painstakingly crafted a suicide note to Willard. She reminded him of how much she had loved so many things in the life they shared: their children and grandchildren, music, conversation, walks in the park along the river. She would miss them all, but him especially. She did not want him to blame himself for what she did. She cherished his caring ways and his respect for her stubborn independence. She asked him to respect her difficult choice to end a life that once overflowed and was now drained of its meaning. She knew he would miss her. And she pleaded with him to reach beyond missing her and embrace the fullness of the years he had left. When she was done with the note, Ida took her own life at age seventy-one.

Willard loved her for her stubbornness. He had watched as she persevered through those last years and months, far beyond the point in her illness that he himself could have endured. He read her decision to end her life as one more excruciating expression of her independence. Yes, it was an agony to go on without her. But he respected her decision and knew she did not make it lightly. And he took heart from her desire that he find his way through his pain to once again enjoy life with those they brought into the world together.

Those who have died, like Ida, often have strong desires for us, too. They want us to live well after they die. They hope that we will thrive, find purpose and meaning in life, succeed, be happy, know joy and love—and they tell us as much. They worry about and pray for us. They do what they can to provide for, and even prepare us for, when they will be gone. They do not want us to be overwhelmed by their deaths or to dwell in the pain of missing them. They want us to hold dear the good in their lives, to use and cherish what they have given. We fulfill these desires lovingly as we treasure their legacies and grant them places in our hearts.

Lasting Love Is Good for Us

Human culture . . . tempers spontaneity with wisdom
inherited from the past and by hopes projected into the
future. . . .
We come home to the fullness of our humanity
only in owning and taking responsibility for
present awareness as well as for the full
measure of our memories and dreams.
Graceful existence integrates present, past, and future.

—Sam Keen

Finding ways of loving those who have died can benefit us in countless ways. Our lives are enhanced as we, individually and with others, feel and express our gratitude to those who have died for all they have given. And we can benefit in any or all dimensions of our lives.

We can benefit psychologically. For example, a child feels good about herself when she remembers how her father gave her so much of his attention, interest, enthusiasm, and affection. A widow faces the challenges of living alone with renewed self-confidence as she recalls how her husband encouraged her to face the prospect of his dying and devoted himself to teaching her how to manage household and financial matters when he was gone. A woman draws inspiration from her dead mother's courage and advice as she copes with the challenges her family faces when her husband is seriously disabled and loses his job. A brother attributes much of his success in rising above poverty and persevering through medical school to his dead sister's undying faith in him. An adopted son who was told the identity of his biological mother only after her death comes to understand himself better as he learns about his heritage from others who knew her.

And in the aftermath of death, we can find renewed meaning and reward in everyday activities and interests. For example, a woman is grateful for her friend's having introduced her to ballet and thinks of her each time she thrills to a performance. Another maintains her dead sister's garden. A young man continues with rock-climbing and senses his friend's presence whenever he completes a difficult and satisfying climb. A father takes up his dead son's interest in the environment and finds satisfaction as he volunteers at a local recycling center.

We can benefit physically. For example, a widower at last follows his wife's advice to see a doctor for a physical examination and begins a fitness program. A woman vows to join Alcoholics Anonymous and quit drinking when her closest friend succumbs to liver cancer. A father stops smoking when his daughter, who had always begged him to do so, is killed in an auto accident. When a widow moves beyond intense longing for her husband's return and begins to connect with all she still has of him, she is no longer drained by incessant weeping, and her energy and zest for living return.

We can benefit intellectually. For example, a daughter takes inspiration from her dead mother's unpublished poetry and short stories and pursues a career teaching literature. A man recognizes that he developed his knack for calculation and delight in mathematical puzzles in evenings spent with his grandfather. A woman remembers the late-night talks with her grandmother and cherishes the wisdom she found in them. A rabbi appreciates how his mother's devotion inspired his search for understanding of life in the human condition and the workings of divine grace.

And we can benefit socially. A young woman appreciates how she was first introduced to many of her lifelong friends by one who is no longer with them. A widower loves children with new intensity and in ways he learned from his wife. A grandson is grateful for his grandmother's advice about how to win and hold the heart of the woman who became his wife. Brothers reconcile as their father had wished. A mother strives to become more like her dead son in his gentle, patient, and forgiving ways with others. Adult children of a couple who died in a plane crash find renewal and satisfaction as they make a point of getting together more frequently and maintaining better contact while apart. Another family devotes part of each year's Thanksgiving holiday to a celebration of lives now ended, by remembering the gifts they still hold from them. A daughter takes up her dead mother's commitment to promote the welfare of abused children in her local community through volunteer service at a shelter. A couple establishes a foundation to support research into dementia in the elderly when both of their mothers die of Alzheimer's Disease.

In these and similar ways, lasting love makes us whole again as individuals, families, and communities. We reweave the threads of our lives, creating newly integrated patterns. We reintegrate the values and meanings of the stories of those who have died into our own life stories. We reinterpret our past lives with the deceased, alter how we live in the present, and project new hopes and purposes into the future. We change, as do our enduring connections with those who have died, with our families, with friends, with the larger community, with God, and even with our life's work.

As we find or achieve wholeness in each of these ways, we define who we are in terms of our continuing relationships, including our relationships with those who have died. We grow in understanding of how much our relationships matter to us. As we give places to lasting love in our lives, we become whole again, but in different ways.

Our lasting love also mitigates, or balances, the pain of missing those who have died. This love helps us to carry our pain. It reassures us that they did not live in vain and it brings comfort and solace as it gives them a new, enriching, dynamic, and enduring presence in our lives. It makes missing them more like loving them while we were separated in life. The motivation to lasting love and enduring connection draws on the best that is in us. It sets us on hopeful paths into futures where we feel powerfully and intimately connected to those who have died. When we cherish their legacies in this way, we connect with the best life has to offer us.

Learning to Love in a New Way

*The earthly beloved, even in this life, incessantly triumphs
over your mere idea of her. And you want her to; you
want her with all her resistances, all her faults, all her
unexpectedness. That is, in her foursquare and independent
reality. And this, not any image or memory, is what we
are to love still, after she is dead.*

—C. S. Lewis

I have told many stories about how we can love those
who have died and how we find enduring connections with
them even though we are now separated. By treasuring their
legacies in all their many forms, we continue to love them. We
cherish the memories and the stories of their lives. We care about
what they cared about. We give them places in our hearts, souls,
and spirits.

Quite often, we do these things instinctively, without thinking
or deliberating. Some of us establish enduring connections within
traditions that encourage and guide us. Some of us have lost
touch with traditions but could return to and find support from
them still. Others of us establish enduring connections outside
traditional contexts.

Extreme longing for those we miss or intense pain sometimes
blocks our paths to lasting love and enduring connection. Sometimes we are simply blind to the possibilities. Most often, we fall
short of our aspirations because we do not know how we can
make the transition from loving in our loved one's presence to

loving after death has separated us. Our instincts take us only so far. Others only rarely support us on our quest, much less guide us onto hopeful paths, or show us steps we can take.

In what follows I will share the stories of people who have walked hopeful paths to reach deeper lasting love, who have found rich and enduring "living memories." I will help you see how their practical, soulful, and spiritual lives were enriched by their ability to build these living memories. I will show you how they were able to find their paths, avoiding the pitfalls that could cripple them. With imagination and courage, we can find similar paths and take similar steps, as individuals, families, and communities. We can further the interests of those who have died, give them a symbolic immortality, and fulfill their desire that we live well in their absence.

II

Transitions to Lasting Love

Taking Leave and
Opening Our Hearts

*The memory of your dear Father, instead of an agony, will
yet be a sad sweet feeling in your heart, of a purer, and
holier sort than you have known before.*

—*Abraham Lincoln*

Bryan was nine when his best friend, Larry, died suddenly
and unexpectedly. Larry's parents had him cremated immediately and
without ceremony. Bryan, naturally, was hurt terribly by the death
of his friend. His own parents, Fran and Bob, comforted him as best
they could.

Bryan was distressed about not knowing where Larry was. He
wanted a place to go to be with him. He asked his parents to assure
him that if he were to die, they would bury him where other kids
could find him. They said they expected he would live to old age.
But they also promised to do what he asked. Bryan thought it would
be great to have a large stone that kids could climb on. Fran and Bob
agreed that, if they had to, they would make his grave a place that
would be fun for kids to visit.

In the months that followed, Fran noticed that Bryan made many
drawings of two boys riding on a roller coaster. She asked if they were
Bryan and Larry. He smiled and said they were. She saw in the
drawings how much Bryan missed Larry. At the same time, he remembered the good times they had together. The drawings seemed
like Bryan's way of making his own memorial for Larry.

Tragically, Bryan also died nearly a year later in a drowning accident. With the help of the funeral director, Bob constructed a pine casket, and Fran painted a small picture on its side of a roller coaster with two boys riding in it. Remembering the difficulty Bryan had with Larry's death, they encouraged family, friends, and parents of Bryan's friends to bring their children to calling hours and the funeral. After they told those who came to calling hours about the meaning of Fran's roller-coaster painting, several of the children placed drawings, notes, small toys, even some of Bryan's favorite candy with Bryan in his casket.

At the funeral, the minister acknowledged the presence of so many children, welcoming them and tailoring her remarks to them. She explained that in one way funerals are about saying good-bye to those we love, something that can be very hard to do. We come together in sadness and sometimes cry. But we can also find comfort from others who love the same person we love. She also reminded the gathering that funerals are in another way about beginnings, about new ways of holding those who have died through our memories of them.

She encouraged everyone to think of favorite stories about Bryan and to speak when the spirit moved them. Bob and Fran began with some they had planned to share, knowing the minister's plans. Others followed their lead, including Bryan's grandparents, aunts and uncles, some of the children, and their parents. No one seemed to notice or to care how long the sharing lasted. There were many tears. There was laughter. And they remembered Bryan well.

They then went to Bryan's graveside. They followed a sheet Bob and Fran prepared and sang several of his favorite songs together. They prayed for him together. In turn, each placed a daffodil on his casket. Bob and Fran then joined staff from the funeral home in lowering Bryan into the grave with their own muscle power. Those who wished took turns putting small shovels of dirt in his grave.

Fran and Bob were also true to their promise to establish a grave for Bryan that children would enjoy. They searched for a cemetery that would permit a large stone on a grave, and they found one, but *it was too far from home for them to visit regularly. And it was too far for children who knew Bryan to come and play. They buried Bryan in a nearby cemetery and had his name and the dates of his birth and death engraved on his grave marker. They added a depiction of two boys riding a roller coaster.*

Fran and Bob visited Bryan's grave often, alone and together. They wept, spoke to him, and prayed over him. Sometimes they left flowers or a small toy. A few times they were pleased when they found other parents with their children there. And at these times they remembered Bryan together. Sometimes the children chimed in with their own memories; sometimes they played. On other occasions Fran and Bob smiled when they found that others had left flowers, children's drawings, or playthings on the grave.

Ceremonies of separation, including rituals, informal gestures and activities, and memorialization, are most familiar as the things we do in remembrance in the liminal times and circumstances immediately after someone we love dies. We find ourselves in chaos and disarray. Like Fran and Bob, we are suspended between an old order that can no longer be and a future order yet to emerge. Ceremonies offer some order and meaning in the midst of the chaos of our lives. They can support us while we take leave of life as it has been in the presence of those who have died. And they can help us to begin to see how we can still be touched and moved by loved ones even though we are now apart. Ceremonies of separation can support us in both these ways when we experience episodes of intense hurt in days and years ahead.

Some ceremonies of separation are planned, formal, and public rituals, like the calling hours, funeral, and graveside service Fran and Bob had for Bryan. Processions, prayer services, memorial services, entombments, and cremations are familiar rituals to most of us.

But many individuals and families add spontaneous, informal, personal, or private gestures within such formal settings. We lay a bouquet of flowers beside a casket. We share a story about the deceased in a receiving line or during a service. We pause beside the body of the one who died. We place a memento with him or her. We pray silently in a funeral home, during a memorial service, or at a graveside.

Other ceremonies take place outside formal contexts altogether. We light candles at home or in places of worship. We record our feelings and thoughts in a journal or diary. We write a memorial poem. We listen to or sing a special song. We retreat to a quiet place to meditate or pray. We meet informally for a remember-when session.

Often during ceremonies we begin to memorialize those we love. We mark their passing with gravestones, monuments, plaques, eternal flames, tombs, urns, or niches in cemeteries, mausoleums, columbariums, or other locations where we place their physical remains. We dedicate theater seats, park benches, church pews, or collections in their honor. We mark where they died. We contribute to causes or institutions they held dear. We give to funds related to the causes of their deaths. We contribute to hospitals or hospices that cared for them. We plant something in special places in their memory. We donate their organs so that others might see or live. We name our children after them.

The memorial gestures, actions, and events in ceremonies of separation rely heavily on symbols for their power. Privately and together we use objects, language, and music. Some resonate with our pain and sorrow. Others, like Fran's painting on the side of Bryan's casket, evoke the life now ended. Still others affirm the ties that bind us together as families, communites, and co-inhabitants in the human condition. Symbols affirm values and meanings we hold dear—and they help us move through suffering and change.

Many of the things we do and the symbols we use simultaneously help channel our emotions and support our remembering. Flowers express our care, our sympathy for those most immediately affected, and the melancholy truth that even the longest life blooms only briefly. And they speak of our affection for our loved ones and the beauty and wonder of their lives. Music resonates with our deepest feelings. And it reminds us of those who have died and of special times in our lives. Eulogies or less formal storytelling reveal our sorrows even as they vividly capture aspects of the lives we remember. Moments of silence are filled with both our deepest feelings and fondest memories. We express our feelings and offer remembrances directly and symbolically in condolence books, guest registries, cards, letters, knowing glances, warm embraces, shared tears, phone calls, conversations in quiet corners and public places, and gatherings before, during, and after formal rituals and ceremonies. Lasting memorials express and hold our sorrows. And they often symbolize our desire never to forget our loved ones or something about them that we cherish.

Our worlds, like Fran and Bob's, stand still when someone close to us dies. We suspend life as usual as we begin to experience the full force of what has happened. Loss casts us into emotional turmoil. We miss those we love in sadness and sorrow. We agonize as we take leave of what can no longer be. We dread entering the next chapters of our lives shadowed by their absence.

Our experiences, gestures, and tributes in ceremonies of separation can help us move through our suffering. They can provide a sense of closure on the life we shared as we acknowledge the finality of death. They can give us pause to feel and express the powerful emotions that separation arouses. As we do these last things for those we love, we assuage our feelings of helplessness. Ceremonies are among the first steps we can take to leave the worst of the hurt behind us. We expect too much if we expect that they will end our hurt. Instead, they help us to acknowledge and express it.

Many of us feel our pain most acutely as we spend our last moments together with the bodies of those we have loved. We see them in calling hours or in an open casket. We touch or kiss them for the last time. We speak quiet goodbyes. We feel their weight as pallbearers. We witness their burial, entombment, or cremation.

We feel and express our hurt and anguish privately and publicly. Many of us hold our hurt within or shield it from public view. Many of us remain silent as we witness events and the ritual performances of others. Some of us weep quiet tears. Many bring our sorrows to God in private and public prayer. Still others of us sob, wail, and express our emotions openly.

Some of us go to memorials to cry, give voice to our sorrows, meditate, contemplate, or pray. We can use these places as reservoirs for our hurt. We can lay down our burdens as we "let go" there or find release, peace, or consolation. Some of us more easily return to daily life and carry the residue of pain that remains deep inside, knowing such release is available.

Ceremonies also provide opportunities for us to receive and give emotional comfort and support to one another. We can sit with, stand alongside, and hold one another as we share the life-shattering experience, the history, and the emotions. We can reassure one another that we are not alone by the fact of our presence and in what we do and say. We can feel the power of shared grief. Its healing and uniting force permeates our intimate moments and public gatherings with those who mourn with us. Public ceremonies can respond to our longing for the embrace of family, friendship, and community. Traditional symbols, gestures, objects, sounds, and settings can enable us to feel at one with others who have mourned before us.

Our experiences, gestures, and memorializing in ceremonies of separation can also help us to see how we, like those present at Bryan's funeral and graveside, can still be touched and moved by those who have died. Ceremonies can support us as we look back in time to when the presence of those we love enriched us. We can pause to remember lives of family members or friends now ended. We can bring to mind and acknowledge meanings and values we found in their lives. We can pause to reflect, contemplate, and mediate on what we have known and cherished in sharing life with them. We can remember them in prayer. We can talk with one another about them. We can give thanks for the lives of those no longer present, praise, and pay tribute to them.

Lasting memorials can become a focus for continuing interactions with those who have died. We can experience our visits to memorials as opportunities to be close to those now gone. In those typically quiet, safe places, it can feel comfortable and fitting for us, alone or with others, to sense their continuing presence in our lives. We can remember them tearfully or laughingly, and even reminisce with them. We can tell them about events in our lives and our thoughts and feelings. We can sense how they would react if they could speak. We can praise and express our gratitude, share our hopes, or pray with them.

Ceremonies of separation can lead us to hopeful paths where we can simultaneously carry the pain of separation and love those who have died in new ways. We can realize that their legacies remain with us and that we have memories to cherish. We have practical influences to embrace. We are, and ever will be, different for having known them. We can draw inspiration from them. We can open our hearts and consider how to sustain connection with them as we keep their legacies alive in us in the days that follow. We can find comfort and consolation as we take the first, tentative steps toward lasting love.

Missed Opportunities

It was as if God gave us our baby back so we could say good-bye.

—Mother of a stillborn child

We sometimes miss or abstain from ceremonies of separation. At other times we omit them altogether and do nothing to memorialize those who have died. We go on without pausing to take our leave and thus miss the opportunity to remember and pay tribute. We miss the comfort and support ceremonies give us as we feel and express our hurt. And so we lose the chance to take vital first steps toward loving in separation.

Sometimes we miss out on the benefits of ceremonies inadvertently. Sadness and the ending of the life of someone we all care about bring us together. But we also find ourselves in the middle of rare and welcome reunions. We may spend most or all of our time catching up on the details of our own lives and may be so glad to see one another that we keep the death and the life now ended in the background. We may prefer a happy focus to a sad one. Or the momentum of the event may distract us from remembering.

One family I know has found a way to avoid repeating this pattern. The Rileys had left too many funerals without acknowledging their hurt, giving and receiving comfort, or sharing memories of those who have died as they would have liked. They now acknowledge their joy at seeing one another with a reunion dinner and evening the night before each family funeral. They allow themselves to celebrate meeting again and delight in one another's company. This lessens their distraction from what brought them together.

In the days that follow, they turn their attention to ceremonies of separation. They feel sad together. They reach out to each other and comfort those most immediately affected. And they take full advantage of the time they have to exchange memories of those who have died.

Sometimes we keep ourselves at a physical or emotional distance from ceremonies of separation because they may seem too painful. We often evade ordinary good-byes for this reason. We may fear embarrassing emotional displays or losing control altogether. We may fear that others will not understand or will fail to support or comfort us. We avoid these ceremonies by not appearing at all or by numbing ourselves with drugs or alcohol. But ceremonies of separation when another dies are not occasions for ordinary good-byes. The loss of presence in this life that death entails is final. We risk far greater pain and prolonged anguish when we leave good-byes unsaid or undone when this kind of separation is thrust upon us.

Sometimes well-intentioned others try to protect us from the pain that leave-taking entails, and this often only compounds our anguish.

When Cecilia took an overdose, she was brought to a hospital and eventually referred for a psychiatric consult. The overdose came, as had several other episodes of serious emotional distress, on the anniversary of the stillbirth of her baby eight years earlier. At that time her husband, Renaldo, hospital staff, and a funeral director decided it was best that she neither see the baby nor know the details of the disposition of his body. The therapist connected the overdose with the stillbirth, and Cecilia agreed she needed to do something to address what still troubled her about it. She was angry about the decisions others made for her. She felt she had not said good-bye to her son, Roberto.

The therapist hesitantly approached a chaplain about the possibility of helping with a funeral. The chaplain recognized the power of ritual and agreed to help. A funeral home set the scene near a gravesite with flowers and a child's coffin with a baby blanket inside.

Both parents attended the simple services. The chaplain, having talked with them, was able to speak of both their pain and anguish and of what Roberto meant to them. They opened the coffin. And as she pulled back the blanket, Cecilia swore that she at long last saw the face of her child. The parents wept together and held each other close. They closed the coffin together. Renaldo carried the coffin to the grave and swore that he felt the weight of a baby within it. Cecilia felt for the first time that Renaldo understood, shared some of her hurt, and loved Roberto as she did. Both said it was as if God returned Roberto to them temporarily so they could hold him, say good-bye, and return him to His loving arms. Even long after death ceremonies of separation still help us to heal.

Sometimes we may avoid ceremonies of separation because we misread our own needs for ritual support in this time of separation and transition. We may not fully grasp how rituals, formal or spontaneous, provide stability and order in the midst of chaos and disarray in our lives. We may fail to appreciate the power of symbols and symbolic gestures to help us move through and transcend our present suffering and reconnect with the legacies we still hold. We may fail to appreciate how actively participating counters our feelings of helplessness and passivity in the face of events beyond our control. We may think ourselves more emotionally and socially independent than we really are, underestimating the power of shared grief to comfort and console us.

Sometimes we are excluded from ceremonies of separation because our grieving is dismissed as nonexistent, insignificant, or illegitimate. We may experience our grieving as "disenfranchised." Others may fail to recognize that the very elderly, young children, and the retarded, demented, or otherwise mentally compromised among us also grieve.

When Barry was five, his grandfather Aubry died. His mother, Belinda, and her family expected Aubry's death for a long time. They visited with him often as lingering illness consumed him. Their parents brought Barry's cousins to see Aubry in the last weeks of his life. But Belinda felt that seeing his Grandpa the way he was and saying good-bye would be too difficult for Barry, the youngest grandchild. When Aubry died, Belinda and the others saw little need for a funeral. They had Aubry cremated immediately as he had wished and did not claim his ashes.

Barry's first major loss confused him. The last time he saw Aubry he was very much alive. Where was Grandpa now? His parents' abstract answers didn't help. Barry became visibly anxious. And his temper flared regularly as it had rarely done before.

Belinda approached the funeral director who had handled Aubry's cremation to ask if he could help. With her permission, he talked with Barry. He then suggested that it could help if Belinda secured the others' permission to bury Aubry's ashes. A grave could make it easier to explain where Aubry was. It would be a concrete place Barry could see and visit. Belinda agreed that it could help Barry and admitted it might help her to deal with vague feelings that it "wasn't right" to just leave Aubry's ashes at the funeral home. The others agreed to the burial.

Barry joined his parents, aunts, uncles, cousins, and a minister for a graveside service. He cried in Belinda's arms and whispered "Good-bye, Grandpa" through his tears. He asked his parents to bring him to visit Aubry the next three Sunday afternoons and stayed for brief visits. He was no longer visibly anxious and his tantrums ended.

Others may disenfranchise us as they dismiss the significance of our relationships with the deceased or discount the value of what we lose. This can happen when we lose homosexual partners, extramarital heterosexual partners, stillborns, miscarried or aborted fetuses, loved ones who are severely afflicted or handicapped, pets, prisoners, co-workers, or those from our past, including former spouses, companions, or friends.

Zach, a student in one of my workshops, knows the pain of such exclusion. His parents divorced when he was a teen. He was forced to choose between them and went to live with his mother. His father remarried and began a second family.

Several years later, Zach's father died. Zach was in his early twenties when he appeared at calling hours for his father. He was told by his father's new family that he was not welcome there. They also made it very clear that they did not want to see him at the funeral. Zach was stunned and deeply hurt. He did not wish to make a scene. He withdrew, deferring to their pain. Fortunately, the funeral director saw what had happened and called Zach aside as he was leaving. Together, they found ways for Zach to have time with his father outside the formal ceremonies. Zach was able to do what he needed to without the knowledge of, and without adding to the distress of his father's new family.

Others may find something repugnant about the death itself, for example, in the case of suicide, murder, violent or mutilating death, or in a controversial war like Vietnam. When others are unwilling to acknowledge our hurt and fail to provide social support or even sanction us, disenfranchisement compounds the challenges we face in grieving. Our feelings of abandonment, alienation, guilt and shame, anger, depression, helplessness, and meaninglessness intensify. We may sense that others are oblivious to the good that we found in lives now ended.

Like the Civil War, the Vietnam War divided America against itself. We disagreed profoundly over whether we should be fighting at all, the draft, troop buildups, objectives, strategies, and atrocities. Perhaps most unfortunately, we divided over whether sacrifices in a losing cause, or in what many thought to be a misguided and meaningless conflict, could be meaningful. For the first time in American history, veterans returned home to a country that failed to open its arms in a welcoming embrace. Families and friends buried and memorialized their own. But many sensed that the country was indifferent to their personal losses. They were joined by veterans in their search for a public memorial that would acknowledge and commemorate these losses.

The Vietnam Veterans Memorial, a V-shaped black granite wall that bears the name of every American killed in the war, year by year, was dedicated in 1982, eight years after the war ended. Families and friends of those who died, veterans, and visitors have come to see it as a much needed, belated tribute to the war's participants. The monument has amazing healing power for the nation, veterans, and families of the dead. The V-shape symbolically suggests a terrible wound in the earth itself, the ground on which we live and together survive those listed there. The nation's loss is made tangible and visible. So many, so many names.

None who visit the memorial can fail to think of the horrors of war and of what those who came back alive witnessed and carry within. Many approach the wall to search for the names of individuals whom they knew personally. They weep, pray, and leave flowers or messages. They come alone, or, more often, with friends, family, or fellow veterans. Many sense the nation's embrace of their sorrows and of the sacrifices of those they love.

We pay a price when we miss the opportunities that ceremonies of separation and memorialization provide. We may compound our grieving as we remain suspended in our private suffering. We may hesitate with an uneasy sense that there is something we need to finish before we go on. We may prolong or delay leave-taking and thus compromise the reshaping and the redirecting of our lives that must follow. We may make it more difficult to find a hopeful path toward lasting love.

Frozen Scenes

You cannot understand life and its mysteries as long as you try to grasp it. Indeed, you cannot grasp it, just as you cannot walk off with a river in a bucket.

—Alan Watts

When someone we love dies, we can easily feel as if our world and our very selves are falling apart. An event beyond our control shakes us to the core. So much of what we have taken for granted is no longer possible. Our daily life is in pieces. Our hopes and dreams are shattered and we feel disconnected from others and no longer at home in the world. Our pain cuts deeply. We sense that we can never be the same persons we were. It can seem as if our hearts are broken. A profound change in our world calls for profound changes in us. The death undermines our sense of security. The enormity of the event and the challenges it presents make us fearful and anxious. The death clarifies how tenuous our hold is on the world and what we care most about in it. How vulnerable we feel!

We long for safety and stability in the midst of chaos. We want security and order in our lives. A temporary retreat from our new world can provide stabilizing refuge—a time and place to feel and express our grief and be comforted. It offers an opportunity to take stock and ready ourselves to shape, and move into, a new order in our lives.

Usually, within a relatively short time, our will and pain move us to return to the flow of life and begin to meet the challenges at hand. We begin making changes, however tentatively and painfully, in a world that is so different without our loved one. We do so at our own pace and in our own way. We find some security and stability in parts of our life patterns that remain viable; within our families, with friends, and in our communities as we together reshape and redirect our lives as survivors; as we hold onto some things that were important to those who have died or return to places that still hold special meaning for us; and when we learn to treasure the legacies of those who have died. We begin again to trust that life can bring satisfaction and have purpose and meaning.

Sometimes, though, we do something far different from catching our breath in the face of enormous change and challenge. We attempt to create security and stability by rigidly imposing our wills on ourselves and the world around us.

Tanya was a young woman who still lived with her parents when her father was killed in a car crash. Nearly two years after the accident, she still insisted that her mother change nothing at home. It was as if she were making the world itself, or at least the corner where she lived, a memorial to her father.

Virtually everything Tanya's father left behind was to stay just where it was when he died: his clothing, his workshop and tools, unfinished projects, his desk and its contents, his books and magazines, his shaving kit, even his toothbrush. She pressed her mother to hold to a daily routine that remained just as it had been. When her older siblings came to visit, she demanded that they, too, comply with her wishes. She insisted that holidays and birthdays be marked exactly as they always were. She controlled the others with flare-ups directed at any who dared to question what she wanted.

She looked at me with clenched fists and tears welling in her eyes and said, "It's bad enough that Dad had to die. I don't see why anything else has to change."

Sometimes, like Tanya, we go on as if a temporary retreat from reality is a sustainable way to be in the world. We desperately try to establish stability and order in our lives. We resist any change in our surroundings or ourselves. Or we take command of smaller parts of our worlds and attempt to freeze them in place. We convert a dead child's room into a shrine. We refuse to use, touch, move, give away, or sell a bed. We sanctify a corner filled with a parent's, companion's, or child's belongings or creations. We immobilize a car. We insist that a holiday be celebrated as it always has been, despite the crucial absence of a central character in the celebration.

We court danger when we do these things. We introduce rigidity where there was none before. We petrify our life surroundings. We wrap ourselves in all that is familiar in the hope that we can hold "close" those who have died. But, ironically, we fix in place remnants of what was, but obviously is no longer. It becomes painfully clear that the one thing we cannot do is meet our loved one again in the frozen sets of our lives. Their lives are no longer vital forces there. As we hold things and places still, we strip them of their dynamic flow and power. They no longer move, inspire, nurture, or sustain us. As we cling to once easy and purposeful routines, they become obsessively repetitive. As we unbendingly walk through celebrations as before, they lose all spontaneity.

We often don't stop at freezing our physical surroundings. We powerfully resist allowing any new feelings, actions, thoughts, expectations, or hopes into our lives. We struggle to engage in life as much as possible as before, working around the emptiness as best we can. We resist going in new directions without those we love by our sides. We block the rhythm of our lives and transform them into unending ceremonies of separation.

We may fear the unknown. Or we may fear that we will fall apart emotionally if we allow ourselves to move and change.

Sensing our own vulnerability, we defend ourselves by refusing to change our life's pattern or direction in a world that requires it. We may insist that "the only difference is that she (or he) is not here." But our insisting does not make it so. His or her death is not a simple fact. Its effects ripple through our life patterns and life histories and those of our fellow survivors.

When we persist in resisting change in ourselves or our surroundings, we stall in coming to terms with the reality of what has happened. We may be tempted to believe that "I am dealing with it." And it is not that we are doing nothing. Often our efforts require more and more time and energy. They can become all-consuming and exhausting. However, they do not take us to a better place. They do not bring the comfort, stability, and safety we want. Instead, we find ourselves becoming hypersensitive, increasingly agitated, and anxious as we strain to hold everything and ourselves together.

Ultimately, we cannot succeed. We attempt to control the flow of life itself, to make ourselves invulnerable. The wall we build against that flow most likely will develop leaks and eventually burst. Or we may so isolate ourselves from others that life will find a new course and leave us behind in a stagnant pool.

We typically freeze the world or ourselves in place without considering how we affect our fellow survivors. None dare question what we do. We demand complicity. We angrily resist disagreement, even discussion, or attempts by others to change what has been touched by those who have died.

When we do these things, we stifle interaction and strain ties with our family and friends. We risk alienating them and isolating ourselves. At the very least, this compounds our hurt. It can also add to our losses, if our anger or manipulation drives others away. They, in turn, also lose us.

It is one thing to set our own pace as we come to terms with our surroundings. We can steady ourselves in our own, private routines as we wish. We can take our time as we approach and deal with things, places, or occasions that are especially challenging and deal with them in our own ways. We can ask, and reasonably expect, others to be patient and respect our feelings and needs. We can also join with family and friends to decide together how best to deal with things, places, routines, and occasions that matter to us.

But if we act as if we are the only ones challenged by aspects of our surroundings, or as if only our wants and needs matter, we may offend others and lose their comfort and support. It is plainly not fair to insist that our need for stability and order take precedence over all else. Failure to respect our fellow survivors in these ways can, and often will, hurt them. They may or may not tolerate and forgive us. In either case, we will have been a very difficult presence in their own difficult circumstances.

Family and friends may defer to us in fear of angry words, explosive behaviors, or ugly exchanges. If they recognize how much we hurt, they may decline to confront us. They may not only defer to us but also offer attention, patience, and sympathy. These may tempt us to remain immobile in a world that ultimately demands that we move and change.

We need and deserve others' sympathy and comfort as we grieve. We also sometimes need help and support from family members, friends, survivor groups, or professionals. They can aid us in moving away from helplessness or inertia toward active engagement with our new lives, and onto hopeful paths.

We are especially fortunate when we find others who have walked or otherwise know paths out of mourning and despair. When they become trustworthy companions to us in our grief, they provide some of the safety and security we need. They can help us rediscover familiar sources of security and stability in our lives or find new ones. They can assist us in appreciating how love is dynamic and ever changing and that it cannot survive stagnation. They can help us explore how to find places in our hearts for lives now ended.

Even when we begin to fall into rigid patterns, our spirits remain remarkably resilient. Aversion to continued agony and stagnation itself moves us. Belated recognition of the futility of freezing life helps us change direction. We can seek to hold those who have died in memory in ways that do not drain us, or them, of life. Hope of finding lasting love with the person who has died can provide our most powerful incentive. Ceremonies of separation or memorials we create with others can be among our first steps toward healing.

We go too far when we attempt to fix in place, or make memorials of, the world or potentially vital corners of it. Permanent memorials fix something in place off center stage in our lives. They help us to remember lives now ended even as we find a new rhythm of life in an ever-changing world.

We go too far when we fix our attention permanently on the experience of loss and, in effect, make our own lives perpetual ceremonies of separation. Effective ceremonies fix our attention momentarily. In them, we pause to acknowledge what has happened and absorb the first sharp pangs of the hurt it brings into our lives. As we remember and pay tribute, we take our first halting steps in the transition from loving in presence to loving in separation.

Investing Ourselves
in Ceremonies

It was my job. I was his son. It was my love.

—Roy Nichols

Darnell needed blood transfusions for his hemophilia. One transfusion infected him with HIV and the virus gave him AIDS. While Darnell was still alive, his parents, Floyd and Dinah, joined with others to call for greater public awareness of the plights of those who had the disease and those who loved them, the dangers of the epidemic, and the need for more effective response.

Darnell died while still a young boy. Many from the AIDS community as well as family and friends joined Floyd and Dinah for Darnell's funeral and burial services.

Floyd and Dinah welcomed the opportunity to make a memorial panel for the NAMES Project AIDS Memorial Quilt. As thousands had with other panels, they invested Darnell's with their love. Floyd helped with the planning, sat and remembered with Dinah, and held some pieces in place as she did the sewing. They chose Darnell's favorite color, red, for the background. They placed Darnell's name and the dates of his birth and death at the top. Together they decided on a cross for Darnell's love of God, a rocket ship for his love of science and science fiction, and a cocker spaniel for his love of Sparky. For themselves, they added the words, "We will always love you."

Common threads of love tie Floyd and Dinah and fellow AIDS survivors to those whose lives they cherish and to one another in shared sorrow. Those threads are woven symbolically into each individual panel of the memorial quilt that represents something of the character of the one who died and others' love for him or her. Common threads of sympathy and compassion tie the dying to one another and unite their survivors in a community of survivorship and a sense of collective loss. Those threads are woven symbolically into the quilt in the ties that bind the panels together. How powerfully healing for Floyd and Dinah was the experience of weaving those threads into the quilt with their own hands.

No one can grieve for us. Nor can anyone stand in for us as we feel the pain of separation. Grieving is an active process of coming to terms with what has happened to us. We experience the full power and support of ceremonies of separation when we, like Floyd and Dinah, join in planning for them, participate actively, and choose or use symbols that bear our own meanings. The more we invest ourselves personally in ceremonies of separation, the more directly we engage with the pain and in the movement from loving in presence to loving in separation. As we do these last things for those we love, we also do them for ourselves and our grief.

We can, and often do, find support in grieving when we witness the ritual performances of others, identify with them, and resonate with the symbols they use. Sometimes, though, we find such rituals empty and sterile. We may feel distant from or unmoved by the proceedings. We may feel that others' expectations and choices, rather than any of our own needs and preferences, are reflected in what we see and hear. We may not identify with what those performing the rituals are doing or saying. The symbols others have chosen may not speak to us. We may feel disconnected because we are spectators rather than participants.

Typically, when someone we love dies, we feel passive, powerless, and helpless in the face of events beyond our control.

Watching and listening to others perform rituals, especially when they have planned them without taking our needs or preferences into account, can reinforce these feelings. We can counter these feelings in several ways. We can try to become part of the planning or at least ask that our suggestions be considered. We can ask to participate in public ceremonies if we wish and suggest ways we would like to be included. If these efforts fail, we can seek ways to say and do what we feel we need to alone or with close companions outside the context of formal rituals. We can plan and participate in our own simple ceremonies of separation.

Roy Nichols, then a funeral director, was often a guest in my classes and workshops. He captivated us with stories of how he helped families and individuals find ways to participate meaningfully in ceremonies of separation.

Roy had been a funeral director for over ten years when his own father died in a hospital in 1973. Roy's mother and brother were there, and Roy held his father's hand as he died. They wept. Roy was far from home, so he called a funeral director from nearby. When the men came from the funeral home, Roy, without explanation, asked them to stand aside as he positioned the cot and lifted his father's body onto it himself. He felt a sense of desertion as the two strangers turned to leave, his dad with them.

Another funeral director did the embalming, but Roy did everything else. He filled in the death certificate, notified newspapers, contacted the cemetery, arranged for the church with the minister, and notified family, friends, and neighbors. He knew how to do many of these things because he was a funeral director. But, he says, he did them because it was his dad, and he was his son.

In the days that followed he and his family participated fully in ceremonies of separation. They came from long distances. Attending to the details and sharing responsibilities renewed closeness among them. They had an impromptu prayer service the night before the funeral along with clergy and friends. They joined in a circle that included his dad's body in a casket. They spoke openly about his life and death and their own senses of mortality and immortality. They tucked him into his casket and closed it themselves. They carried him to his grave, lowered him into it, and shoveled the dirt in themselves. In Roy's words, "We closed out his life ourselves."

This event was not only an emotional turning point for Roy, it also changed his understanding of his role as a funeral director. He wondered how often he had been the stranger in others' lives. How often had he done things for sons, daughters, parents, and spouses that they might meaningfully do themselves? How often had he made decisions for them on the assumption that they would find it too difficult?

Roy resolved to refocus his funeral practice on the needs of those he was helping to take their first steps in grieving individually and together as families and communities. He vowed to make it clear to them that ceremonies of separation are theirs to shape and experience as they choose. He came to believe it was his professional obligation to provide them with every opportunity they might want to participate.

I always had to tell my classes and workshops that not all funeral directors, clergy, or others whom we might approach for assistance in ceremonies of separation do what Roy did. Few feel, as he does, that we have a right to be told about the full range of ways we can interact with the bodies of those we love and participate in ceremonies. Few establish the atmosphere of permission that he did.

Many, however, are very receptive to initiatives and requests from the family to be more involved. They are happy to work with us to decide what might be most meaningful. They, like Roy, recognize the value of participation.

Unhappily, many others still practice as Roy did before his father died. They believe their role is to plan and do for others on the basis of what they take to be in their best interests. Their paternalism is often very well intentioned. But they often leave those they serve as passive witnesses to what they do and say on their behalf. Sometimes, sadly, they even discourage initiatives and deny requests when people ask to be involved.

I will always admire Roy for his courage to change course in his funeral practice because of his own personal experience as a bereaved son. Many responded warmly to him when he came and told his stories. And many returned to me later and told me how they used his wisdom when those they loved died. They took initiatives and found great meaning in even the simplest participation in ceremonies of separation.

Choosing Our Own Ways

*What matters is not what life does to you but rather what
you do with what life does to you.*

—Edgar Jackson

We must gauge for ourselves what balance between
spectator and participant roles is appropriate in ceremonies of
separation, including creating memorials. Total immersion, like
Fran and Bob's when Bryan died, is not for everyone. But even
modest participation can make ceremonies of separation more
meaningful. We can look for opportunities as they arise in our
own experiences.

Roy Nichols told stories of how he began to offer options
very early in his talks with those who came to his funeral home.
They could do something, like contacting the newspapers or
arranging with churches, or he could do it for them. In a little
while he would ask them what they decided.

Sometimes, they said "yes" to all his open invitations, divided
responsibilities, and totally immersed themselves. In their own
ways, and in terms of their own needs, styles, and preferences,
they planned and did virtually everything themselves, as Roy and
his family had.

At the other end of the spectrum, some mourners declined
virtually every opportunity to take part in the ceremonies they

planned. Even then, they were actively engaged in deciding to witness rather than participate—no one else had decided that for them. And Roy had established an atmosphere in which they knew it would be okay to act spontaneously as their needs and spirits moved them.

Most often, those who came to Roy chose to participate in some ways and to leave the rest in others' hands. Some notified newspapers and telephoned friends. Some parents cleaned and dressed their dead children. Some held and rocked them while planning the arrangements or during calling hours or funerals. Daughters and sisters did their mother's or sister's hair or makeup. Many selected special items of clothing or jewelry and some placed these on or with the one who died. Often mourners found ways to talk to, pray over, look at, touch, hold, kiss, spend time with, or say good-bye to the bodies of those they loved. Many placed notes, letters, poems, or mementos with their loved ones. About a third closed caskets themselves. A few even built wooden coffins with Roy's help.

Some assumed roles during calling hours and wakes, standing in receiving lines, making sure that guest registers or books of condolence were signed, seeing to the physical and emotional needs of others. Some held informal gatherings, remember-when sessions, or prayer services.

Some served as pallbearers or found other roles in processions. Some buried or entombed their loved ones or scattered their ashes in places that held special meaning. Others donated their bodies, or parts of them, for medical use. Some participated actively in burials or cremations, while others symbolically threw dirt or flowers into, or on, fresh graves. Many added personal touches to designs for grave markers, established memorials at home, or in other creative ways memorialized those who died.

Many found ways to personalize and shape public ceremonies. They chose music to be played or performed it. They chose readings and prayers, and some read or led them. A few presented eulogies or spoke more informally about their memories of, and love for, the family member or friend who had died. Some invited any in attendance at public ceremonies to join in tributes, give voice to their feelings, offer prayers, or the like, as they felt moved at the time.

Many of the opportunities for participation that Roy invited people to consider were extremely painful. He told us that he recognizes that it is only human to seek to avoid pain and difficulty. He also said that he believes that sometimes doing what is hard can also be very meaningful. This may be especially so when it supports our grieving, which is itself difficult.

He said that if he, or anyone, were to ask someone for immediate decisions about hard choices, most would turn away from likely painful opportunities. So he deliberately put those he counseled in positions where they did not have to decide immediately. The interval gave them time to pause, entertain second thoughts, and sometimes choose to do difficult things themselves. For some, it became clear that they could perform these rituals better themselves or that it made sense, given the relationship they had with their loved one. Many felt they would be in a better place themselves emotionally if they did it.

Roy observed that few would choose at first blush to close a casket. That simple physical movement is an emotionally and symbolically charged gesture of finality. Like few others, it can bring home the reality of the loss of presence. Roy regularly told people that when the time came to close the casket he would ask them if they would like to leave immediately, stay with the body a while and then leave, stay and watch him close the casket, or take their time and, when they were ready, close it themselves. Few left immediately. Between a third and half closed the casket themselves.

Roy was very firm in his feeling that he had no right to make any decision for another about the value of potentially very painful experiences and gestures.

Roy told us the story of a widow whose husband had been burned terribly in a plane crash. He knew it would not be easy for her, but Roy felt an obligation to let her choose whether she wanted to see her husband's body. He gave her a day to make up her mind. Had he asked her on the spot, she later said, she would have turned away from such a painful experience.

When he asked her the next day, however, she chose to see her husband. To prepare her, to avoid shock and trauma, and to give her a chance to change her mind, Roy asked her permission to tell her in explicit detail what she would encounter. She still chose to have the experience.

She brought in a flight jacket and placed it on her husband's charred remains in the casket. Painful as this was, she no doubt found it a most meaningful gesture.

Another of Roy's stories illustrates how even very modest and spontaneous gestures in ceremonies of separation can mean a great deal to us.

In his usual manner, Roy repeatedly gave a widower choices of either doing things for himself or having Roy do them. The man deferred to Roy every time. Roy then did his "funeral director thing" of doing for others.

The day of the funeral, Roy offered the man the choice of driving the hearse to the cemetery. He declined. With his permission, Roy offered the same choice to the man's son. He accepted. The widower then decided to ride with his son. Roy would follow in a separate car.

On the drive to the cemetery, the lead car took a "wrong turn." The son drove to a section of town with broad lawns, to the home where the couple had lived for over thirty years. Driver and passenger changed places in the hearse. The widower drove up on the couple's lawn and then twice around the house. Only then did the processional head for the cemetery. The widower found within the atmosphere of permission Roy had established an opportunity to do something that had meaning for him.

Among the most affecting stories Roy ever told were those about children. They have worlds to relearn, too. Often deaths are unprecedented events for them, and they depend on adults in so many ways for support and guidance in finding their ways as they grieve.

Children do well when their parents and others make it clear that their experiences matter, that they are cared for and welcome by their sides. They do well when they are helped to understand and their questions are answered: When they are told what happened and about ceremonies of separation honestly, in words they understand, and in ways that do not mislead them into fantasy, and when others give them opportunities to see, hear, and explore for themselves.

Children are helped to deal with their hurt when others open their arms to them, do not hide their own feelings, and make it clear that it is okay to be sad or feel whatever they are feeling. Like adults, children do well when they are helped to deal with their own helplessness in the face of circumstances beyond their control—when they are told that no one will force them to do anything they do not want to do, and that they will be given choices about whether and how they might want to participate in ceremonies of separation.

Most often children choose to be present with their parents at the ceremonies. Some opt to see those who have died, to touch or kiss them. Others place toys, even loaded squirt guns, drawings, or notes with the bodies. They choose to help in preparations for when visitors come to their homes. They take charge of registration or condolence books. They aid other children who come for calling hours. They help select what clothing is be used, especially when a brother or sister has died. They pick a piece of music for calling hours, a funeral, or a graveside service. Some choose to ride in the hearse to the cemetery, to place a flower on a coffin, or to throw dirt into a grave. Some insist on staying until graves are filled to ensure that "everything is done right."

Conflicts about Ceremonies

Aren't I special, too, Mommy?
—A bereaved brother

🌾 *Olaf, Inge's husband, died when he was seventy-four. Before he died, he often spoke with her and their children about what his funeral would be like. He knew there would be crying, but he hoped not much. He knew that someone would talk about him, and he hoped they would at least be fair. And he said that he didn't want any women soloists. He knew Inge loved sopranos, but he couldn't resist adding, "I'm afraid I might hear the screeching and not be able to get up and walk out."*

When Olaf died, Inge made the funeral arrangements herself. She asked her pastor to invite a soprano from the church choir to sing one of her favorite hymns. She was sure Olaf had been joking just to tease her and that he would neither hear nor be distressed.

The soloist's beautiful singing comforted Inge. But Lars, Inge's oldest son, resented his mother's decision. When he spoke with me he said, "I can't understand how she could do such a thing when Dad was so clear about what he wanted. How could she be so selfish? I'll never forgive her."

When George's wife, Agnes, died, he and their children agreed to go ahead with the arrangements the couple had made through their local Memorial Society. Neither Agnes nor George wanted the "fuss" or the expense of a traditional funeral. Both believed they would have little difficulty getting on with their lives without ceremony. And they wanted to spare one another and their families the pain of a public good-bye. So, Agnes was cremated immediately and there was no funeral. George took the urn containing her ashes and placed it on a closet shelf at home.

It wasn't long before several of George and Agnes's friends told him that it felt like "something is missing or not finished." They asked his permission to plan a gathering to remember Agnes and close out her life together. George recognized that others might have needs that he had overlooked and welcomed their overtures. He checked with his children, and several admitted they had some of the same feelings.

Two weeks after she died, Agnes's family and friends joined in a memorial service for her. One friend organized a bulletin board with photos of Agnes and her friends. Her children prepared a family photo album to be passed around. Arrangements were made for a piano, and a friend played several of Agnes's favorite songs while the others sang along. Several told stories about Agnes, how she had touched their lives, and how they would remember her. George spoke about Agnes's illness, her last days, and how much he loved her. He said it felt good to learn how much the others loved her, too. And he voiced a suspicion that somehow Agnes had overheard them all and was pleased they came together as they did.

After consulting with his children, George chose to bury Agnes's ashes in a nearby cemetery. That way family and friends could come to pay their respects or visit whenever they wished.

We do not come to terms with loss alone. This may comfort and console us, but it also complicates our grieving and relearning the world. Each of us walks an individual path in grieving. But our paths intersect frequently since the worlds we experience include many of the same things, places, and other people. We also walk collective paths in grieving—we share responsibility and have our own parts to play as we transform the ties of love and association that bind us within our families and communities.

Our ways of dealing with our losses mutually affect one another. It hurts to see others hurting. We worry about each other. We wish we understood better what separation means to others, or that we were understood better by them. We may or may not be available to support and comfort one another. We want to keep our families and communities intact.

We experience many ceremonies of separation together. Effective ceremonies support us as individuals and as families and communities during our grief. But our desires and expectations about individual and collective grieving as we plan such ceremonies of separation will almost inevitably conflict.

We can disagree on so many things. Who is to have a say in what is done? How do you take into account the needs of young children? Will there be calling hours, a funeral, a memorial service, a committal ceremony, a wake, or any formal ceremonies at all? The timing and location of such events are also at issue. What is to be done with the body of the one who has died? What activities, gestures, and symbols will be included in ceremonies? Who, if anyone, will participate actively and what will they do? Should there be a memorial, and, if so, of what type?

Sometimes we resolve conflicts about these matters smoothly and find our way through supportive ceremonies, as George and the rest of Agnes's family did. Sometimes we agree to disagree without difficulty. Often we come to impasses, as Inge and her son Lars did after Olaf died. Interaction breaks down and we fail to make decisions that satisfy us.

We compound the tragedy of loss when we allow disagreements about ceremonies and memorials to come between us. Heated conflict, new tensions, lingering ill will, and even permanent splits can result. When they do, we add more bad memories to those of the death itself and the anguish that followed. We put unfinished business in place that can interfere with our remembering and cherishing the legacies of those who have died.

To avoid such consequences, we need sensitivity, tolerance, mutual respect, and skills in communication. We must recognize that each of us is affected differently by the death and that we can work to understand, tolerate, and respect differences. We can find ways to say and do what we need to privately and not concern ourselves about what others think. Often we can juggle schedules so that some can do what they feel they must while others stay away. We can appreciate how we find different values and meanings in music, readings, traditional practices, symbols, gestures, and participation. We can understand that we vary greatly in how we carry and express our hurt, give and accept support and comfort, remember and pay tribute, find peace and consolation, and understand and hold the legacies of those who have died.

We can recognize that we may need to change our previous expectations of one another and the roles we play in our families and communities and that no one among us alone controls the shape of family and community grieving or the ceremonies and memorials that support it. We can take care to include as many as possible in decision-making. When it is not practical to include all in planning, we can do our best to take into account the desires and needs of all who will witness, or might want to participate in, what we plan. We can seek ways for all to participate actively who wish to do so and we can use whatever abilities we have to cooperate, negotiate, and compromise as we bear in mind what seems best for our families or communities.

The potential for hurt, conflict, and disagreement is especially acute when we sometimes decide to memorialize at home.

I have often heard my wife, a specialist in sibling bereavement, tell a story about a home memorial for a dead child. The mother chose to permanently display drawings by her dead daughter, Amy, on the wall in the family eating area. The father deferred to his wife's pain and wishes.

Adam, Amy's surviving younger brother, asked if some of his drawings could also be put on the wall. His mother said, "No, that is a special wall because Amy can't make any more pictures for me. You can make Mommy a lot more pictures." A discussion with Adam brought his hurt to the surface. He said it made him feel as if he wasn't good enough to be thought as special as his sister since he was still alive to draw other pictures.

There is no problem when we sometimes simply delay dealing with places in our homes and their contents until we are ready. But sometimes we inadvertently make them into ineffective memorials when we begin to treat them as inviolable means to preserve connection to those who have died. We need to be careful not to petrify our intimate life surroundings, to strip them of their capacities to move, inspire, nurture, or sustain us. Places permeated with absence make poor memorials. They become repositories only of pain and do not nurture our souls or spirits.

Sometimes, like Adam's mother, we make a personal decision to establish memorials in clearly shared spaces in our homes. We may insist that a portrait or favorite chair remain in place and be treated as sacred. We may choose to display a prized possession of the deceased, like a favorite piece of clothing, something he or she made, or a beloved plaything, in an entrance hall, living or family room, or kitchen, where it had never been before. We may create something and insist that it be displayed where others will see it daily. In any of these ways we intrude without permission into the lives of those who live with us. We force them to have experiences whether they want them or not.

When we make unilateral moves at home, we presume dangerously. What we do on our own in especially sensitive areas or in shared spaces is almost inevitably hurtful and destructive. Others must live under the same roof with whatever memorials we establish. We need to know and take into account how what we do may affect them. Acting on presumption can drive us apart and add to our sorrows in the very places where we long most to come together and find peace and consolation.

We may fairly safely choose to establish a memorial in a private place in our home, say in our own bedroom or in an office or hobby space that everyone recognizes as ours. We may place a cherished photo or other object, or cluster several of them, where we and we alone are likely to encounter them regularly. We can use items that have been ours all along or secure agreement from others to use objects that we have held in common. We can create something that suits us. We can allow others to enter our private spaces unintrusively, if they, too, choose to visit the memorial we establish. We can recognize that others may want personal memorials of their own.

We can also successfully establish memorials in shared spaces in our homes when we plan together, agree about them, and are sensitive to how they will affect all who live with us.

In How We Grieve, *I tell the story of Bill and Diane, a couple whose three young children, Ann, Mike, and Jimmy, and Diane's sister, Mary, died in a terrible accident in their own home. They chose to build a new house because the site of the accident was filled with haunting memories and visions.*

When I visited Bill and Diane in their new home several years later, they showed me a memorial display for their dead children in an entrance hall. It consisted of several shelves of pictures with a few mementos from their lives.

Bill and Diane had two more children, born after the others had died. They were very sensitive about not treating them as replacements for those who had died and about helping them to understand that there are other members of the family who lived before them. The memorial display also included pictures of their living children and items that they wanted on the shelves alongside things from their older sister and brothers. Bill and Diane told me that they hoped the memorial would say to their children, living and dead, "We love you all. You are each very special to us."

III

Memories

Holding Them in Memory

And Hamed lived again—in the hearts of all who remembered him.
—Sue Alexander

The direct simplicity of a children's story can touch adult hearts as few things can. Sue Alexander's *Nadia the Willful* is a perfect example. It charms and moves me whenever I read it. I ask those in my audiences to close their eyes and listen as I recite the engaging, full text aloud to them.

Nadia was a Bedouin girl who lived in the desert with her father, the sheik Tarik, her mother, and six brothers. They called her Nadia the Willful because she was stubborn and had a fiery temper. The oldest brother, Hamed, was her father's favorite son. Only he could tame Nadia's temper and bring her to laughter. She followed him wherever he went.

One day, Hamed mounted his father's stallion and rode off in search of grazing land for the sheep. He never returned. After extensive searching, Tarik realized that Hamed was dead, claimed by the drifting sands. He told Nadia. She screamed and wept, crying repeatedly, "Not even Allah will take Hamed from me!" until Tarik insisted she be silent. Both were inconsolable.

Tarik sat silently, alone in his tent. He spoke to no one for days. On the seventh day he came out of his tent and assembled the clan. He proclaimed that from that day no one was to speak of Hamed or even mention his name. He would punish anyone severely for reminding him of what he had lost. All were afraid. All obeyed.

Nadia, too, fell silent. But she could not help remembering Hamed. She passed her brothers at play and remembered games Hamed taught her. She passed women weaving, talking and laughing, and remembered stories Hamed told that made her laugh. She saw shepherds with their flock and remembered Hamed's love for a black lamb.

As she remembered, Hamed's name came to her, but she did not speak it. As her silence persisted, her unhappiness grew. She cried and raged. Others avoided her. Her loneliness increased.

One day she passed her brothers playing. She corrected them as they made wrong moves in a game Hamed had taught her. She spoke his name. Her brothers looked around in fear that Tarik may have heard. He was nowhere in sight, so they asked her what Hamed had shown her. Speaking of Hamed eased the pain of missing him. She had similar experiences with the women weaving and the shepherds. They were afraid at first. But the women then laughed as she told Hamed's tales. And the shepherds told their own stories of Hamed and the little black lamb.

Nadia's mother warned her and reminded her of Tarik's promise of punishment. She didn't know how to tell her mother how talking about Hamed eased her hurt, so she said simply, "I will speak of my brother! I will!" The more she spoke of him, the more clearly she could remember Hamed's face and voice, the less she hurt, and the less angry she felt. She found peace. Others who listened and spoke with her could also see his face and hear his voice.

One day a shepherd came to Nadia's tent and called out about "Hamed's black lamb." Tarik, not Nadia, emerged from the tent. Fiercely, he declared that the shepherd must leave the oasis by sunset, never to return. Nadia protested, but Tarik responded, "I have spoken." The shepherd prepared to leave.

Returned to silence, Nadia's memories began to fade, her pain intensified, her temper heated, and peace left her. Unable to stand it any longer, she went to her father. "You will not rob me of my brother, Hamed!" she insisted. Tarik glared. Speaking before he could, Nadia asked Tarik if he could see Hamed's face or hear his voice. He told her that he could not though he sat for days on the spot where last he saw Hamed and tried to bring him to mind. Nadia's father wept.

Nadia then explained that there was a way and asked Tarik to listen. She began to speak of her brother, walks they had taken, talks they had had. She went on about the games, Hamed's stories, and the way he calmed her when she was angry. Her memories were rich and varied. When she finished, she asked her father again if he could see Hamed's face and hear his voice. Tarik nodded and smiled through his tears. Nadia said, "Now you see, there is a way that Hamed can be with us still."

After some time of quiet reflection, Tarik, in a voice once again gentle, asked Nadia to bring his people together. When they came, he proclaimed, "From this day forward, let my daughter Nadia be known not as Willful, but as Wise. And let her name be praised in every tent, for she has given me back my beloved son." Kindness and graciousness returned to the oasis. Hamed lived again.

We, like Nadia, her father, and the others in the story, have so much to cherish in those we love and the lives we share with them. We know and love them so variously, no two of us in identical ways. Each of us gives and receives in unique daily life patterns and histories with them. They also hold distinctive places in the patterns and histories of our family and community.

Death wrenches their physical presence from us; we can no longer share life with them as we once did. But death does not extinguish our deep desire to cherish them and what we found in life with them. As Nadia knows instinctively, and as she teaches her father, we can fulfill that desire only if we remember. Memory returns them to us in our separation. We can once again see their faces, hear their voices, and love them still. When we actively bring them to mind or reminisce, we can redeem the best of them and our lives together. Only through memory can we consciously acknowledge, explore, appreciate, and cultivate their legacies.

Sometimes the pain of missing those we love can overwhelm us, as it did Nadia's father. When it does, we may do as he did. We may, in effect, declare that the past shall be treated as if it never happened. We refuse to speak about it and come down hard on those who remind us of it. We then choose, though not deliberately, to avoid the pain of loss and separation at the expense of not remembering. We cut off conscious access to all that we still hold dear of those who have died. We remain different for having known them, and we have much to be grateful for, but we choose not to bring these things to mind. We compound our own bereavement and separation. We deprive ourselves of the riches our memories can bring us.

Sometimes our experience is like Nadia's. Others around us signal, forcefully or subtly, that they prefer silence about those who have died. This can suggest that those we loved were barely noticed or are easily forgotten. The larger world seems determined to "return to normal," as if they were never here. When this happens, the world feels cold and terribly indifferent just when we crave warmth and compassion. Our unhappiness grows as the silence exaggerates our sense of separation from those who have died.

When even those closest to us appear determined not to speak of the dead, we feel alone in our grief. We can sense, however wrongly, that we were the only ones touched by those who have died or that no one loved them as much as we did. Sometimes we feel guilty as we join this complicity of silence and succumb to its pressures. We hold our hurt inside and leave memories unspoken to meet others' expectations and avoid censure. Where silence prevails, we again compound our bereavement.

Memory brings aspects of the past into present awareness. When we remember those we love, we reconnect with them even as we continue in new and unexpected directions. This connection is fragile when compared to connection in their presence—but it is nevertheless substantial and precious.

Conscious remembering and shared reminiscing enrich our present living. And they enable us to carry much of lasting value into the future. Memory allows us to reclaim and revive our appreciation of those we still love and the gifts they continue to give us. We can cherish their legacies here and now. We take delight in having known and loved them. As we cherish them, we experience again the praise, gratitude, and joy they bring to our hearts.

Unfinished Business

I only hope you can forgive me for not doing better with my fears of letting go.

—A bereaved mother

The last conversation Jessica had with her son, Shawn, haunted her. She had been sharply critical of his refusing to turn down the stereo in his room. And she couldn't resist launching into an old refrain about his leaving the room in disarray. Shawn had lashed back at her. He insisted he "needed space" and that he was more responsible than she seemed to think. He said he sometimes wished she would just get off his back. In the middle of their argument, Shawn's friend honked his horn in the driveway and Shawn stormed out the door. He died in a car crash later that night.

Jessica loved Shawn dearly. She wanted to remember the delights of raising him and the many wonderful times they shared. But she could not forget their last moments together.

One afternoon she decided to write a letter addressed to Shawn. She poured out all that was in her heart. For her part, she was sorry. She asked him to forgive her for making such a fuss over what really was "his space." She wrote,

I hope you know deep down that I was probably upset by something I never told you. Your room was the first declaration of your inde-

pendence. It reminded me that I had to let go of you one day. I'm not sure I've ever been ready for that. I was holding on to mothering my little boy, and you were on your way to being a fine young man. There is really nothing for me to forgive. You were doing what all young boys must do. I only hope you can forgive me for not doing better with my fears of letting go.

She went on to tell him how much it hurt to think that he left this world with their last moments on his mind. She closed with

I know you may not have gotten past those last words when death took you. But I want you to know that I believe you would have had you lived. I know your heart was too good for that not to be so. I will love you always. Thank you for being such a wonderful son and loving me. May peace be with us both.

—Mom

The next day Jessica brought her letter to Shawn's grave. She wept as she read aloud what she had written to him. It said what she needed him to know. As she read, she imagined Shawn saying what she needed to hear in return. He understood, and, yes, he loved her. She felt peace between them.

When she returned home, Jessica sealed the envelope and placed it in the back of the scrapbook of Shawn's life she had been assembling over the years. The last conversation and its extension at the graveside were part of her life with Shawn. The letter about them seemed to belong in that scrapbook. Sealing the envelope meant to her that she was now done with that conversation. She had put away the pain and anguish it aroused. In the days that followed, more pleasant memories of life with Shawn began to flood Jessica's thoughts.

I think again of the story of Bill and Diane, whose three young children died in their home in an accident while Bill and Diane were away. Bill told me he was troubled by a memory about the week before they died. He had taken his family to church and his son, Jimmy, wanted to sit in the front row. For some reason, Bill felt *uneasy. He ushered everyone into the second row. Jimmy stood through most of the service, leaning toward, and more than once nearly falling into, the front pew. It was one of his last wishes and it hurt Bill to remember how he had denied Jimmy such a simple thing.*

When the priest and Bill were planning the funeral, the priest said he was concerned that it might be difficult for people to confront so many caskets at the front of the church. Bill insisted that they be there. He told me it was his way to belatedly grant Jimmy's wish.

Often there is unfinished business between us and those whom we have loved and who loved us in return. This is especially so when death is sudden and unexpected, but it can be part of any loss experience. Questions remain unanswered. Exchanges are left in suspense. We resent or disapprove of something they did or said; we regret something we did or said. They have hurt us—we have hurt them. Unresolved tensions linger in the air and we wish we could have said good-byes. We wish that they, or we, had said "I love you" more often.

Unfinished business unsettles us. It may even deeply distress us, especially when we leave it unfinished. Preoccupation with it can easily cloud our memories of all that was good in our relationships with those who have died. Unwelcome memories of unfinished business crowd out other happier memories we would welcome.

Some of us deal with unfinished business in ineffective ways that can even perpetuate our hurt. We may find it hard, or refuse, to acknowledge troubling or painful episodes in our relationships. We may ignore them or discount their significance. We may attempt to swallow or bury them and succumb to pressures not to "speak ill of the dead." We try in these ways to put unfinished business out of mind just because memories of it and the feelings they arouse are unwelcome.

When we act this way, we leave our unfinished business un-finished. We suppress our hurt and distress rather than addressing or resolving it. It lingers in the background of our experience and can reemerge at times when it is least welcome. It can interfere with our remembering and cherishing the legacies of lives now ended. We need to seek ways to lay what troubles us to rest. As a friend is fond of saying, "Bury it dead, not alive."

In order to deal with unfinished business, we must first honestly acknowledge that we are troubled about how things were between us and we need to identify specifically what troubles us. Sometimes that is obvious, as it was for Jessica and Bill. Sometimes it is not. When it is not, it can help to review what it was like when those who have died were alive. We can take notes as we do, either in our heads, or (better) on paper.

We can begin by remembering what we liked or admired about those who have died, recalling all the good we have known in them and in our relationship. Most often, as it did for Jessica and Bill, the good will far outweigh what troubles us.

We can then more easily remember irritations, disappointments, difficult episodes, slights, and heartaches. As we do, we need to remind ourselves that mixed feelings come with the territory in most, if not all, close relationships. Even the finest characters have flaws. Even the best relationships have knots and loose ends. Loving someone is compatible with not approving all that he or she did or said. And, of course, we sometimes fail them. They and we, as Jessica and Bill came to realize, are only human.

For each detail we identify that troubles us, we can use our imaginations to think of ways to relieve our hurt or find some resolution or closure. We can seek answers to questions that plague us from other sources. It may turn out that only the deceased knew the answer. If so, our imaginations may enable us to understand how they would have answered. Jessica's imagination assured her that Shawn would forgive her for what she had said. When we cannot find answers, we may have to seek ways to let go of our need to know.

Like Jessica, we can say things we feel we must in interaction with the deceased at a funeral home, at calling hours, during a service, at a graveside, or during visits to a cemetery. We can create a setting, perhaps with the help of photographs of them, where we can easily imagine conversing with them. We can then say out loud what we feel we need to say in order to let go of what troubles or hurts us. We can also imagine what the deceased would say or what we might need them to say to find peace and consolation. We can address those who have died in prayer, forgive or seek forgiveness, or open ourselves to whatever we feel we need to find comfort and closure.

We can write notes, letters, or poems to those who have died about our concerns. We can say, as Jessica did in her letter, all we want to about how we feel, what hurts, what we wish or hope for. As we write, we can experience and express powerful emotions. The way we choose to close a letter can be very effective in enabling us to let go of what we write about. It is a good idea to keep a copy of what we write. We can then review or amend it later or choose to share it with a friend, family member, or counselor.

Often we can, like Bill, take opportunities in funerals or ceremonies to address unfinished business and loosen the grip of troubling memories. Or we can think of ways through rituals of our own devising to let go of what troubles us. We may, like Jessica, focus on something we have written or an object that represents the hurt we feel or what arouses it. We may be able to find such symbolic objects, or we can create them. We can spend time with these objects and allow ourselves to feel and express our hurt. When we are ready to let go of the hurt, we can, as Jessica did with the sealed envelope and scrapbook, do something with the object that symbolizes our letting go of what it represents. We can find ways to give it to those who have died: for example, by putting it in a casket or bringing it to a gravesite. We can burn it, bury it, cast it to the wind, set it adrift on a body of water, or whatever works best for us.

We can tailor similar actions or gestures to fit our own circumstances and our unique relationships. We can choose to do them privately. Or we can decide to be in the company of others who are willing to support our actions. We can free ourselves from the terrible "if onlys" that unfinished business brings. We can tame unwelcome memories. And when we do, we open ourselves to welcome memories. We free ourselves to remember more clearly, and cherish, the good we found in life with those who have died.

Negative Ties That Bind Us

Intimate relationship has become the new wilderness that
brings us face to face with our gods and demons.

—*John Welwood*

Sometimes unfinished business centers on far heavier matters. Some of us have known serious, long-standing troubles in our relationships with those who have died. Where there was reason to hope for, and even expect, love, some of us have felt a lack of love, affection, attention, or care.

Some have endured gross insensitivity, disrespect, indifference, imbalance in give-and-take, or ingratitude. Substance abuse or destructive family patterns may have compromised or even ruined what could have been so much better. Sometimes we become unusually dependent on those who have died—to the point at which some of us have merged our identities with theirs, deferred to them on almost all decisions, or allowed them to manage nearly all details of our lives. Some of us have struggled with another's attempts to control, manipulate, dominate, or even possess us. Some of us have been abused and actually harmed physically, sexually, or psychologically. Still others have compromised, hurt, or seriously harmed those who have died.

None of us needs to be sad over the loss of what has hurt us. It is only human to feel great relief when truly terrible relationships seem to have ended. But we don't leave such relationships untouched. Our relief in no way signals that we are free from the effects of what hurt us. Negative ties to those who have died can continue to hold sway in and distort our lives, often in ways that are very hard for us to detect, and we need to disentangle ourselves from such ties. Doing so can be one of the most challenging aspects of grieving.

When negative ties preoccupy us, we become mired in the hurt they still arouse. When we try to put them out of mind without freeing ourselves from them, they often insidiously compromise our efforts to learn how to be and act in the world without those who hurt us or whom we have hurt.

We and others who truly care about us can recognize when negative ties still hold us. Powerful feelings of anger or guilt may begin to preoccupy and consume us. These feelings may interfere in our lives with family or friends; we may become hostile or self-destructive.

If we were victims of serious abuse or neglect, we may feel passive, helpless, depressed, humiliated, unworthy, ashamed, or hopeless. We may allow others to begin to victimize us. We may begin to abuse others. We may witness, or participate in, continued substance abuse. Or we may see how family or community patterns that supported physical, emotional, or substance abuse are still in place. If we were overly dependent, we may feel overwhelmed and abandoned, deeply insecure, unprepared or unable to function, helpless, or furious at having been left behind.

We may begin to fervently long for the return of the one who died as the only way to address or resolve conflicts. Or we may grow ashamed of our powerful feelings or our part in the troubles. We may begin to swallow our feelings or join others in keeping secrets. We may feel profoundly unhappy and sense we are drifting into despair.

We must find ways to let go of the negative. We have to free ourselves from what could perpetuate it and learn better ways of living with those who survive with us or enter our lives later. If we cannot let go of the negative, we will not reclaim whatever saving grace existed even in deeply troubled relationships. There may have been good times before or after the worst times or even nuggets of peace and goodness in fleeting moments in the midst of what was most troubling. How poignantly tragic if we cannot relinquish the negative in those rare cases where there may be nothing redeeming even after we search long and hard!

In either case, holding onto, or being held by, the negative leaves us only in undesirable enduring connections with those who have died. No lasting love will be found in such dark places. Nor can we make it appear retroactively where it was not present. If there is love to be found or reclaimed, we must free ourselves to look for it.

When we acknowledge seriously negative ties and their hold on us, we can sometimes deal effectively with them on our own. This is especially so when we see clearly that there is much to love, much that we can reclaim from even highly ambivalent relationships. Some of the ways of completing unfinished business I have already discussed can prove very useful, even in addressing extreme anger or guilt. However, the more serious the troubles we have known and the more they have dominated our relationships, the more daunting are our challenges. The likelihood increases that we will need professional help in disentangling ourselves from negative ties.

Many of the troubles I have mentioned are among the most difficult for any of us to deal with effectively on our own. This is especially true when serious abuse, substance abuse, or unusual dependence has occurred. Some of us sense when we first acknowledge that there was significant trouble in our relationship that we need professional help and it is best to seek it then and there. We are aware of what troubles us, and we are ready to work with another to address it.

Some of us need to struggle on our own first before we can bring ourselves to obtain help. We slowly begin to see when we are not doing well. Intense feelings may persist and preoccupy us after good faith efforts and we may feel that we are stuck and making little or no progress. We may come to realize that the problems are too severe or complex for us to deal with alone and that they are not singly our problems but ones that infect life in our family or community. We may sense that we are unable to clearly identify some of what holds us. We may feel self-destructive. If any of these are true, we had best concede that it is time to seek professional help.

When we turn in this direction, we should avoid those who insist on principle that we must relinquish all ties to our dead loved ones. It is not that simple, even where serious trouble has permeated our relationships. There is no reason to let go of what we can truly cherish and treasure of lives now ended, even when that may be precious little. Often the prospect of finding a small saving grace in a very difficult history can motivate us to work through and break the destructive hold of all the rest. A good professional can walk this road with us.

Only rarely will our relationships have been totally, utterly destructive and then completely letting go may be desirable. This can be extremely challenging and painful. The lingering effects of such negative ties can be especially hard to detect and deal with. When we suspect we must walk this path, it is especially important that we do so with a competent professional who can help us recognize our needs and support us as we do what we must.

Horrific Memories

Only then did it come to me—I could hate what Juan did
to end his life but still love Juan.

—A bereaved father

Hector approached me during a break in a presentation I was making to a group of bereaved parents. He said his situation was different from most since his teenaged son, Juan, had committed suicide. The group had been unable to identify with or listen sympathetically to many of the distinctive aspects of his grief. He told me of his two-year private struggle to come to a realization he now thought obvious. He guessed it had taken that long for it to come into his head and then make its way into his heart.

"At first," he said, "I hated what my son did. I hated him for doing it to himself and to me and his mother. God, how it hurt! It will probably always hurt. My insides were churning constantly. I couldn't get my mind off what he did with that gun."

"But," Hector went on, "one day I saw that I hated what he did because he took a life I dearly loved. And I wished he had loved it more. I think that was probably the turning point, though I didn't quite realize it then." He went on to tell me how hard it was to accept that Juan did not want to live. He blamed everyone, including himself. But, ultimately, he concluded that it was Juan's decision, and no one else was to blame.

He continued, "At that point, I felt so sad for Juan, not just sorry for myself and his mother. Feeling sorry for him reminded me how much I loved him, how much I still wanted to love him. Only then did it come to me—I could hate what Juan did to end his life but still love Juan. It took a while for this to sink in. But as it did, I began to remember all that I loved about Juan, the fun and how good it was to have him in my life."

"I want you to know," he said, "I think that realization saved my sanity. I'll never stop loving Juan. But that doesn't mean I have to approve what he did. It seems easier every day to let that be as awful as it is. And it's easier to be grateful for the time he was with us."

Sometimes, as Hector's story shows, there is something horrible associated with the deaths of those we love. Our minds fix on the horror to the virtual exclusion of all the good we hold in memory. We cannot help ourselves—we agonize over the dark emotions the horror arouses.

Sometimes we witness in person what horrifies us. We see them die abruptly or in agony. They die alongside us in accidents, disasters, or war. We come upon their dead bodies unexpectedly; we are face-to-face with the results of violence or mutilation. Often what we witness is thrust upon us without warning, and images of what we have seen, heard, touched, or smelled plague us.

Sometimes we do not witness the horror in person. Those we love die in ways that terrify us. They may perish in ways I have already described, or they may be murdered or suicides. Our imaginations take us to the horrific scenes nonetheless. Often media coverage thrusts unwelcome scenes in our faces.

Sometimes well-intentioned people try to protect us from seeing those who have died because, in their judgment, it would not be good for us. A mother is not allowed to look at or hold her stillborn child. A widower is restrained from seeing or touching his wife's body "because it is not viewable."

Paradoxically, this can make matters worse. It can lead us to imagine far more horror than there really is. And not being given a choice can itself add to our distress and tendency to become preoccupied with what must have happened. Yes, we can be traumatized if we are not told what we will experience in enough detail. But we are rarely, if ever, traumatized if we are prepared well, choose freely to encounter even the most difficult scenes, and do not confront unexpected horror. Those who try to protect us have in most instances seen for themselves without trauma.

I don't need to rehearse the details of stories I have heard to make clear what I mean by horrific experiences. True horror can grip us. When it does, we are held captive by dreadful memories, real or imagined. Often we become and remain extremely agitated, hypersensitive, or hypervigilant. The scenes may replay in our sleep. Preoccupation with the horror blocks out other memories. In the grip of horror, we are unable to recover the good we have known in the lives of those who have died. We cannot cherish them unless and until we loosen that grip.

Some of us manage, like Hector after a very difficult struggle, to free ourselves. But as horrible as Juan's suicide was, he did not witness the act. Nor did he see Juan's body until after a funeral director had prepared it for viewing. Hector's journey could have been even longer had he come upon the physical horror without warning. He may not have made it at all without help.

Some of us who survive the horrific deaths of those we love find help and support in groups comprised of people with similar experiences. We can find specialized groups like those for survivors of suicide, veterans, or parents of murdered children in most large metropolitan areas. Their members listen willingly to much that the rest of the world seems unwilling to hear. Simply being heard and knowing that others have known similar agonies proves immensely helpful for some. Such groups are less successful, however, when we are in the thrall of the horror we have witnessed directly or imagined vividly.

When we are preoccupied by horror surrounding the death of those we love we are experiencing what is known as post-traumatic stress. Along with the preoccupation we may experience the nightmares, extreme agitation, hypersensitivity, or hypervigilance I have mentioned. All these debilitate and divert us from grieving our losses and relearning our ways in the world in the absence of those who have died.

When horrible memories grip us in posttraumatic stress, we need professional help to extricate ourselves from it and the debilitation it entails. We owe it to ourselves and those we still love to seek such help. When we commit to it, we put ourselves on hopeful paths. Those paths will take us where we can recover the full range of our memories of our loved ones. Only then can we cherish them despite the horror that took them from us.

Memories and Dying Days

It is incredible how much happiness, even how much gaiety,
we sometimes had together after all hope was gone.
How long, how tranquilly, how nourishingly,
we talked together that last night!

—C. S. Lewis

My father died in the hospital in 1969. His life had been difficult after a stroke in 1965 and a debilitating surgery shortly thereafter. My mother and grandmother cared for him at home. But he was in and out of nursing homes and hospitals throughout the period. I helped take care of him when I was home from college the first two years after his stroke. I was then away in graduate school the last two years of his life and able to visit only infrequently. Though he was obviously deteriorating, there was never a time when death and dying were discussed openly. There was a great deal of mutual affection, yet it was not easily or often expressed. Much of what could have been said remained unsaid.

I remember my last visit before Dad died. Mom called to tell me that he was quite ill and had been admitted to the hospital again. She made it clear that if I came, it would be my last visit. Though incredibly weak, Dad, as usual, was glad to see me. Our conversation was minimal. Quiet time predominated. He seemed surprised at my visit, since I had visited him at home not long before. Yet, he acted not so surprised. It was as if he knew why I had come without saying as much. We talked some about the weather and, of course, about sports, especially baseball.

Our parting was on the surface indistinguishable from any other. Neither of us was able to find a voice for what we ached to tell one another. I'll never really know if his saying good-bye to me touched him as deeply as my saying good-bye to him. I can still see the unspoken desperation in his eyes nearly thirty years later. I felt so small not knowing how to respond.

Dad died a short time after my visit, at the age of seventy-three. Though I still felt small for that weak good-bye, his death did not devastate me. He had lived a long life and been a modestly happy man. His final suffering, though prolonged, was not intense. He died quietly and painlessly. I was relieved his ordeal was over. Yes, I hurt, and I knew I would miss him. My tears came relatively easily, and they comforted me.

I had known and loved Dad for twenty-four years. I realized how fortunate I was to have had a father in my life and to have known him at all. Yet, perhaps the most difficult part of his dying was wanting to have known him better. He had lived the greater part of his life, nearly fifty years, before I was born. Much of his life's story was obscure to me. I knew some of the major events. But there were, and still are, large gaps. I knew, and still know, little of how he experienced those events or how they made him who he was. He had never talked much either about external happenings in his life or what was happening inside his skin. That pattern continued through his dying days and my last moments with him.

When Dad died, my young head filled with wonder. What did his seventy-three years mean to him? What was it like for him to realize that his life was coming to a close? Did he sense that he was saying good-bye to everything he ever knew or cared about? What did our twenty-four years together mean to him? What did they mean to me? Does everyone leave as much unsaid as we had? What would dying be like for me one day?

I carried the wonder with me as I returned to my life's routine. I finished my graduate studies and began teaching philosophy. A few years later, I introduced a course on death and dying, primarily for students who would enter the helping professions. My wonder, no doubt, partially motivated my turning in that direction. I knew those I would teach would want wisdom about being with the dying and their families. I knew I didn't have it, but I knew we could search together. It is the sort of thing philosophers are supposed to do.

That search has taught me many things about how the dying and their survivors experience their last times together and what they think when they are alone. I long ago realized how fortunate Dad and I were to have any time together at all. There was nothing horrific. We shared some peaceful silence, and it was always clear that we loved one another. So many would give almost anything to have as much to remember. I have learned to live without answers to some of my wonderings, especially about what his life and our last meeting meant to him. I have also learned how dying days and what we remember of them can be far richer than the thin memories I carry from that last meeting.

We will remember parting moments with those who are dying for the rest of our lives. And we can love them well while they are still with us. We can interact with them in ways that will make it easier to continue loving them when they are gone. Illness and physical conditions, established characters and inter-action patterns, and our abilities to communicate all impose limits. Within them we can make and recover memories to cherish. We can look toward the future together in ways that will aid our loving them when they are gone.

We can imagine a time several months after death comes. We can think what might then seem unresolved or otherwise troubling about our relationship with the dying. We can ask ourselves if we prefer to tolerate the irresolution of unfinished business then in order to maintain well-established norms of communication, candor, and honesty between us now. Perhaps we will feel constrained by such considerations, perhaps not. If not, we can do all we can to come to terms with the unfinished business we identify and the distressing feelings it arouses in us and them. We can try to resolve conflicts and heal rifts between us. We can forgive omissions or offenses or seek forgiveness. We can find ways to do or say to one another what we feel we must while they live. It is not impossible to address unfinished business after those we love die, but it is usually far more difficult. It is always hard when it remains unfinished.

When we are intimates of the dying, we typically draw closer to them. Often we join with health care professionals to care for them. As we do, we contribute to their quality of life. We can come to feel that we are "doing all that we can do" as family members, companions, or friends in difficult circumstances. This helps minimize our feelings of helplessness, regret, or guilt both before and after they die.

When others in our intimate circles join us in giving care, we can come to appreciate how they share our love for the dying. The dying, in turn, often recognize the depth of our care and concern, and benefit from our ministering directly to them.

When caregiving is effective, the dying can remain themselves within the limits that their illness and debilitation allow. And we can know good times with them. There can be much to be grateful for in the experiences we have together, even as illness progresses and death approaches. Their simple presence means so much to us. We may share extended conversation and enjoy richly varied exchanges or only briefly illuminated moments. Embracing warmly, touching softly, holding a hand, wiping a tear, looking into each other's eyes, praying together, listening to or singing a favorite melody, or sharing silence can be precious to us. We can speak our hearts to them even when we are unsure if they can hear us.

It can be difficult to carry memories of illness, debilitation, and deterioration, as well as the hardships of caregiving, sacrifice, and disruption. But we can balance them with memories of the good times that we found together: the moments of joy and laughter, the meaningful things we managed to say and do for one another, the ways in which we touched one another.

Leave-taking is perhaps the most difficult experience any of us will face, a vitally important act as the end of life approaches. How I wish I had learned about leave-taking before Dad died. Unsaid good-byes can haunt us for years. So, too, can guilt over clinging when the dying are ready to let go. Effective leave-taking brings closure to our time together, eases our transition to life without our loved one, and aids the dying in their transition into death. We can communicate leave taking in words of acceptance of the inevitable, remembrance, gratitude, and love, or gestures that convey the same meanings.

It helps when we recognize that leave taking is about separation and not about ending our love. With this in mind, we can imagine a wider range of things to say or do to acknowledge the meaning of the presence that is coming to an end and to express how our love will continue.

We can take beginning steps with the dying that can help us make the transition from loving in presence to loving in separation. With them, we can review the life now ending and our lives together. And we can anticipate the future.

As we review the past, we remember cherished experiences. Memories of good times bring delight, joy, and laughter. We recall things we have cared about together. We remember lessons in living that we have learned from and with them. We realize how we and our intimate circles have been different because they have been with us. We remember how they have inspired us to strive and to deal with adversity.

Reviewing memories and stories with the dying enriches us, expands what we know of them, and multiplies our delight in all we have shared. Sometimes, if the dying are able and willing, we can tape or otherwise record the store of memories that come to us. Remembering together deepens our appreciation of the extent and value of what we will still have of them when they are gone. We can tell them we love them, affirm the meanings of their lives, praise them, and thank them for all that they have given us while they've been with us. They can express gratitude for the time they were here and thank us for sharing life with them. These expressions can console and comfort us deeply.

As we anticipate the future, the dying can tell us how they would like us to further their interests after they die. They can voice concerns about our well-being and wishes for us as we grieve. We can tell them how we will remember them and cherish their legacies. We can pledge to try to realize the hopes they have for us as individuals, families, and communities. We can assure them that we will do our best to balance the pain of missing them with our love for them.

Remembering at the Time of Death

What is the value of the life of a virtuous woman?
—The beginning of a eulogy

Memories of lives now ended are very much on our minds at the time of death. We remember what life was like with those who have died and how and why we love them. We remember our last moments with them. Ceremonies of separation, formal and informal, support and encourage our remembering privately and together with others.

A number of years ago a colleague and I made a film about funerals. We interviewed several people about funeral and memorial services and heard many stories about remembering in such ceremonies.

We spoke with Jim and his wife Pat one afternoon. Jim's elderly mother and father had died a week apart of natural causes. The priest, who knew Jim's parents and the family well, offered a eulogy at the first funeral. The priest remembered well. His remembering helped those gathered to focus on what they could cherish in the life now ended.

The priest, snowbound in the East, was unavailable for the second funeral a week later. His assistant did not know the deceased or the family. Jim was a shy man of few words, unaccustomed to speaking in public. Yet when he was given the option, Jim decided it would be best if he gave the second eulogy. He wanted to do it for his parents and for those who didn't know them as well as he did.

Jim said, haltingly, that he told his audience what his parents meant to him and how he loved them. It wasn't easy for him, but he was glad he did it. Pat went on to say that Jim's talk of "my Mom and my Dad" reminded everyone of what brought them there. She said his speaking was "a gift" to all, especially their young children. Their grandparents had lived at some distance, and the children only knew them from occasional visits. Jim's words told them who their grandparents were in his eyes. His obvious love for them also revealed a side of their father she felt they needed to know.

A few years later, my colleague showed the film to a class. He heard a gasp when Jim and Pat appeared briefly on the screen. When the film ended, to his amazement, one of their children, who was coincidentally enrolled in his course, confirmed everything her mother said. She had no doubt that she would always remember what her father did for her and the others who were there.

A friend's Aunt Ruby was an elderly woman who had never married. She lived the life of a virtuous woman. No one knew anything of her to the contrary. When people wanted advice on the proper thing to do, they sought it from Ruby. She wasn't arrogant about it; it was something in which she took quiet pride.

When Aunt Ruby died, the minister who knew her well was out of town. The assistant minister was to do her funeral and give her eulogy. He took seriously his responsibility to help people remember. He interviewed the family to learn what kind of person Aunt Ruby was and was careful to always refer to her by her last name. He listened well, and the family felt reassured. He left the interview with the distinct impression that he must remind people of Aunt Ruby's virtue.

The funeral went well, until the eulogy. Even that began well. He started with a reading from Psalms: "What is the value of the *life of a virtuous woman?" His audience was relieved. He had clearly done his homework. He and the text continued, "Surely it is greater than rubies." A few gasped. Then others could not help laughing out loud at the awful, inadvertent pun on her given name.*

I need not state the moral of the story. No doubt the minister's listeners had an experience different from Jim's listeners. There is no substitute for personal knowledge of those we remember.

Our memories vary richly. And we begin well when we allow memories to flow freely at the time of death. The characters and lives of those we grieve have many aspects—none of us knows them all. When we remember together, we can hear how they have touched others in similar ways. Or we discover how they touched others differently in their many roles in the world. There is room to disagree, and to agree to disagree, about what we have seen in those we love. The more we learn, the more treasured memories we have to carry with us.

Often conversation in the days after death is filled with memories of our last moments with the dying. Caregivers often wish to unburden themselves of the difficulties they faced, to tell others who will listen patiently. As they tell and retell their stories, they can sift and find the good moments in the last days. They can bring them to the fore and begin to let go of the difficult times. They can then more easily remember the good times before the difficulties began.

I learned a valuable lesson about remembering at the time of death from Helen, a frequent visitor to my classes and workshops.

Helen's daughter, Mary, died suddenly at age three. As I did with other bereaved guests, I asked her to speak of her experiences at the time of death and to offer any advice she could about what others can say to someone who is grieving.

Helen first told of a neighbor who called to invite her over for coffee shortly after the funeral. She wondered if Helen would like to see pictures she had of Mary at play with her own daughter. Helen could not resist and cried when she saw the pictures. But she was ever so grateful to have seen them. Her neighbor told her how much she and her daughter liked Mary. They remembered her together. And Helen was able to see Mary through another's eyes. She felt less alone in loving her.

Helen said that we should not be afraid of making grieving persons sad. They are sad already. Nor should we be afraid of reminding them of those who have died. They are thinking of them constantly. It is far sadder when, in its silence, it appears that the world chooses not to remember someone they cannot, and will not, forget. She urged those who do not know what to say to offer to share a memory, now or at another time when the bereaved may prefer to hear it. She said the memories shared with her, and the warmth in the sharing, meant more than any other words from those who sought to comfort her.

I have asked many bereaved persons about Helen's advice, and none has disagreed with it. When I'm asked about what to say, I relay her advice. But often the question is, "What can we say when we haven't known those who have died?" I add that we can then tell grieving persons that we wish we had known the deceased better. And that their sadness suggests they loved them very much. We can say that we would like to hear some of the story of the life now ended if and when they would like to tell us. If they don't go on to tell us immediately, we can assure them we will ask again later.

Fragile and Fleeting Memories

Preserve your memories;
They're all that's left you.

—Paul Simon

Married to Alonzo for less than a year, Latitia was expecting her first child. Unable to afford prenatal services, she knew enough to take good care of herself during pregnancy. Nothing suggested the baby might be in trouble. Her labor came earlier than she expected, but she assumed she had miscalculated the date of conception. When Zo drove her to the emergency room, they took her promptly to delivery.

She first sensed that there was serious trouble from the looks on the others' faces as she delivered. She knew it when she heard no cries from her baby and they covered it and rushed it to another room with no explanation. She quickly became desperate for answers. "What happened? What's wrong with my baby? Why won't anyone tell me anything?" It didn't help that the doctors first approached Zo in the hallway. When she heard him cry out, she nearly leapt to her feet and was restrained by a nurse and her own physical weakness and pain. ·

The doctor and a weeping Alonzo came to tell Latitia that the baby was stillborn. She asked to see and hold her child. The doctor said he "didn't think that seeing her would be a good idea." Incred-

ibly, Zo nodded in agreement. What did he know that she didn't? Her mind began racing with visions of grotesque deformity. She insisted she had a right to know why they thought seeing the baby was not a good idea. Sensing that she would not be denied the information, the doctor explained as gently as he could that Latitia's baby girl had been born anencephalic: She had no brain, and a major portion of her skull had failed to develop.

Latitia began to panic. She wanted to see her baby and hold her. She knew that was her right as a mother. Still, she feared they would refuse her that consolation no matter how she protested. She determined to calm herself to increase her chances of persuading them she could handle anything She said, "I have been carrying this child and expecting to have her with me for the rest of my life. Now you are telling me I can't even see her and hold her for a few minutes? I can only have a memory of you telling me she is too pitiful for me to look at? Who are you to take what little I have of her away from me, too? If she has a face, I want to see it. I need to see my baby."

The doctor assured them that their baby had a face. It was just that so much of the back of her head was missing. Latitia asked if there wasn't some way a nurse could wrap her in a blanket so she could see her face and hold her without having to look at the back of her head. The doctor conceded that there was.

A nurse brought Latitia's child to her a few minutes later. She felt the weight of the girl in her arms. The child's face looked nearly perfect in her loving, tear-filled eyes. Latitia held her child alternately in her glance and close to her breast for several precious minutes. She showed her to Zo. He told Latitia how grateful he was for her courage in insisting that their child become real as it had in those minutes. Only then did Latitia let Zo cradle the baby in his arms. They decided to name their daughter Mina as they had planned. And to give her a proper funeral and burial.

I know of no story about a memory as fragile and fleeting as this one. So much so, in fact, that neither Latitia nor Zo would have had any concrete memory of Mina at all if Latitia had not insisted as she did. Such memories are beyond price. And yet, so many mothers and fathers of miscarried and stillborn children have been deprived of what Latitia fought for and won. Fortunately, many today work hard to make such precious memories available.

By contrast, most of us are privileged to share life, and full life at that, with those we remember. We have so many more memories to cherish. But we can lose our hold on them, too, unless we take measures to preserve and protect them.

We miss terribly those we love in a world filled with their absence. At the same time, their absence is palpable precisely because we remember them. The things, places, activities, experiences, occasions, and meetings with others that remind us of their absence also remind us of the presence we have lost. The world, then, is also filled with memories of them. By no means a substitute for their presence, and far less tangible, our memories are precious nonetheless.

Because they are intangible, our memories have ways of slipping away. They vanish as soon as we turn our attention elsewhere. Unlike all the things that arouse memories when we first encounter them, our memories may not be there when we return. If they are when first we return, they may fade as we return again and again, as we grow accustomed to the absence of those who have died. If we do not return at all, the memories will have to come from somewhere else. If we wish to remember again, we may need to make conscious efforts to revive what previously came to us spontaneously.

Memories come in a rush when we first meet the world transformed by our losses. Our memories can seem to blur together, to cancel one another. The flood can overwhelm any particular memory and threaten our hold on it. We may want very much to hold special memories but sense that we are losing our grip on them. We may fear we will lose memories permanently.

The pain of missing those who have died may prompt us to flee from or avoid the scenes in which their absence affects us most powerfully. We may put away, or even get rid of, things that remind us of them. When we distance ourselves from the pain, we also distance ourselves from what stimulates the memories we cherish. If we hastily discard or abandon sources of memory, we risk regret and may compound our losses.

We want to remember without so much pain. And we know those we love want us to remember them. So we fight against the tendencies of memories to slip through our grasp. The less the pain of missing them dominates, the clearer our path is to remembering. We more willingly and comfortably approach the area where we have felt their absence most acutely. We are more receptive to the memories that come to us there.

And the world often surprises us with memories that come back to us when we least expect them.

I think again of Helen, whose daughter Mary died when she was only three. Several years later she and her husband, Roger, went to the Indiana Sand Dunes for a holiday. Only after they had been there for some time did Helen begin to cry unexpectedly. She explained to Roger that she had just remembered promising to bring Mary to see the dunes. She said her sadness quickly dissipated. She and Roger went on to enjoy the dunes with a sense that they were there "as Mary's representatives."

Like Helen and Roger, we will have first encounters with parts of our worlds where memories occur spontaneously. They will also come when we experience familiar things, places, activities, occasions, and others in a new light. And they will happen when something about the entirely new and unfamiliar resonates with something about those we love or the lives we knew with them.

We need not stop at waiting passively for memories to come to us—we can more actively seek them out. When we approach what has seemed most haunted by the absence of those we love, we can concentrate on recalling more and more of the welcome memories that things, places, activities, and occasions hold. We can interact with fellow survivors to recover as much as we can of what we remember together. Yes, we may cry as we realize more of what we miss. But our tears pass away, and our memories remain. We can take delight even as we weep.

We can take measures to secure and hold the memories that come to us and that we recover. We can hold onto, or go to, what arouses our fondest memories. We can carry mementos, such as photographs or jewelry, with us, keep them or other things in drawers or private places, or display special objects wherever it suits us and others who may be affected by them. We can live in or revisit special places and take time to remember privately or with others. We can bring those we love to mind, alone or together, on occasions when they used to be with us. We can remember as we return to, and enjoy again, experiences or activities once shared with them. We can tell stories of them, their lives, and our lives together.

We can use many aids in remembering. Many of us have scrapbooks, photos, audio and videotapes, and home movies of those we love. Sometimes they leave letters, journals, or diaries that tell us much of how they experienced their own lives and life with us. Often, in their wills, they leave us legacies that they hope will help us to remember them. Some of us listen to or make music or read favorite passages that move us to remember.

We can record our memories in our own diaries or journals. We can write short stories about experiences we hope never to forget. We can seek out fellow survivors for remember-when sessions in which we reminisce together and exchange stories of the life now ended and our parts in it. We can make audio or videotapes of these sessions. We can combine our private remembrances in joint collections. We can create family or community archives. We can elaborate in any of our records about the satisfactions, rewards, and meanings we find in our memories.

We can set aside times to revert to memories. We can remember during graveside visits. We can deliberately pause on waking or when we retire at night. We can regularly recall them in quiet meditation or in our prayers. We can remember them with our fellow survivors on holidays, birthdays, or anniversaries.

We can invent our own special rituals for remembering and feeling that they are close—and sometimes they provide ample clues as to how we might do this.

I think of a story told by John R. Aurelio in his book Returnings. *Emil had an unforgettable zest for life. Rarely the center of attention, he was nevertheless "a presence" wherever he went. He had a knack for making everyone feel special and infecting them with his love of life and simple things. At a family cottage on a lake, he insisted that the sun never set unwatched. He would roust everyone from the dinner table or whatever they were doing and drag them, if necessary, to give the setting sun an audience. Invariably, they fell silent in awe of its simple beauty.*

Emil died of a heart attack early one December. All who knew him were devastated. The next summer many happened again to be at the same family cottage. They were busy with other things when someone noticed the sun was setting. "Look everybody. It's an Emil sunset," someone cried out. Aurelio concludes his story,

> *Without even being summoned we all dropped what we were doing and went outside to watch the blazing sun go down. No one spoke. At that moment, we all knew that Emil was actually there with us. He was present to us because he had left us the sunset as his sacrament and we all knew it and felt it.*

Incomplete and Partial Memories

His friends' stories gave me more of my son to love.
—A bereaved mother

In 1985 I gave a talk on *"Grief, Love, and Separation"* in Jerusalem. I took exception to prevailing theory at the time and urged that lasting love was both possible and desirable. When I finished, an Israeli woman entered the discussion. She thanked me for being the first to reassure her about her efforts in the time since her son had died. When I asked her to elaborate, she told a remarkable story that helped me realize I was on the right track in understanding mourners.

Her son left home in the city when he was a young man and went to live in a Kibbutz on Israel's northern border. He lived there for several years and made a life and friends. I do not recall whether there had been many visits between them during those years, only that his mother found the separation difficult and wished he lived closer. One day, tragically, a mortar shell flew across the border from the north and killed her son. In the year since his death, she had missed him terribly. She said she had cried often and at times bitterly. She had no tears that day when she spoke to us.

She wanted most to tell us that she had begun keeping a journal in which she recorded memories of her son and her thoughts and *feelings about his life. It helped her through the emotion of her loss. She also told us she had made several trips during that year to the Kibbutz. She sought out her son's friends, several of whom she had met or learned of through his letters and phone conversations. She wanted to know more about her son's life in those years. She exchanged her memories of times less familiar to his friends for their memories of times less familiar to her. She learned about his daily life, his likes and dislikes, his interests, his maturing character, his friendships, what his friends loved about him, their fondest memories of conversations and things they did together, what his home, family, and homeland meant to him, his aspirations, hopes, and dreams. She recorded what she learned in her journal.*

Some in her family, along with some friends, worried that she was obsessed with her son's death. They urged her not to make the trips and to get a grip on herself and go on with her life. She said she did not feel preoccupied with what had happened. Her efforts seemed to her more life-affirming than death-denying. She had made only a handful of trips during the year and planned, at most, one more. She found the exchanges extremely meaningful. Remembering was part of her life, but not all of it by any means.

She felt that his friends welcomed the opportunities her visits gave them to remember someone they also loved. She was grateful for their generosity and kindness and warmed by the feeling of community she found with them. Best of all, she felt that she knew her son better than she ever had. She holds his life to be among her most precious gifts. The journal moved her beyond merely missing him. It enriched her understanding of the story of her son's life that she will always cherish. And it helped her to give her son a place in her life beside those she holds dear who survive with her.

As we recover and hold memories of those we love, as this mother did, we reconnect with pieces of their lives and aspects of their characters. With enough pieces, we have the makings of stories. The stories of particular experiences, incidents, and aspects of character allow us, more or less, to form narratives about their lives as wholes. And we begin to cherish their life stories, and them through the stories, when they are no longer with us.

Sometimes, as this mother's family and friends did, others worry about or even discourage us from seeking and giving these memories a significant place in our lives. We can avoid trouble when, like this mother, we seek to add to our store of memories in ways that enrich our lives as well as when we try to find a comfortable place for remembering in our lives that neither pre-occupies us nor compromises our relationships with others. We simply do not want to forget. And we hope that others will welcome remembering as part of the new balance in life we find for ourselves.

Often our memories are incomplete and partial—gaps in them may reflect gaps in our histories with those who have died. Or simple forgetfulness may block access to much that we could cherish if only we could recall. It can take fresh encounters in the world pervaded with their absence to jar our memories. Mis-perception or misunderstanding at the times we now recall may ground our misremembering. Or selective memory may distort what we remember.

Our memories may be incomplete or partial for yet another reason. Our situation as survivors is much like that of the blind men who encounter separate parts of an elephant. In the well-known parable, each comes to know only the one part and gives a quite different description of what an elephant is.

Each of us accumulates distinct memories as we grow to know and love those we survive. We have different interactions and histories with them. We may even experience the same events in different, complementary, or contradictory ways. We piece together quite different stories about them and each story has its own validity. Unless we misperceive, misdescribe, or deliberately distort, it is a true report of our experiences. Unless we have been deceived, it is true of those we love.

Our stories only appear to contradict one another to the extent we mistake the aspects of those we love for the whole of their characters or lives. When they are accurate, our stories complement one another. If we can overcome tendencies to believe we have the best, or the only, true account of those we love, we can combine our stories. When we do, we can learn a great deal from one another about the complexity of the character and details of the life story we each love and cherish in our own ways.

When those we love die, we do not cease wanting to know the details of their lives. Much eludes our most accurate memories. But we can improve on our incomplete and partial memories in several ways. We can work to free ourselves from influences that inhibit our remembering or distort what we remember. And we can open ourselves to sources that can revive or enhance what we remember.

Sometimes more information about those we love simply comes to us. We find something they have held onto all their lives, like old letters, a diary, photos, other writings or creations, treasures, or souvenirs, that speak to us. Family and friends go out of their way to bring memories or mementos to us. Someone speaks casually of something new they assume everyone knows about our loved one. Long forgotten or unknown relatives or friends introduce or reintroduce themselves into our lives and bring memories with them.

We can do much on our own to deliberately seek information that fills gaps in our memories and in the stories of their lives. We can concentrate on those we love in quiet surroundings free of distractions and allow memories to flow freely. We can return to places where we shared life together or that promise to remind us of what we may otherwise have forgotten. We can review personal or family records. We can discover clues and follow leads suggested by the artifacts they leave behind. We can become like

Alex Haley and do detailed searches through public records and the like.

We can exchange stories of those we love with one another. We can take the initiative or welcome others' initiatives. With those who live close by we can reminisce whenever the spirit moves us. We can call or write those who live at a distance. Like the Israeli mother, we can seek out and approach others who have not been close to us to trade memories of our loved ones. We can establish regular times to remember with others who knew and loved them.

Whenever we meet to remember, we often bring something new to the table. Something since last we met prompted someone to recall elusive details. In response, another may confirm the memory or recall something different or related. Often new memories emerge in conversation in other ways. Someone tells an old story with a new emphasis or in greater detail. This triggers another to recall something else we had forgotten. Someone brings an old or recently discovered memento that floods others with fresh memories.

Remembering together fills gaps in the stories we hold and cherish of those who have died. It broadens our grasp on the fullness and richness of their lives. It assures us we have not loved alone. What we give and receive adds immeasurably to our personal, family, and community legacies of memory.

In all these ways, we can open our hearts to remember. We can be receptive to what comes to us. We can deliberately seek to overcome the limits of our own incomplete and partial recollections. And as we do, the stores of memories and stories we keep in our hearts grow. We come to know those we love better. We have more of them to love.

Richly Meaningful Memories

All our affections, when clear and pure, and not claims of possession, transport us to another world; and the loss of contact, here or there, with those external beings is merely like closing a book which we keep at hand for another occasion. We know that book by heart. Its verses give life to life.

—George Santayana

Bryn and Violet eagerly awaited the birth of their third child. But Ellie came too soon, in the twenty-second week of Violet's pregnancy. She was so tiny. And she had serious respiratory difficulties. The doctor told them that she would have to struggle mightily to survive. She assured them she and the staff in the neonatal intensive care unit would do all they could to pull Ellie through and allow her to go home.

Ellie lived only ten days. Either Violet or Bryn was by the side of her incubator every hour of her short life. They watched how she struggled. Though they could not hold Ellie, they were encouraged to touch her gently and speak to her. They did so for hours. They sang every lullaby they knew. And they prayed that God would hold her in his arms and protect her. They hung on every word the doctor offered them, first with realistic and then with desperate hope as Ellie's condition worsened.

When Ellie died, Violet and Bryn were able to wrap her in a blanket, hold, and kiss her for the first time. The hospital provided a rocking chair and privacy, and told them to take all the time they *needed. Bryn phoned Violet's parents, who lived nearby and were watching Ellie's brother and sister. He told them what had happened and asked them to bring Tim and Jane to meet their little sister. Seeing how easily and gently their parents interacted with Ellie, Tim and Jane first touched and then took their turns holding and rocking her as did Violet's parents. Bryn had asked his father-in-law to bring his camera, and they took the only pictures they would ever have of Ellie and her family. There was much crying but also incredible warmth and closeness.*

Several days later, with the help of a chaplain friend, Bryn and Violet invited family and close friends to join them for an informal funeral for Ellie. Ellie was there wrapped in a blanket as she had been in the hospital. First Violet held her, and then others did as the spirit moved them. They sang hymns and lullabies together and prayed. But mostly Bryn and Violet took the lead in talking about Ellie. Only they had been with her through the ten days of her life. They talked about their hopes and expectations and how they hurt when they were dashed.

But, more than anything, they wanted to introduce Ellie to those who would never see her alive. Her ten days were brief but full. They talked of the quiet times when they just watched and wondered at the fire of life they sensed in her. Her warmth when they touched her. Her features and movements while sleeping and while awake. How she resembled her sister and grandmother.

They spoke of her struggle for breath and life itself. What they imagined her life would have been had she lived. Some of what they said to her and how she responded when they caressed her. How good the doctors and nurses were with her. Her perseverance and courage. How knowing and being with Ellie helped them to see that sometimes the smallest things in life are among the most precious.

They told of the day the chaplain came to baptize Ellie. How they trusted she was in God's hands when he did. How good it was to sing some of the same songs with their family and friends as they had sung to her.

They spoke of how wonderful it was to hold and kiss Ellie at last. They passed the pictures around that they took in the hospital. They asked those who gathered with them to tell them about their feelings for and thoughts about Ellie and her short life. As many did, Violet and Bryn felt and expressed their gratitude for the support they experienced when Ellie was alive. They told the others how good it felt to know that they were now not alone in knowing and cherishing the story of Ellie's life. They thanked the others for welcoming Ellie into their family and community.

Violet and Bryn taught those who were privileged to be with them, and me when I learned their story, that even the shortest human life is rich in meaning. We need only to attend to it and look within ourselves to begin to appreciate all we can find in it. Fortunately, most of us share many more days with family and friends than Bryn and Violet had with Ellie. When those we love die, we, too, can remember and make the legacies of meaning in their lives our own.

We remember those we have known and loved so variously. We recall what our senses gave us of them. What their faces and bodies looked like. How they moved and did all the things they did. The sounds of them, especially their voices. How it felt to touch and be touched by them. Even smells and tastes come back to us. We recall the sensory starkness or richness of scenes we witnessed and lived with them.

We remember more than what our senses told us. We recall the colors, textures, the ups and downs, of their emotions. Their laughter and tears and what brought them on. We remember their interests, preferences, habits, dispositions, motivations, projects. Their successes and failures. Their pride, shame, and guilt. We recall how they were when with us and with others, intimates and strangers. We remember their strengths and weaknesses, their virtues and vices. We remember their courage and fears. How they carried themselves in the world. We recall their beliefs, convictions, and principles. What they stood for, and how it shaped their lives. We remember their hopes, dreams, and disappointments.

We remember the flow of their lives, the unfolding of their life stories. Some of our memories are like miniatures or snapshots of simple and precious or troubling moments. Others are more like newsreels or home videos that capture whole scenes, events, occasions, or experiences. Some memories are like short stories or documentaries that treat themes and trace connections across several episodes. Others are like novels or epic poems that encompass grand developments across their lifetimes.

Memories and stories frequently evoke the same responses in us now as they did when those we love were alive. Sometimes we recall the most intimate aspects and moments of our lives together. In our closest relationships we share our lives uniquely. We remember signals and gestures, "in" jokes, quiet confidences, hurts, and secrets that we never disclosed to others. We recall what we said and did in times and places that were ours alone. Some of our feelings of intimacy come over us again as we remember the special closeness, flavors, textures, temperatures, rhythms, and flow of the life we shared. We carry these memories and feelings as silent companions in life.

We can return alone or with family and friends to enjoy again what we love about those we remember. We can still delight in the good times we shared. We smile and even laugh to ourselves about everyday meetings and exchanges, simple pleasures, precious moments, unforgettable sights and sounds, fun and laughter, celebrations, joyous occasions, craziness and absurdity, good fortune, successes, hopes and dreams realized, and peak experiences. We connect with the good in them, the good they did, and all they gave to us and others. We can admire, appreciate, praise, and honor them again.

Our memories and stories bear reviewing and retelling. They are like other beloved stories in many ways. They fascinate us.

They draw us to them and we return to them with open hearts. This returning freshens and revitalizes them and our hold on them. Often we find something new to love or ponder in them.

We can explore endlessly the rich meanings that the beloved stories of our loved ones contain, the light and the shadows. This allows us to deepen our understanding and appreciation of the narratives and those who lived them. Particular moments or episodes reveal more of their significance, beauty, and nuance. Overlooked patterns, connections, and sequences come into view and the subtle unfolding of familiar themes in their lives becomes more obvious. New themes and tones intrigue us. Some of the finer aspects, complexity, ambivalence, and depth of their character draw our attention. Newly recovered details or perspectives may change our understanding of the stories exchanged and may reveal why those we remember were the way they were. We may gain insight into what has puzzled us. We may discern things that help clear the air of what has troubled us. Sadly, we may also see heartbreak or tragedy that previously eluded us.

Remembering together adds more than further delight in memories. We enjoy one another as we share our smiles, laughter, pleasure, and enthusiasm for someone we all love. We grow in understanding of one another and of ourselves. We come to see that none of us holds a privileged perspective on the lives or characters of those who have died. When we agree that we all love them, we can agree to tolerate and carry differing views of them. We come to see and appreciate how those we love helped make us what we are when we are together, fully human and in some ways like them because their lives touched ours. The sense that they are still with us warms us and brings us closer. We join in savoring their legacies.

Our love moves us to recover and cherish our memories and stories in these ways. Cherishing involves more than adding to our memories. We treat them as precious and preserve them. We revert to them often, whenever we need or wish to, alone or with others. We delight in and appreciate them for their own sake. We explore them lovingly and open ourselves to the deeper meanings they hold.

We cherish those we love in and through our memories of them. Cherishing is the way we still hold and love them in our hearts. We hold them dear and treat them with affection, flaws and all. We treasure the satisfaction, reward, and meaning we find in them. And with such rich memories, our hearts are filled with delight, joy, understanding, and deep gratitude.

The Dance Continues in Memory

We are "taken out of ourselves" by
the loved one while she is here.
Then comes the tragic figure of the dance in which
we must learn to be still taken out of ourselves
though the bodily presence is withdrawn,
to love the very Her, and not fall back to loving our past,
or our memory, or our sorrow,
or our relief from sorrow, or our own love.

—C. S. Lewis

In the concluding chapter of How We Grieve I tell the story of Kathryn. Her husband Mark died from an inoperable brain tumor when he was thirty-eight. His legacy to her included their two children Josh and Sarah, both under five when he died.

Mark expressed concern that Josh and Sarah, being as young as they were, might forget him. He longed to be part of their lives after he was gone. Anticipating his death before the holidays, Kathryn wrote all on their Christmas list, explained that Mark was dying, and asked them to send remembrances of his life. Nearly a hundred responses came from family and friends all across the country, including photographs, extensive memories, stories that Kathryn had not heard, and expressions of affection and gratitude. She gathered them together in scrapbooks and shared them with Mark and the children on several evenings before he died. Together they provide a vivid and permanent record of the meanings that those who loved him found in Mark's life. Mark told Kathryn it was the most wonderful gift he had ever received.

Since his death, Kathryn rereads these books to renew her appreciation for Mark. And she brings them out to read with Josh and

Sarah. Over the years Kathryn comes to see how Mark has become a living presence in their lives.

When we, like Kathryn, Josh, and Sarah, return to memories and stories of those we love, we keep them alive in our hearts. This is not simply a play on words or a misleading figure of speech. They are no longer physically present—and we miss that presence terribly. They are nevertheless present in our lives, as themselves, as long as we remember them. They remain the same persons who once lived their lives with us. We remember the flesh-and-blood, independent reality of those lives, something that never was and never will be a product of our imagination or a fiction. Their reality triumphs over any image we carry of them. We still love those real people. Their remembered presence is as real as their presence in our hearts and lives when they were alive and merely separated from us. In both instances, memory substitutes for perception as the primary medium through which we welcome their presence. They still "take us out of ourselves" as they hold our attention, move us to laugh and cry, influence what we do, nourish our souls, and inspire us.

They are in our hearts as a living presence. C. S. Lewis suggests in *A Grief Observed* that the pattern of interaction between us and those we love is like a dance. I can imagine no metaphor more full of life and life-affirmation. The embrace of those we love when they die is like the continuation of a dance where the partners are apart.

Those we love are ever-changing, dynamic, and flowing like the music that moves us. We love our companions in the dance of life as we commit ourselves in trust and a will to be with them through change and growth. We attend to their movements and the rhythms of their lives as they attend to ours. We move together through harmony and discord. We are alternatively passive and active, receptive and responsive, in a free exchange of movements and replies. We embrace one another in mutual care. We appreciate the separate parts we have in the dance. We do together what neither of us can do alone. The dance continues while we are apart, when time and distance separate us. We continue to attend to and respond to one another. We sustain this connection when those we love die. And we continue the dance in our hearts.

Kathryn lives with Mark in her heart. She talks with him at the cemetery, while alone as she fingers his ring, as she prepares for the day before the mirror, and as she closes the day in prayer. She delights in him again whenever she reviews the scrapbooks with Josh and Sarah. She carries on an internal dialogue with him while she makes important decisions about her own or the children's lives.

Mark encouraged her to seek further training in nursing administration after he was gone. She draws strength from him as she returns to school and pursues her studies. She feels his influence as she perseveres through the hardest times, when she feels the combined burdens of schoolwork and raising their children. She thanks him when she receives her degree and takes her first post. She thanks him again later, when she joins a nursing faculty.

Every year, during the holidays and on Mark's birthday, Kathryn takes out the scrapbooks and shares parts of them selectively with Josh and Sarah. Each time they see new things in the stories and remembrances and have new questions about their father. Their intense interest touches Kathryn. They seem to be getting to know him better. They occasionally refer to him in daily life and sometimes ask her to tell them more about Daddy. Whenever this happens or she sees some of him in what the children do, she tells Mark that night in her prayers.

To her amazement, Mark had talked with her candidly about her marrying again. He even wrote her a letter urging her to think about how important a companion in life might be for her and a father figure for Josh and Sarah. Immediately after he died, remarriage was the furthest thing from her mind.

Five years later, after finishing school and beginning her new administrative career, she meets Jim. He is also widowed, but childless. They hear each others' stories and those of their first spouses. They acknowledge their sadness. They come to feel grateful that the other was so touched and shaped by the earlier marriage. When Jim begins to talk of marriage, Kathryn realizes how much she loves him. She returns again to her internal dialogue with Mark. She takes out his letter and rereads it. She sees how sincere his wishes were for her and their children. She feels no disloyalty. She senses only warm acceptance by Mark of the changes she plans in her life. In Jim, she sees a wonderful companion for her and a stepfather for her children. She thanks Mark for his blessing and eagerly accepts Jim's proposal.

Kathryn and Jim work hard to build their new relationship. At the same time, they respect the legacies of their previous marriages. They accept that each will often recall their first spouse privately or with family and friends who knew them. They willingly support one another when the pain of missing them comes to the surface or they meet a new challenge in grieving. Jim encourages Kathryn to continue the holiday and birthday remember-when sessions with Josh and Sarah, though he prefers not to be present. He loves Josh and Sarah as if they were his own, but he respects their needs to be Mark's children.

As Kathryn, Josh, and Sarah have learned, our relationships with those who have died are dynamic. We blend private remembering and internal dialogue with them into our new life routines. We carry them with us as we move in new directions in life. We find places for discussions about them with fellow survivors and others who enter our lives after they die. We make places for our continuing relationships alongside relationships we already have and develop with others. We adjust the balance among our relationships just as we do when our relationships with the living change.

Sometimes we sense, as Kathryn did with her second husband Jim, that we can talk with others about the places we give to our continuing relationships with those who have died. We can then better understand and respect each others' experiences, wants, and needs. We can find a new balance among our relationships through open negotiation and compromise.

But not all our relationships with family and friends are as easy as Kathryn's is with Jim. Sometimes it is hard to be open and candid. Others' sensitivities and even jealousies can drive our seeking new balance underground. We will always be different for having known those who have died. And we can always remember and appreciate them. But our desires to accommodate living family or friends dictate that we must guard our lasting love and remember silently, in private, or when the others we want to accommodate are not present.

We and our life circumstances change in the years after those we love die. We remember them from different perspectives and against the background of changing interests, desires, and needs. We recall or learn new things about them. We become ready or able to see different things in them and in their lives. We return to memories and stories of those we love at different points in our lives. We may return deliberately for specific purposes. We may want to refresh our memories and understanding or search for new detail or insight. We may return to records of remembrances to help others, especially growing children, come to know those we love and who even love them. We may establish personal, family, or community rituals on holidays, birthdays, or anniversaries to keep memories alive or strengthen common bonds of love among us. At others times, events in our lives or aspects of our circumstances remind us of those we love and their continuing importance to us.

When we keep those who have died in our lives through memories and stories about them, their foursquare, independent reality regularly shatters any illusions that we have or ever had them as possessions. We again stand before them in wonder as we do before other mysteries in life. There is always something more to them than what we have known and loved so far. Life stories and memories are by their very nature open-ended—they are never finished. They stimulate, provoke, and move us in expected and unexpected ways. They are full of surprises that delight, perplex, sadden, trouble, or challenge us. The meanings we find in them are inexhaustible. The more we learn about those who have died, the more we realize that we will never fully understand or appreciate the complexity of their life stories or the depth of their characters.

We continue to build still richer and fuller relationships with those we love on the basis of the fertile memories and stories we keep. In them we find the legacies of their lives. As we review what we remember, we begin to see the many ways we are connected to those we love. We learn how they are already in our hearts, at the centers of our lives, in other places besides conscious memory. We also begin to sense how, if we want, we can sustain, cultivate, and deepen our identification and connection with them. We can use what we remember about them in ways that honor them and influence our practical lives, ways we will now explore.

IV

Practical Life

They Are with Us in Our Practical Lives

When I go to that corner, I can just sense what he would do. Sometimes I do it his way, sometimes I find my own way.

—A bereaved friend

Max and Gabe were lifelong friends. When they left the army, Max went to work for a large corporation based in their home city. Gabe joined his father in an antique business. Max and Gabe took turns as best man in the other's wedding. They became godparents to each other's children. Their families visited, played, and celebrated together. Max and Gabe continued to fish and hunt in season. Max drew Gabe into golf. Gabe persuaded Max to join his Monday night men's chorus.

Both men provided well for their families, and talked often about their work. Max envied Gabe's ability to work with his Dad and interact daily with his customers. Gabe repeatedly tried to persuade Max to join him and his father in the antique business. But each time, Max declined. Max wondered what he would have to offer. Although he loved old things, he knew little about buying and selling for a profit. He worried that if things did not go well, he could complicate Gabe's relationship with his father or even spoil their own friendship.

Max was downsized out of his job after twenty-five years, mostly in middle management. Shortly thereafter, Gabe's father succumbed to a major stroke. Gabe wanted to keep the business going, but after a six-month struggle, he realized he couldn't manage alone. At last, he persuaded Max to join him. Without Max, he would have to sell the business. Gabe wanted him as a partner as well as a friend. Max's management experience would be an asset. Gabe would teach Max all he needed to know about antiques, something he wanted to know more about anyway. If things didn't work out, they could both turn in new directions with no hard feelings. Max used most of what was left of his buy-out from the company to buy in as Gabe's partner.

The partnership could not have been more successful. Max delighted in the more personal and hands-on aspects of his work, and his flair for management proved invaluable. He slowly but steadily began to master the subtleties of assessing the value of antiques and negotiating purchases and sales. Max and Gabe prospered together through the next five years. Max wondered why he had ever hesitated to join Gabe. They shared delight as their children graduated and began to marry. Their leisure time together provided a wonderful balance. Working side-by-side capped it all off beautifully.

Then, without warning, Gabe died of a heart attack at age fifty-three. Max was devastated. Though his family comforted and consoled him, Max felt a great emptiness at the center of his life. Gabe was so many things to him at once. How could he ever manage without him?

At first, the pain of separation nearly overwhelmed Max. Gabe's absence was obvious in so many places and on so many occasions. But gradually, and to his surprise, Max began to sense that Gabe was still with him. He didn't want to go so far as to say that he actually met Gabe or felt that he was watching over him. But there was much in his experiences that led him to understand how some people might want to talk that way.

It began when he returned to work a week after Gabe's funeral. He very much wanted to keep the business going. He knew how much it meant to Gabe. He also wanted to do well for his new silent partner, Gabe's widow. He had come to love the work, and he felt deeply grateful to Gabe for all it meant to him. He had no doubt about managing the financial end of things. But he worried about his newly acquired and still developing knowledge of antiques.

The first day Max couldn't put the "Open" sign in the window. He retreated to the back room where he and Gabe had their desks and prepared new acquisitions for display. There, Gabe had taught him the business. He stayed in that room all day. He wept as he tried to gather his thoughts and develop plans for going on without his partner. Occasionally, he sat at Gabe's desk and poured through the stacks of papers and catalogues. As he did, he found his head cleared and it was here he did his best thinking.

In the days and weeks that followed, Max returned often to Gabe's desk, which he began to call "Gabe's corner." There was a need for the desk space anyway, he told himself. But, truthfully, he realized that he could easily connect with Gabe there. He found Gabe's perspectives and ideas accessible. When he sat in his chair, the ideas that came to him were like advice from Gabe. And he could test his own ideas against Gabe's instincts. He could easily imagine, and almost hear, Gabe's voice and its concerned, delighted, and encouraging tones. Max had acquired skills and invaluable experiences in his five years with Gabe. Still, he needed and valued the help he found in Gabe's corner.

Max is now convinced that he owes much of the continuing success of the business to Gabe. It was more than a year before he told his wife and, at her insistence, Gabe's widow, of this secret of his success.

Max feels in many ways as if he is Gabe's representative as life in their two families unfolds. He misses him when the families get together. But he also realizes that, were it not for Gabe, he would not know so many of the delights of these occasions and activities. He is grateful for the privilege of knowing his friend's family so well and of sharing the responsibilities of watching over his children. He follows some of Gabe's ways with children as he now interacts with the grandchildren Gabe never saw. And he is pleased to see how well

Gabe's family remembers him and continues to enjoy doing so many of the things they once did with him.

Max avoided fishing and hunting for the first year after Gabe died. He didn't feel right going without him, and the business took much of his time. When he returned to familiar streams and their old duck blind the next year, he knew they could never be the same without Gabe. But he now feels close to him in those places. He uses some of the time there in internal dialogue with Gabe to tell him about recent events and life in their families. The pleasures of the quiet waters and marshlands have come back. He recalls and uses some of Gabe's tips about casting and calling the ducks. Now and again he "catches one for Gabe." Max's schedule crowds out his golfing. But he continues with the men's chorus and is grateful for Gabe's bringing him to it and helping him make new friends there.

We remember, as Max does, so much of what those we love did and said when they were with us. We recall where our family members and friends put their energies and invested their efforts. We know what work mattered to them, what they were trying to accomplish, and the satisfaction they found in their labors. We recall what they did in their free time and when they were at play. We know their interests and preferences and the delight and satisfaction they found in using their minds and bodies. We remember their distinctive ways of speaking and interacting with their families, friends, colleagues, and strangers. We remember how we respected, admired, appreciated, and delighted in what they did and said.

We remember the things we did together, how we worked, played, and shared our family and social lives with them. We remember how what they did and said colored and influenced our everyday lives. We and others notice how we came to be more like them in practical ways.

I have already spoken of how we feel helpless when we realize that we cannot bring those we love back. Often, however, we, like Max, know a different helplessness. We are at a loss as to how to carry on without those who have died. What are we to do now? Are we capable of doing what we learned to do with them? Can we find purpose in work we shared or delight in an activity we enjoyed together? Or will the pain of missing them be too much?

Some of us believe that those who die continue to play active roles in our lives. We believe that they exist in another realm, or on a different plane close to the reality we know. From there they literally watch over, protect, and benefit us as guardian angels or spirits. They grant us favors, bring good into our lives, support, encourage, and cheer for us. This belief speaks to our helplessness in managing without them. It assures us that we are not alone as we continue in their absence as individuals or as families.

Many of us, like Max, hesitate to go so far in describing what we believe. But our experiences provide us with a basis for understanding how someone would choose to speak as if they had a guardian angel or guiding spirit. We feel that our deceased family members or friends are still with us in what we do and say. We feel and welcome their continuing influences.

What they did and said still motivates us. We experience their continuing support as we use material legacies to do things that would be otherwise beyond our reach or far more difficult. We do and say some things out of feelings of responsibility to them. We find access to their advice and counsel, follow some of it, and pass on the rest. We use lessons they have taught us that strike us as valuable. We identify with some of their interests and cares. We sense how they still contribute to our practical lives, individually and in our families and communities. These experiences also speak to our helplessness in managing without those who have died. In them we recognize, make use of, and cherish their practical legacies.

When our family members and friends are alive, we do well to avoid becoming overly dependent or relying excessively on them in our decisions and actions. We go too far when we strive to follow them in everything we do. It is no different when they die. If we had such trouble in being our own persons when they were alive, overcoming that difficulty becomes unfinished business for us after their deaths. We can learn to choose and act by our own best lights, following those we love selectively. But Max had no such difficulty in taking responsibility for his own life when Gabe was alive. And he shows no signs of having any such difficulty after his death. If we have been our own persons in life with those we love, we can responsibly accept and use their practical legacies after they die without fear of compromising ourselves.

Our practical inheritances are not always as rich and varied as Max's. But most of our family members and friends have touched us in some ways that can make lasting differences, great or small, in what we choose to do and how we do it. We can, like Max, gratefully acknowledge and gracefully embrace these differences. And as we make their practical legacies our own, we give those who have died yet another place in our hearts. We meet them again where we feel the pulses of everyday activities, in long-term projects and concerns, and in interactions with others in our practical lives. In what we do and say, we find a new way to keep them in our hearts.

Acting on Promises

Please look after your younger sisters for me.
—A dying mother's request

Carla was the eldest of eight children. As so often happens in large families, she helped her mother with the younger ones, and took on more responsibilities as she grew. She wondered if her mother, Marti, loved her as much as the others. She didn't feel as much of her warmth, and sometimes felt pushed to do too much around the house. Still, she loved her siblings, especially the surprise of the late arrivals, her twin sisters, Maria and Linda, born when she was eleven.

Carla's father died five years after the twins came. Carla had adored him, and the loss was crushing. Her mother, too, was devastated. The insurance made it possible for her to go on without having to return to work before the children were grown. A sister and brother-in-law who lived nearby offered invaluable support and assistance. Marti relied even more on Carla, but Carla became distant, irritable, rebellious, and hard for her mother to reach. She continued to do her part at home, out of love for her brothers and sisters, but she longed to escape. She married at nineteen, moved with her husband to another city, and started a family of her own.

When Carla was in her early twenties, her mother became gravely ill. Carla took her two toddlers with her and returned to Marti's side as she lay dying. They reconciled. Carla apologized for being so difficult when her father died. Marti assured Carla that she loved her as much as the others. She hoped Carla recognized her love in her entrusting her with so much responsibility. Carla saw it when Marti said it, but told her it was hard to feel it when she was younger. Marti said she wished she had shown her more affection and regretted not being able to reach and comfort her when her father died. They cried together. Carla felt closer to her mother than ever before. Difficult as her mother's dying was, the time they found together was precious to them both.

Marti told Carla how much she loved her new grandchildren and how much it hurt to think she would not be there to watch them grow. She shared her worries about the children she was leaving behind. Four were still at home, including the twins, then age twelve. Marti had arranged with her sister and brother-in-law at the time her husband had died to take the children if anything happened to her. She was confident that they would provide a good home for them and see them through school. But she was concerned about her youngest. They would be without both their father and mother through the teen years ahead.

Marti asked Carla, who knew them best, to do what she could to be there for the twins in those years. Carla assured her that she would. Marti then asked Carla to promise to look out for her youngest sisters as long as she lived, to be watchful and caring as their mother would have been. Again, out of love for her sisters and respect for her mother, Carla promised. Marti died a few days later with all of her children and her two grandchildren nearby. Carla was determined to remain faithful to her promises and to go wherever they led her.

It took some juggling because of commitments to her own growing family, but Carla managed to maintain close contact with her twin sisters through their teen years. She spoke often with Maria and Linda on the phone. They came for long summer visits the first several years *after Marti died. Carla could still remember what it had been like for her at their age, and they valued her ideas as those of an older sister, not a parent. They loved playing with Carla's children. They helped her with them as Carla had helped their mother when they were young. Eventually, the pull of teen interests kept them home longer during the summers. Still, they visited regularly through those years. Carla felt good about doing as her mother had asked.*

Maria and Linda finished school and Maria married and began a family of her own. She stayed in touch with Carla. Maria's children seemed like both a niece and nephew and early grandchildren to Carla. She spent as much time with them as her busy life allowed.

When the twins were thirty-five, Maria's husband was killed in an auto accident. Like her mother, Maria was widowed with a young family. Carla comforted Maria as Marti would have. She saw how difficult her own grief made it for Maria to reach out to and comfort her children. Carla did her best to support them, as she wished her own mother had been able to do when her father died. In the years that followed, she remained in close contact with Maria. She welcomed Maria and the children on frequent, sometimes extended, visits to her home. Carla was both sister and mother to Maria.

Linda lost her fiancée in the Vietnam War. She began to abuse alcohol. Her bitterness and drinking made her alternately irritable and abrasive, cool and distant. She resisted Carla's and Maria's attempts to comfort and console her. In the years that followed, Linda led a troubled life. One series of outbursts and attacks drove Maria out of her life. But Carla was determined to remain true to her promise to her mother, no matter how often Linda insulted and abused her.

It seemed to Carla that Linda had known too many losses and that it was too much for her. She drifted from temporary companion to temporary companion, and job to job for two decades. Carla maintained contact with Linda through those years, but was never able to get close to her. She waited for her as Marti would have.

Finally, Linda acknowledged her alcoholism and the devastation in her life, joined Alcoholics Anonymous, and sought professional counseling. She began to put her life back together. She welcomed Carla's support and begged her forgiveness for all the trouble and heartache she had brought into her life. They began to find a closeness they had not known since Linda had left her home with their aunt and uncle. Maria kept her distance.

Two years later, and twelve years after Maria's husband was killed, Linda fell ill with liver cancer. Carla invited Linda to come to live with her and her family, now nearly grown. With support from the local hospice, Carla nursed her dying sister through the last months of her life. She persuaded Maria to come to her dying sister's side for a tearful reunion and reconciliation. Carla offered Linda an undying love. In part, she stood by her as a sister. In part, she remained true to the promise she made to her mother.

Those we love often have strong feelings about what they would like us to do after they die. Many of us, like Carla, make promises to them before they die. They may, as Marti did, enlist us to look after those they love. They may ask us to carry on with efforts they have begun: to take over a business, continue a professional practice, manage some property, execute their will, run a household, maintain a garden, or see their projects through to completion. Or they may ask us to do something they believe will benefit us: to seek more education, change our work, find a life's companion, overcome a destructive habit, change our ways with others, or modify our spiritual practices.

Promises obligate us, even after death. We are never obligated to make promises, but we are obligated once we do. So we need to exercise good judgment as we weigh requests to make them. Sometimes those we love ask us to promise to do things we are unable or unwilling to do. We are honest with them and true to ourselves when we decline such requests. It is far easier to work through the difficulty and awkwardness of declining than to live with promises and commitments we cannot or will not fulfill.

When we are unable to follow through on what they ask, we can fairly and easily explain why. We can apologize for our lack of ability, resources, or authority. We can sometimes promise to try our best, stopping short of promising success. We can perhaps help them to find someone else who is capable of what they ask. At other times we may be able to promise to do our part along with others.

When we are unwilling to commit ourselves, we may be quite uncomfortable when it comes to explaining why. We may be capable of doing what they ask, but regard it as requiring too great a sacrifice. Or we may think that what they ask is inappropriate. They may ask that we compromise or set aside concerns that are vitally important to us, never love again, or deprive ourselves of what brings us joy and happiness.

Denying heartfelt requests is never easy. But it is no more difficult than when we deny such requests when we expect those who make them to live. We can acknowledge the depth of their feelings, express regret at our differences with them, or give some account of why we feel we cannot promise. We can tell them we prefer to live with the tension now than with failing them after they are gone. We can offer to explore alternative promises we would gladly keep, including promises to further other of their interests.

Often we promise because we care about what those who ask us to promise care about, just as Carla cared about her twin sisters. Our promises then firmly commit us to going where those cares take us. Like Carla, we cannot always foresee how far we will have to go to fulfill them, but we affirm our intentions to stay the course. Sometimes, we promise in ways that require some self-sacrifice on our part. We promise out of respect for those who ask us. We honor them as we act out of a sense of responsibility to them. We love them as we keep our promises to them.

Using Their Advice and Counsel

Thirteen years ago I lost a brother, and with his spirit I converse daily and hourly in the spirit and see him in my remembrance, in the regions of my imagination. I hear his advice, and even now write from his dictate.

—William Blake

Kim looked up to her sister, Sandy, who was two years older. She followed Sandy in nearly everything she did: volleyball and softball, schoolwork and social life. Far from minding, Sandy thrived on the attention and chance to show her younger sister everything that excited her. Sandy was successful and popular. She was proud of Kim as her life took a similar shape.

As they grew up together, each came to think of the other as her best friend. They confided everything, especially late at night when Kim came to visit in Sandy's room before they went to sleep. They spoke about things they would never think of talking about with their parents.

The summer she turned fourteen, Kim was at once excited and anxious about entering high school in the fall. She knew she could rely on Sandy's advice and counsel, and she sensed she would need it more than ever.

In late June, while riding with some friends just recently licensed to drive, Sandy was killed in an auto accident. Kim felt betrayed by fate and abandoned by her sister just when she needed her most. She wanted to do well in the coming year because that was what Sandy would have wanted. At the same time, she had doubts about whether she could make it without her.

Through that summer, Kim crept into her sister's room and spoke with Sandy at the close of day as she had so often when she was alive. Her parents kept the room just as it had been before the accident. It was not difficult to sense that Sandy could still hear her there. Kim told her about events of the day and about her expectations and fears. As she did, she began to remember some of Sandy's advice about high school. She grew more confident that she wouldn't have to manage entirely without her.

Kim continued her nightly discussions with Sandy during the school year. And she thought of her often during the day whenever she faced something new. She told me she thought of Sandy as her "guardian angel." She could often imagine what Sandy might advise. She could almost hear Sandy's voice telling her about similar experiences, the choices she made, and what she said or would say about why she made them. Kim said she even introduced Sandy to her boyfriends and found she saw them with fresh eyes with her sister's help. It wasn't the same as having Sandy there in the room, in the hallways at school, or rooting for her at her games. But Kim did not feel nearly as alone in that room or those places as she had feared.

Ruth was married to Otto for nearly forty-five years. As was common in their generation, Ruth worked outside the home until the children came. She then did the greater part of raising them and keeping house. Otto filled traditional roles as breadwinner, financial manager, and amateur repairman. Ruth and Otto devoted their spare time to music, movies, and wine.

When he was sixty-four, Otto learned he had melanoma. Treatments were at first effective, but then the disease took him on a relentless course toward death. He and Ruth spoke honestly and lovingly about what was happening. They made every day count until the end.

Otto was naturally worried about what life would be like for Ruth without him. She told him not to worry. But she did not mask her anxiety well. Otto insisted that she let him help her prepare for being a widow.

Otto put their financial house in order. He walked Ruth through the papers she would need to manage on her own. They practiced balancing the checkbook. He explained about their accounts and investments, and how to keep tax records. He made lists, and Ruth added notes as he elaborated.

Otto also reviewed maintenance procedures for the house and car. He showed Ruth how to do some simple repairs. He wrote out instructions for others and lists of places to call for help. Again, Ruth took notes.

Otto was aware that Ruth knew well her own tastes in music and film and could continue to enjoy them on her own. But he had always shopped for wine and made the selections. He listed their favorite white, red, and sparkling varieties. He urged Ruth to continue his subscription to a wine lovers' magazine. He explained how he used it to spot promising vintages and good buys.

Otto died just over a year after his diagnosis. And while Ruth knew her life would never be the same, she was grateful for Otto's concern about practical matters. Because of his care, she managed quite nicely with the things she had practiced, using Otto's guidelines and her notes. She felt protected by him still, even though she now had learned to take care of herself.

We can, like Kim and Ruth, remember and use some of the advice and counsel those who have died offered us. In this way they participate in our practical lives just as they did when they were alive. We still respect their good judgment, and we follow their advice when, in our own view, it makes good sense. We appreciate their concern and interest in our doing well and the skills and know-how they gave us.

And we are grateful on those occasions when their advice proves useful. We sense that they still support and walk with us as we face daily challenges. Sometimes, their advice doesn't work out for us, and we set it aside and act by our own lights.

Our situation is similar when we respond to wills that specify what those who have died would like us to do with what they leave us. Occasionally, they stipulate conditions we must meet in order to inherit and it can seem that it would have been better had they discussed these matters with us before they died. It would be easier now to view the directives as advice rather than as a set of orders.

We can view some directives and conditions in wills as well-intentioned advice and counsel. They may reflect advice we have heard and long intended to follow. We may then conform with them, appreciate the intentions, and feel supported as we would have had they given us the benefit without conditions.

Some directives and conditions seem only to be attempts to control and manipulate us; nevertheless, we may conform. Or we may decline to conform and either forego the benefits or contest the will. No matter what we do, we will likely feel some resentment and tension with the one who has died. We can hardly feel that they support us in what we do in such circumstances.

But, we are not limited to advice actually spoken or offered. We are also familiar with the general tenor and drift of the advice they gave us. We have observed them in circumstances like the new and unprecedented ones we now face. Like Max, we can sometimes simply take new challenges to places where we feel close or connected to those who have died. We can experience ideas that come to us there as if it were advice from them. Or, like Kim and Kathryn, we can often place ourselves in dialogue with them. We can recall the tone and temper of their voices. We can see what things would look like from their points of view. We can come away with a strong sense of what they would advise. We can feel their continuing support and encouragement.

Ruth also found she could sense what Otto would advise in unprecedented circumstances in this way. She took her problems with her and sat in her favorite chair next to his in the family room. When she closed her eyes and imagined him beside her, she could hear his gentle voice making suggestions. She didn't always agree with him, but she knew he still cared. Sometimes, as she enjoyed a glass of wine in her chair, she toasted the man with the reassuring voice.

Doing Things Their Way

In all things we learn only from those we love.

—Goethe

    Dean's grandparents' farm was less than an hour's drive from the suburb where he lived with his parents. His family didn't need a holiday, birthday, or anniversary as an excuse to get together, though they never missed one. He loved his grandmother, Edie, but he couldn't get enough of his grandfather, Nathan. Dean followed him everywhere, and Nathan loved him every minute they were together.

Nathan had a way with Dean that made him feel like he was the center of his world. When he played or talked with Dean, Nathan gave him his undivided and rapt attention. He looked at Dean with warm, loving eyes that said he delighted in simply being with him. He drew cartoons while Dean watched and giggled, and he showed him some simple ways to make up his own cartoons. He motioned for Dean to sit beside him when he seemed unhappy or hurt. He had a way of listening that assured Dean that he really understood him. He lifted Dean into his arms or onto his shoulders so he could see what everyone else was seeing. He made up bedtime stories that were better than any in the books his parents read him. Later, when Dean was too old for bedtime stories, Nathan still made a point of closing the day with him in quiet conversation about the good things that had happened during the day.

From the time he was three until he was fifteen, Dean spent a month each summer at the farm. Nathan taught Dean to love animals. He raised grain, not livestock, but there were many animals on the farm: a milk cow, a few chickens for eggs, cats to chase the mice, and golden retrievers as pets. Nathan showed him how to approach and care for the animals. He taught Dean how to train the dogs to obey and do an occasional trick. He took him to county and state fairs each year. As he grew older, Nathan showed Dean how to use tools, run some of the farm machinery, and tend the large vegetable garden he and Edie maintained. Nathan had many "secrets" about how to do things, and he shared them with Dean.

Nathan shared Dean's love of sports, especially baseball. Nathan came to as many of his games as distance and time allowed. Over several summers, Nathan first taught Dean how to slide without hurting himself and later how to throw a curve ball.

When Dean was thirteen, Nathan showed him parts of the journal that he kept. Nathan told Dean that he began the habit when he was given his own grandfather's journal when his widowed grandmother died. He recorded his daily life. He wrote notes to himself about experiences that had special meaning for him so that he wouldn't forget them and so he could review his thoughts later. He carefully observed how other people treated him and one another and tried to learn from what he saw and heard.

Dean began to keep a journal of his own. Like his grandfather, he became a keen observer of human behavior. He took special care with entries about Nathan and his ways with others. He came to see that his grandfather made everyone believe they were the center of his world when he was with them. It seemed to have everything to do with how he looked at them, gave them his undivided attention, and listened with understanding. He vowed to do his best to be like Nathan in these ways.

We, like Dean, learn many things from those we love. Sometimes, as Nathan did, they take time and trouble to teach us skills, help us develop our abilities, and refine our routines. They explicitly share techniques, secrets, tricks, and shortcuts and help us learn their ways of doing things.

At other times, we learn by observing what they do. We notice their habits and dispositions, the routines they follow, the strategies they develop. We learn from them by example. Sometimes, we consciously follow their example; often, we become like them in what we do without even realizing it.

We learn selectively from different people. Some, like Nathan, are very capable in many things, and, like Dean, we share many of their interests and follow them in many ways. Others are also capable, but our interests do not overlap with theirs as extensively, or their ways do not particularly suit us. So we follow them in far fewer ways. Still others are not as capable in much that they do, but we still learn some things of value from them.

We watch and listen as our family members and friends do their work, perform chores, or take care of everyday business. Different ones teach us how to build, maintain, and repair things. To develop good work habits. To manage our time. To manage our money. To maintain a household. To see and create opportunities and make the best of them. To improvise and make do with what is available. To lead others. To follow. To cooperate and win others' cooperation. To be a team player and promote team spirit. To respect and care for our environment.

We learn from those we love as they walk the world around them and enjoy their time away from work. Some teach us how to delight in simple pleasures. They or others show us how to open our senses to the wonders around us. To savor precious moments. To pursue and reach peak experiences. To play games and sports. To exercise and care for our bodies. To maintain our health and well-being. To do and make things with our hands.

To draw, paint, or sculpt. To sing or play a musical instrument. To dance. To tell stories. To value silence and solitude. To reflect, contemplate, meditate, or pray.

We learn from family members and friends as they interact with others. Some show us how to enjoy the company of others. To appreciate the gifts others offer us. To delight in conversation and activity together. To nurture and comfort a child. To keep love alive with a spouse or companion. To maintain friendships. To welcome and entertain guests in our homes. To respect others. To make others laugh or smile. To protect ourselves and those we love. To break tension and diffuse anger. To mediate disputes and resolve conflicts. To support others in times of crisis. To comfort those who are less well off. To care for the sick or the elderly. To find satisfaction in volunteer service.

We may not be as aware as we might like of such practical legacies. We can remember what our loved ones have explicitly taught us and what we consciously admired in their ways of doing things when they were alive. But we may sense that we can and want to learn more from them or that there are things we have already learned, but are only dimly aware of. When this is so, we can do our best to remember activities and experiences with those we love that we enjoyed or found especially meaningful. We may or may not have a journal like the one Dean kept in which he recorded events, and reflected on his life with his grandfather Nathan. But we can create a similar record of what we now remember. We can then explore the activities and experiences we recall and seek practical lessons in living from them. We may find we are already doing some things the way they used to, or we may search for what we like and resolve to try to do them their way as best we can.

We can also discuss and explore what we remember of those we love with others who also knew them. Together we may remember even more that helps us to see how those we love did what they did. We may find other ways of using these practical legacies as individuals and in our families and communities.

Nathan died when Dean was in his late twenties. By then, Dean had accumulated over a dozen years of journal entries. In the days and weeks that followed Nathan's death, Dean pored through his journals looking for entries about his grandfather. He was not at all amazed to find how many things he had learned from him. He had trained his own golden retriever. He used many of Nathan's secrets in home repair and gardening. He could still throw a wicked curveball in his summer league. But, most of all, Dean appreciated how he was already raising his own children in ways that reflected how Nathan treated him when he was a boy.

Following in Their Footsteps

In all of these things, he feels still married to Lorna and comfortable as he walks the path they set off on together.

—A widower's story

Cliff was at first a carpentry contractor and then a successful home builder. His wife, Lorna, was a social worker who specialized in work with children. They tried to have children of their own but to no avail. Still, they wanted to contribute together to the welfare of children.

When they were in their mid-thirties, Lorna thought of how they could combine their talents and find ways to work with agencies that address problems of homelessness for children in third-world countries. Cliff could use time in the winter months, his off-season. Lorna could allocate her vacation time at first and, if things began to work out, go on a part-year schedule where she worked. Cliff responded enthusiastically to her idea and plan.

For several years they went to locations around the world and did what they could. Cliff worked side-by-side with others in home construction. He learned from local workers about available materials, traditional building styles, environmental constraints, and the like. He learned to adapt what he knew to diverse conditions, and he passed many of his skills on to others. Lorna joined in providing social services to the children and their families when they had them, *or others who cared for them when they had no families. They came to love many of the children as if they were their own. Cliff, especially, came to realize what it meant to care for children in ways he had never known. He had never felt as close to Lorna as when they joined together in this work.*

When Cliff was forty-four, Lorna collapsed at home one night. Two days later, without regaining consciousness, she died of a brain aneurysm. In the first months that followed, Cliff tried to keep his sorrow at bay by pouring himself into his homebuilding business. It kept him busy, but he wanted more. Though he was lonely, he remembered Lorna easily and richly, and he vowed he would never marry again. He decided that he could find the meaning in his life that he craved by continuing in the work they had started together.

In the years since Lorna's death, Cliff has expanded his efforts on behalf of homeless children, and developed a network of home builders who contribute their services in the third world. He has contributed increasingly large portions of his earnings to the agencies he has worked with and devoted more of his own time to work in the field and to interaction with the children. In all these efforts, he feels still married to Lorna and comfortable as he walks the path they set off on together.

Like Cliff, we often follow in the footsteps of those we love after they die. We make their work our own. Sometimes, like Cliff, we continue in work we shared with those who have died. Sometimes, we carry on with work begun by them that we joined in later, as Max did when he followed Gabe into the antique business. At still other times, we pick up where they left off as we take on new responsibilities and make them our own.

But it is not always easy or appropriate for us to try to follow them.

Ben ran a successful group of department stores. He gave his sons Harry and Leonard positions of responsibility with the firm and hoped that when he died one of them would carry on after him. Ben died in his mid-seventies while still at the helm of the company. He willed it to his sons, but neither was suited to assume Ben's mantle of leadership. Harry very much wanted to follow his father. He knew the merchandise well. Sadly, he lacked the abilities to make sound business decisions or manage a complex organization. Leonard, on the other hand, had these abilities but wanted to cut back on his work commitments. He preferred to sell his share of the firm, operate a small specialty shop for a few years, and retire early.

Leonard refused his brother's pleas to remain as his partner. He arranged to sell Harry his share and wished him well. Harry struggled on his own. He hired poor managers. The business faltered. As much as he wanted to be like his father, Harry concluded after several years that he did not have the right stuff. He decided to cut his losses, sold the business, and also retired.

Following in another's footsteps requires several things at once. We need to align our will with theirs. We have to want to make their work our own, not simply because they hoped we would but because of a similar desire within us. If our heart is not in the endeavor, we will almost surely fail. Or, even in success, we may be quite unfulfilled and unhappy. Leonard wisely passed on the chance to follow Ben for such reasons.

We risk compounding our suffering if we let our hearts take over where our heads should prevail. Having the desire to follow in another's footsteps is not enough—we need the talents and abilities. If we don't have them, we need the will, capacity, and resources to acquire them. We may also need to be sufficiently like those we choose to follow in character, temperament, or disposition in order to find success along the same path. Harry was not honest with himself about his own limitations. He added personal disappointment and business failure to the pain of his grief. We can avoid similar trouble only if we honestly assess our own shortcomings and abilities.

Sometimes the combination of will, ability, and character or personality suits us to the work. We follow in the footsteps of those we love not out of feelings of responsibility to them alone but from powerful motivation to be like them in the work we do. Just as Cliff carried on Lorna's labor of love, we can make their vocation or calling our own. And if we put our hearts into the work, we can be filled with the same satisfaction and derive meaning from the work as they did.

Making Their Cares and
Interests Our Own

*The cares and interests hold familiar places in
our lives and hearts again, in part because
those we love helped us to make room for them there.*

—*Author*

Max took over Gabe's antique business. But he also took
up fishing and singing in a chorus because of him. Their families
visited, played, and celebrated together. Carla followed Marti in
her devotion to her twin sisters. Kim followed Sandy into volleyball and softball. Dean became interested in animals, household repair, gardening, baseball, and keeping a journal because
of his grandfather Nathan. Like them, we often follow those we
love in other ways besides in the work we do. We make their
cares and interests our own.

We introduce one another to activities and experiences all the
time. Sometimes we decide to try new things together. Often
we find comparable satisfaction and meaning, though we may
do and experience them in different ways. We don't replicate the
life patterns of our family members or friends, but we weave
common threads of care and interest into them.

Those we love influence our leisure lives. Particular family
members or friends may attend movies or the theater. Participate
in local productions. Delight in music. Sing, dance, or play mu-

sical instruments. Enjoy the arts. Sketch, paint, sculpt, or take photographs. Read avidly. Write poetry, fiction, or nonfiction. Keep journals or diaries. Enjoy spectator sports and even follow the same teams. Participate in sports or physical activities. Enjoy the outdoors by walking, hiking, climbing, camping, fishing, hunting, boating, or bird-watching. Take up hobbies and crafts. Make everything from blown glass to sailboats. Play games and work puzzles. Collect anything from butterflies to antique cars. Enjoy cooking or dining out. Go to flea markets, antique shows, collectors' conventions, festivals, fairs, and amusement parks. Travel widely and visit points of interest. And some of these interests we make our own.

Those we love also influence our more serious pursuits when we are not at work. Because of family members or friends, we may devote time and energy to self-improvement. Give of ourselves to our spouses, companions, extended families, and friends. Join political parties. Support causes we believe in. Work for charities. Attend churches, temples, or synagogues. Volunteer our time and skills to schools, hospitals, centers for children or the elderly, recycling centers, volunteer fire departments, rescue squads, community recreation centers, or libraries. Or join community service, veterans, or professional organizations.

When those we love die, their practical influences are still with us. The pain of missing them may haunt us as we return to doing what brought us satisfaction and meaning when they were alive. But, over time, our pain is most often balanced as the satisfaction and meaning come back. The cares and interests hold familiar places in our lives and hearts again, in part because those we love helped us to make room for them there.

Sometimes we abandon some of these interests altogether after they die, believing that we simply cannot find meaning in them without those we love. We may fear that the anguish of missing them will overwhelm our enjoyment. Or those we love may have played crucial roles, and we cannot imagine anyone else filling them.

But things may be different later. We may go a long way in coming to terms with other challenges in grieving. Others may persuade us to try again. We may find someone with whom we think we could enjoy the activities and experiences that we left behind or who seems suited to the roles that appeared so difficult to fill. Or we may just sense that we are ready to try again. As we revive these cares and interests, we can feel as if we are welcoming those who introduced us to them back into our lives and hearts.

Sometimes those we love tried without success to interest us in activities or experiences that they enjoyed. We could never find the time, or it was simply hard for us to see the appeal or know if we had or could develop the abilities. After they die, we may find ourselves in different circumstances. We may now have the time. We may change and be receptive to what before seemed uninteresting or unexciting and become convinced that it is worth the trouble to develop the abilities. We can then, at long last, try what they had for so long encouraged us to do. Simply trying can be a loving thing to do in their memory. If we enjoy the activities or experiences, we may regret not having tried them before they died. But we can still experience them as welcome additions, part of their practical legacy to us. They, after all, planted the seeds of interest in us.

As we cherish these legacies, we pay loving tribute to those who have died. We remember them as we enjoy activities and experiences as they once did and we sense that they are still with us in what we do. We pay them additional tribute when we introduce others, perhaps our children or friends, to these activities and experiences. We extend their influence and open others' hearts to them.

In all these ways, those we love are with us in our day-to-day practical lives. But they also touch and nurture our souls and spirits—they influence our characters, our ways of being and becoming.

V

Life of the Soul:
Returning Home

Loss and Soul Pain

I know that the thing I want is exactly the thing I can never get. The old life, the jokes, the drinks, the arguments, the love-making, the tiny, heartbreaking commonplace.

—C. S. Lewis

Henry married and made a home and life with Grace for forty-two years. From the beginning, they felt they belonged together. They sensed a special chemistry as they blended their lives— "Better living through chemistry," they liked to say.

Henry and Grace loved one another faithfully and wholeheartedly. They remained their own persons even while something of each found its way deep beneath the skin of the other. They couldn't say exactly how, but there was something more to them together than simply one plus one. They thrived as companions, partners, and lovers as they immersed themselves in the rich details of everyday life and the unfolding of the seasons of their lives. They grew in understanding of one another, themselves, and their special chemistry. They never ceased wondering at how much more there was to understand. They were grateful for one another and all that married life offered.

Grace taught high school history for nearly thirty years. Her enthusiasm was contagious, and the subject came alive in her classroom. She focused on everyday lives in other times and cultures. Her students learned about family and working life and the differences that larger events and cultural changes made in them. She always asked her students to explore their own family histories and develop detailed family trees. She took exception to the usual way of constructing them with the older generations on the top and their descendants arrayed below. "If it's really a tree," she would say, "the roots belong at the bottom. I want you to learn about those roots and how coming from them makes you who you are."

Grace was also a fixture in the community. She led efforts to develop the county historical museum and served as a consultant on several restoration projects. She won consecutive two-year terms on the town council after her children left home. Many were hoping that she would stand for election again when she left teaching. It seemed to Henry that friends and former students greeted her wherever she went.

Henry began as a teller at the local bank and rose to Vice President for Management in the firm that expanded to include several branches throughout the county. Over the years, his own observations and conversations with Grace helped him to see the effects of banking decisions on families, small businesses, and farms in the area. He welcomed the chance to make a difference in his community as he took on more responsibility for setting bank policy. And he welcomed Grace's support as he served on boards for the school system and town library.

Henry and Grace were dedicated in their work. But their home and family were the center of life around which all else revolved. They gave as much as they did to their community because they believed it was an extension of, and support for, the families within it, including their own. They were joined first by three children, Elizabeth, William, and Victoria. They, in turn, presented Henry and Grace with five grandchildren.

Henry and Grace were devoted to their children. They gave them love and affection, each in their own way. Henry was warm and remarkably patient and accepting with them. Grace found it easier to be warm with Elizabeth and Victoria than with William, perhaps *because he was so active and energetic as a boy. She was quick to offer advice and guidance to all. Henry and Grace took an interest in everything the children did. They involved themselves in their school and other activities. Both gave them a love of learning. Grace joined actively in their education and passed on her love of history.*

Grace and Henry's home was filled with storytelling. They listened attentively to their children's stories. They freely shared memories of their own childhoods and often walked the children through family photo albums and scrapbooks. They told stories of their own mothers, fathers, brothers, and sisters: about how they lived, the kinds of people they were and are, and what they did together when they were younger. The family often welcomed the children's grandparents, aunts and uncles, and cousins who had their own stories to tell. And the visitors became characters in the young ones' life stories. The storytelling continued with an expanded cast of characters when the children were grown and brought grandchildren to Henry and Grace's home.

That home itself was remarkable. After ten years of marriage, they bought a barn at the edge of town when Grace convinced Henry of its "potential." For five years they and their growing children invested every spare moment to make it a home like none other. They reshaped it continuously after they moved in. They filled it with memorable moments, laughter and occasional tears, visitors, storytelling, photographs, cherished objects, and souvenirs from their travels. Henry looked forward to life with Grace there when they retired in two years.

Then it happened. One morning Henry pressed the snooze button at the 6:30 alarm as he always did. He reached for Grace and the usual gentle embrace while they waited for the second alarm. His hands trembled and he moaned deeply as he realized that Grace had died in her sleep. She was sixty-two.

Henry missed Grace instantly. She would never kiss or touch him again. Her voice would never whisper his name or speak of the day ahead. He wrapped his arms around her and held her close with her back against his chest. As his eyes flooded, his mind filled with memories of Grace and their family. The thought of never seeing her

again or laughing with her in the home they shared for so long was
dreadful. So, too, was the idea of walking the world without her.
The days ahead at first seemed emptied and impossibly long. His
very soul ached.

Like Henry, when those we love die, we are shaken to the core
of our being, our very souls. We feel uprooted, as if the ground
has been pulled out from under us. We feel wrenched out of and
homesick for the familiar and settled life we knew with our loved
ones that nourished, sustained, and comforted us. We are startled
into recognition, and perhaps ashamed, of how much we have
taken for granted. Where in the remnants of our everyday lives
can we find the grounding and nourishment that will enable us
to feel safe and secure, at home again? Can enduring connection
with those who have died help us revive our souls?

We feel as if our everyday lives have been undone, shattered.
We are at a loss as to how to reconnect with the things and places
and the fellow survivors our loved ones left behind. And how
to reweave familiar threads of caring about these remnants of our
lives with the deceased into the patterns of life and daily routines
we must now reshape. We fear that we cannot be ourselves in a
world transformed by our loss, that immersing ourselves in life
and caring again in familiar ways will no longer bring peace and
contentment. How are we to feel that we belong again in our
life's surroundings? What is the point of caring about others if it
only brings pain? Can we return to everyday life in ways that
reflect how deeply those who have died have touched us and
shaped our souls?

This anguish is soul pain. It is unlike physical pain that comes
with injury or illness. It resonates deeply within us and reflects
some of our profoundest fears. It strikes and lingers in that part
of our hearts in which we seek the grounding, connection, and
love that make everyday life worthwhile. Where we care most
fervently. Where we establish and maintain our integrity. And

where we know the heartbreak of deprivation that loss brings. Soul pain is some of the worst pain of missing those we love.

Soul work is that part of grieving we do as we learn to carry this soul pain. We struggle to find our way back home in a world pervaded with the absence of those we love, and we often draw on their deepest influences as we struggle. But we can mitigate this pain when we find enduring connections with them in our roots, within familiar surroundings, and in the soulful aspects of our own characters.

Choosing How We
Approach Our Hurt

Her absence is like the sky, spread over everything.

—C. S. Lewis

As Henry held Grace close that awful morning, the reality
of separation from her was palpable. A part of him wanted to hide.
But where could he possibly go? He sensed that he would have to be
unconscious not to notice that Grace was no longer with him. Those
who would advise him to "keep busy" or to "put your mind on other
things" would mean well. But, to him, the hurt that Grace's absence
aroused seemed inescapable—he could not pretend otherwise. The
road ahead looked endless. The feelings seemed at times unbearably
heavy. He vowed to himself to stay the course, not run away.

In the weeks that followed, Henry's soul ached in every corner of
his home. Though he knew he never would, it was still as if he
expected to meet Grace there: at the now silent breakfast table. By
the sink brushing her teeth. Searching the closet. At the door as he
left for work. In the hall where they deposited the residue of the day's
business. Beside him as they watched the evening news. Strolling
through the neighborhood at twilight. Reading in her favorite chair
by the fire. Humming along as familiar music came from the stereo.
In their bed at day's end and at the sound of the alarm. Henry only
knew how to live in his home with Grace.

Henry also missed Grace in his larger world. Each child and grandchild reminded him of so many challenges overcome and delights enjoyed with Grace. Each meeting with fellow survivors, including Grace's family, friends, and acquaintances, reverberated with the melodies and rhythms of life shared with her. At work her picture held the corner of his desk, and he recalled why he worked so hard for so long. Familiar parks, pathways, restaurants, theaters, shops and stores, schools, their church, the cemetery, the neighborhood, even places where they always wanted to go but never did, affected him deeply, and at times surprisingly. A laugh in a crowd, the set of a woman's hair, a familiar scent, and for a moment he hoped it had all been a horrible dream. When he least expected it, a favorite tune on the radio, cookies on a store shelf, or the turn of a corner pierced him. Everywhere his world was strange yet tinged with Grace. Henry only knew how to walk this world with Grace at his side.

As it was for Henry, it is painful when we return home to the familiar settings of our lives after a family member or friend has died. As children, parents, in-laws, siblings, grandparents, grandchildren, or friends of those who have died, we may not confront their absence everywhere we turn as Henry did. We may not have lived so intimately with or blended our daily lives as extensively with those we love as he did with Grace. But we do experience their absence. Elements in our life circumstances arouse soul pain within us.

Ironically, the things, places, people, experiences, and activities that arouse our deepest soul pain may be precisely the ones that hold memories, legacies, and connections that can still nourish and sustain us. We may be tempted to flee from what we need the most, those things that, if we can find our ways back to feeling at home with them, have the most to offer us. Tolerating the soul pain may be the price of replenishing our starving souls.

We are wise to resist, as Henry did, temptations to make major, permanent changes in our life circumstances in an attempt to avoid or hide from our soul pain. We risk further uprooting ourselves, inadvertently adding to our losses, and compounding our pain and anguish when, for example, we hastily discard all our loved one's belongings, sell our homes, or move away. We have no need to rush. We can choose our own pace as we experience and express our hurt. There is no "proper" timetable, no set schedule for our struggle to find our way back home in the worlds of our experience. And, ultimately, there are no "right" choices to make.

It sometimes seems as if we hurt the same no matter where we are or with whom. But, though we may hurt constantly, we hurt differently in different circumstances. We notice how some people, places, and things distress us most; we also observe how we feel less distressed in other circumstances.

We can choose when and where we approach what affects us most. Some people, places, or things may seem to us too difficult to face right now, or some experiences or activities too painful. Often we can avoid them or set them aside until we are ready to deal with them and the pain they arouse. When we feel able, we can approach alone or with others. We can approach gradually, stay only a little while, retreat to relative comfort, and return another time. We can force ourselves to stay until our hurt diminishes, happy memories or feelings begin to come back, or we have had enough. We can decide what seems best to do or say. We can express our pain and anguish at the time we feel it most intensely or hold it until later. We can accept or decline offers of retreat, comfort, or respite from family or friends. We can decide together in similar ways when and how, as families or communities, we will approach what hurts us most.

Despite the pain Henry felt there, he knew from the beginning that he wanted to stay in his home. He declined his daughter Elizabeth's invitation to stay with her family for a time. As he expected, the first days without Grace were terrible.

Their bedroom was the worst. He could walk through it to dress himself in the morning. But he slept in the guest room. He would decide later whether to sleep in their bed ever again. After ten days, he determined to try the bed in small doses. He didn't want to part with the bed while his pain controlled him. He forced himself to lie there until he could stand it no longer. He then retreated to the guest room. He did this for another ten days until he spent a night in the bed and actually slept. Then he decided that he would keep it. "If I were to give it away," he thought, "it would feel like giving away part of my life with Grace." He closed Grace's closet. He would wait until his daughters were ready to help him face and sort the contents.

The family room was different for Henry. It, too, was filled with memories. But when he sat in his favorite chair next to Grace's, he felt more comfortably close to her. He remembered good times more easily there. His tears were soothing, not bitter as they were at first in the bedroom.

Early on, Henry found it especially difficult to visit alone with Esther, Grace's widowed mother. There were long silences. Perhaps it was his recognition that he didn't know what it was like to lose a child combined with Esther's reluctance to open that subject. Perhaps it was their mutual recognition of the unspoken pain of losing a spouse. At first, neither seemed to want to hurt the other by talking about Grace.

After some time, Henry expressed his sympathies to Esther in a letter. He also thanked her for bringing Grace into the world and her many kindnesses over the years of his marriage. He added some discreet comments about how difficult it was without Grace. He held back much because he did not want to add to Esther's burden. Esther wrote him and thanked him for his kindness. She, too, was reserved in sharing her pain. But she welcomed what he told her about what he missed of Grace, and she spoke freely of fond memories of her. She said the silence about Grace hurt more than talking about her, but she would understand if he found it too painful. She thanked him for being such a good husband and son-in-law. He felt that the *letters opened the way to more comfortable sharing of memories in person.*

Henry also sheltered his children and grandchildren from the depth of his pain. He saw that they were hurting, too, and felt powerless to help. He knew only how much he wanted them to feel welcome whenever they came to his home. Their simply being with him in the house again warmed him—familiar family noise cut the silence there. The occasional laughter was refreshing and hopeful. They, too, hesitated to speak of Grace when they came together. He sensed they were afraid such talk might upset him. Memories flooded his mind, and he knew they couldn't have forgotten her. It was uncomfortable to watch stifled tears. The awkwardness bothered Henry, and he didn't want to lose the liveliness that always filled his home. He wondered how they could recover it together. At first, he was at a loss as to what to do. He decided to give everyone, including himself, more time.

Henry was disappointed that his friends seemed so reluctant to speak of Grace or to hear his hurt. They couldn't possibly be hurting as much as he was. But he recognized that he, too, had never been very good at such things. He was confident they would come around in time, perhaps when he was more comfortable opening the subjects. Meanwhile, he accepted their occasional invitations to go for coffee or join them for an evening. Their companionship provided some comfort and respite from the loneliness of his home.

Henry resented the pressure to return to work only a few days after Grace died. He had no concentration for weeks. Gradually, however, his focus returned. It is not that the work seemed as important as it once did. But when he lost himself in it for longer periods, the pain at least receded into the background.

We may sometimes conclude, sadly and after considerable effort, that leaving our home, avoiding a particular place, giving away or discarding a cherished possession, limiting contact with someone who survives with us, abstaining from an experience, or refraining from an activity is best. It may become clear that our pain will foreseeably overwhelm the memories in those parts of our world. They seem spoiled by our loss. Letting go in these ways concedes that we have lost more than the one who died. But it can also be part of an honest and appropriate response for us to a world transformed by our loss and the soul pain it arouses. When we choose to do such things, we do not ultimately avoid soul pain. In effect, we choose which soul pain we are best able to carry and how.

We, like Henry, deal with soul pain on our own terms and in our own ways. We cannot make it go away. But through and in spite of it, we can begin to see what remains in our daily lives and life circumstances that can nourish our souls. And we can begin to sense the soulful presence of those who have died.

They Are with Us in Our Souls

A soul mate is someone to whom we feel profoundly connected, as though the communicating and communing that take place between us were not the product of intentional efforts, but rather a divine grace.

—Thomas Moore

Henry never underestimated how precious Grace was to him. He did not call her "Amazing" for nothing. He expressed his gratitude often. Still, when she died, he was painfully aware of how much he never told her. He wishes he could again look into her eyes and tell her all that he has discovered about how much she meant to him. Instead, he begins to tell her at night as he lies awake thinking of her and the events of the day.

Henry tells Grace of how he is finding his way in the home they made together. Surrounded by so many reminders of the life they shared, he feels he still belongs there. It has been their house for thirty years, and so it always will be. Gradually, he comes to cherish the memories that echo there without tears. He is grateful to sense her presence in so many of the things they accumulated and treasured together. He is grateful, too, for the way the walls resonate with their family history.

Henry is determined to fill his home with family life as he and Grace always had. He wants his children and grandchildren, Esther, Grace's brothers and sisters, and their families to feel they belong there, too. But at first it seemed like they all dreaded coming—as if they came because they had to. He thought perhaps they feared his sadness, or even their own.

After several visits, Henry at last finds a way to break through the awkwardness. He begins to tell stories of life with Grace. He talks about memories he associates with things and places in their home. He brings out the albums and scrapbooks. He makes it clear to all that he wants Grace to be with them in memory and in the stories they are so used to telling. He says he wants to hear their stories of Grace, too, along with the other stories he knows are within them. It is not long before the others again feel the warmth that is still in that home. They begin to return to it eagerly and often.

The family members also wish they had told Grace more often about the difference she made in their lives. Henry hopes she somehow overhears them when they speak. But, in case she doesn't, he brings their words to her as their ambassador, sometimes late at night as usual, and sometimes as he sits alone in the chair in the family room next to hers. Elizabeth and Victoria remember and are grateful for her warmth, confidences, and guidance in raising their own children. William had seen her more as a demanding teacher than a warm, accepting mother when he was a boy. But he now values the love that became evident when she supported him through hard times in his marriage. He sees how that love was there for him all along. All three appreciate her constant and ready support, the interest she took in their lives, and her devotion to them. All see what a wonderful grandmother she was to their children.

Henry speaks with Grace about what he sees in himself and in the others that remind him of her. His own love of family and storytelling is most dear to him. He delights in telling her how the others join enthusiastically in the storytelling. The children clearly care as deeply for their own children as he and Grace always have for them. Elizabeth has her mother's often droll but sometimes zany sense of humor, William her tenacity, and Victoria her stubborn independence of mind. They all have some of her uncanny ability to read other

people, to see beneath the surface of their actions to underlying char-
acter and motivation. They seem to be passing these legacies along to
their own children. All are better citizens because of her. They give
back to their communities as if they were extended family.

Henry tells Grace about how he is finding his way in the wider
world they walked together. He misses her in all the familiar places
and when he meets his fellow survivors. But he also feels he still
belongs in these places and with the people they knew. It has been
their hometown, and so it always will be.

Past the initial sadness of missing her in their hometown, Henry
again comes to cherish the memories, sense her presence, and take
heart at the differences her being there has made. When they see that
he is comfortable talking about Grace, others tell him about how she
touched their lives as a friend or teacher or in her work with the
historical society or the city council. They tell him that because of
Grace they experience family life differently and take pride in, and
are more involved in, the community. He senses that she has infected
the town with the love of family and local history that made her who
she was.

We remember, as Henry does, what those we love were like as
people, how they made themselves at home in the world. We
remember how family members and friends immersed themselves
in the details of their daily lives. We recall the things, places,
experiences, activities, and people they cherished. We know
something about the beginnings and unfolding of their life stories. We remember what we glimpsed of their dispositions, mo-
tives, and values beneath the surface of their actions. We recall
some of the strength of their sentiment, attachment, commitment, devotion, loyalty, and compassion. We remember what we
respected, admired, and appreciated in the richness and depth of
the caring and love we saw in them. We sense how we are
different and better for having known and loved them.

We may or may not believe that souls can exist without bodies
or survive after we die. But we can understand our souls as the

animating forces within us that move us to make ourselves at home in the world and draw from and savor the best of what we already have and have become. Our souls are at work deep within us in our desires, emotions, and dreams. Beneath the level of our conscious awareness or intention, they motivate our unself-conscious actions and habits.

In contrast, we can understand our spirits as the animating forces within us that move us to face the unknown, reach for the new, continue to change and grow, and look hopefully toward the future. As we grieve, we simultaneously move in soulful and spiritual directions: We struggle to return home to what is familiar *and* to give new shape to daily life and new direction to our life stories. We will explore movements of the grieving spirit after we have looked more closely at movements of the grieving soul.

Our souls, by their nature, thrive in attachment. They root us in connections with things, places, and, especially, others, weaving and reweaving intricate patterns again and again as our life stories unfold. We thrive in caring and loving, giving and taking, within these patterns. We savor the offerings of the here and now. We become sentimental about and come to cherish much of what our souls weave into patterns of connection.

Within familiar surroundings we nurture and sustain one another. Our souls find grounding in shared histories. We care about and love each other in our own ways. Loving connections with family and friends bring us satisfaction, fulfillment, understanding, empathy, acceptance, forgiveness, sensitivity, respect, reciprocity, warmth, compassion, comfort, peace, contentment, and a sense of belonging.

Much of our sense of who we are derives from the roots we find in the unique patterns of connection our souls weave in our physical surroundings and with those we care about and love. Because our souls work beneath the surface of our lives, we take much of what they accomplish in these ways for granted. Because what they accomplish lies so deep within and pervades the most inaccessible corners of our lives, our souls are ultimately mysterious.

Intimate life with others, our family members, companions, and friends, nourishes our souls as it shapes our daily lives, life stories, and characters. When they die, we can feel that they are still with us in our souls. We find our way back home again among the things, places, other people, experiences, and activities of the everyday life we shared with them. Memories reemerge through the soul pain we experience in the everyday surroundings where we knew them. We miss them there, but we also find sustenance and purpose there. We experience and cherish the resonance of life with them. We see how the next chapters of our life stories are rooted in our past life with them. As we enter those chapters, we appreciate and carry with us the indelible imprints of their lives, great or small, on our souls and those of our families and communities. We make use of deep lessons in living we have learned from them about how to be, not simply how to do. We treasure the irreplaceable gifts of lives now ended that make us ever different for having known them.

As we make their soulful legacies our own, we give those who have died yet another place in our hearts. We meet them again in the familiar rhythms and surroundings of daily life where we feel at home again, in the steady, taken-for-granted pulses of life that still nourish and sustain us. We hold them in our souls.

Meeting Them in Things
They Leave Behind

My grandmother's contemplation of shells has become my own. Each shell is a whorl of creative expression, an architecture of a soul. I can hold Melongena corona *to my ear and hear not only the ocean's voice, but the whisperings of my beloved teacher.*

—Terry Tempest Williams

Dad died thirty years ago. I now have only a few photographs of him. One of Dad and Mom on their wedding day is now on a shelf in our family room. I see more in that photo than just the joy of that day. I see all the years of their marriage as I know them. I see how he was with Mom. And I see how he was with my brother, John, and me.

I expect to have more photos and scrapbook materials when my brother and I eventually sort through the albums Mom now has. When I go through them now, I visit with Dad again, recall what he was like, and find what grounded me and shaped my early years. I also revisit objects in the photos, especially Dad's hats, a console radio, early televisions, favorite chairs, an old dining room set, and Ford cars that are filled with his character and my life with him. In addition to the photos, I expect one day to have a simple, wooden hanging shelf that Dad made for me for the model cars we made together when I was a boy. Such are the few tangible remnants of his life.

My cousin Dick died suddenly while dining with his wife. It shocked us all. Always healthy, vigorous, and physically active, he died in his late fifties. In addition to his wife and children, he is survived by his older brother Don and his identical twin Bob.

His funeral marked a significant departure in the history of funerals in my family. The many I attended while growing up always featured eulogies delivered by clergy, never a member of the family. Many were wide of the mark in capturing the characters of those I knew. Often there was little talk of the deceased even during calling hours, except for some mention of the last days of their lives. This time, both of Dick's brothers spoke from the heart about the brother they knew and loved. Bob even talked about his agony at losing a twin with whom he had been inseparable and strongly identified.

The service also included a showing of a videotape comprised of selections from family videos. It touched on highlights of the story of Dick's life. But it focused mostly on the kind of person he was. He loved his family. He had boundless energy, a zest for life and physical activity, and an incredibly quick wit and delighted in mischief and playfulness with his brother Bob. The vignettes in the tape captured vividly these aspects of Dick's character. It brought laughter into the sanctuary as well as tears.

Photographs are among the most compelling reminders we have of those who have died. Capturing their physical likenesses as the photos do, they remind us vividly of the presence we have lost. But we often see things in photos that lay beneath the surface of the figures they depict—the camera actually does capture aspects of soul.

Some remarkable photos allow us again to look deeply into the eyes of those we love. Others enable us to read much of their soulful characters in their faces, expressions, postures, or clothing, and in the settings of the photos. Often candid, unposed snapshots reveal more than posed or formal portraits. Home movies, videotapes, and audiotapes, like the one shown at Dick's funeral, sometimes enable us to read even more into the movements, gestures, actions, voices, and words of those we love.

Earlier I mentioned Bill and Diane and the tragic deaths of their three children. When I went to visit them in their home, Bill took me to a hiding place above the garage where he had kept some of the children's favorite toys for several years. He told me how they lost themselves in endless play with the toys and how he and Diane cherished the moments they spent watching and laughing with them as they did. When they died he was unable to face or decide what to do with them. He said that giving them away would have been like pretending his children didn't matter to him anymore. He was relatively certain that Diane did not know he had kept the toys.

Bill said he felt the time was coming for a decision. Bill and Diane now had two more young children who were approaching the ages when they would delight in playing with the toys. Would seeing them playing with their dead brothers' and sister's things bring back only pain or also pleasant memories and a special delight and feeling of closeness among all of the children? He was planning to tell Diane he had them and to ask her to help him decide what to do.

We also meet the souls of those we love in the objects they lived with every day, cared about, and cherished, like the children's toys Bill had kept. A desk, table, bookshelf, favorite chair, or bed may hold much history or love. Clothing may reflect soulful aspects of character. Workshop tools, garden implements, kitchen utensils, sewing equipment, art materials, musical instruments, or hobby equipment reveal hands or minds that found satisfaction in the act of creation. Work clothes or shoes, a lunch pail, tools of a trade, a pen, a briefcase, or dayplanner may symbolize dedication to work or devotion to others through it. Cars, boats, bicycles, or other vehicles are often filled with history and character. Sports and leisure equipment, games, collections, or toys may remind us of delight in life and activity, playfulness, fascination, or curiosity.

Their own creations, works of art or craft, or writings are often labors of love. Diaries, journals, albums, scrapbooks, or letters contain much of their character and history. Their watches or jewelry, dishes, silver, glassware, linens, favorite books, keepsakes, mementos, souvenirs, and other personal treasures often hold deep emotion, resonate with significant moments or periods in their life stories, or symbolize their deep attachments to others. Gifts they gave us before they died, or objects they left us in their wills, may become treasured possessions.

We can choose what to do with the photographs, tapes, and things that those we love leave behind. Sometimes we return, as Mom and Henry did, to homes filled with them. Sorting which to keep, which to set aside for a later decision (as Bill did), which to give to others, or which to discard can be a long and daunting process. We can set our own pace and handle these matters in our own way. We can proceed by ourselves or with others' help.

Sadly, we sometimes fight over prized possessions left behind by those we love. Such disputes can compound our suffering and even lead to permanent estrangement within families or among friends. Rarely, if ever, is an object worth such an emotional price.

Sometimes wills forestall such disputes. When they do not, we can do our best to understand and respect one another's histories with the objects in question. We can choose to negotiate and compromise. Valuable photographs and tapes can often be copied. Collections can be shared. Possessions can be divided fairly, bearing in mind that some things have far greater personal significance for some of us than for others. Conflicts between material and personal value can be decided in favor of personal value, with compensation going to other parties if need be. Some especially cherished objects can be shared by moving them from home to home. We can be generous in spirit and even indulge in some self-sacrifice where it seems appropriate. Far better to be guided by good intentions and our imaginations to find creative solutions than to add antagonisms and resentments to the legacies of those we love.

We meet something of those we love within these remnants of their lives. As we keep and cherish or use things they left behind, we come to feel at home again among them. As we continue to care about things that mattered to our loved ones, the sense of continuing connection with them touches our souls. We weave them into the broader fabric of our new life patterns. We carry them with us into the next chapters of our life stories.

Soul Food and Soul Music

The familiar but forgotten smells and tastes restore . . .
a long-dormant element in the soul—
a comforted childhood, a feeling of belonging,
the support of religious and cultural traditions,
and family stories and personalities.

—*Thomas Moore*

Dad was a cook in Wally's Cafe, a small-town restaurant he owned with his brother. He made great soups that we all enjoyed but that he never ate because he refused to eat vegetables. My brother and I were allowed to make our own milkshakes when we ate or sometimes worked at the restaurant. And Dad often cooked at home. Meat and potatoes were the rule when he did, and the steaks were often chicken-fried. He loved fruit pie, especially apple. I think of him whenever I enjoy any of these foods, including an occasional steak without the added chicken-fry. I remember how hard he worked to provide a home for us. His favorite foods take me back to that home with a quiet, gentle man I called Pop.

My grandmother came over from "the old country" in time for the birth of her fifth child, my mother. Life in her home seemed to revolve around the kitchen and the large dining room table with her presiding at its head. I have difficulty remembering her without an apron. She loved German sausage and sauerkraut, dark rye and pumpernickel breads, and cabbage rolls. She also loved strong cheeses I have never been able to approach. She made marvelous

*desserts, including plum and apple cakes, German chocolate cake,
and, my favorite, pastry puffs filled with either whipped cream or
custard and topped with dark chocolate. I think of Grandma whenever I enjoy these treats. I never miss the chance of eating in my
favorite German restaurant in Chicago whenever I return to her
home city. Each time I do, I wish I could return to Grandma's table, see her warm smile, and have her put seconds on my plate one
more time.*

We often find enduring connection with those who have died
in the foods we eat. "Soul food" is an apt term—it conveys
the emotional power that food holds for us. The term does not
apply exclusively to one ethnic group, though it probably orig-
inated with African Americans. Traditional food and drink link
us with our roots in broader cultures and histories that have
shaped us and our families and communities. What we call
comfort food; the foods we return to for special occasions,
holidays, and festivals; and favorite recipes (often handed down
from generation to generation) are staples in most of our do-
mestic lives.

We were fed as children, just as we now feed our own. We
prepare food for one another as adults, sharing a part of ourselves
as we do. Cooking for one another is so commonplace that we
take for granted that it is a nurturing social ritual that goes beyond food. The food nourishes our bodies, yes, but, indirectly,
we are nourishing souls with love and care. Preparing food together saves time and effort, but it can also be a way of loving,
caring, and sharing that draws us close.

We enjoy food and drink with family or friends, or in larger
community gatherings. And when we do, we often rehearse the
happenings of the day. We delight in one another. We talk of
work, family, friendship, and community. We share memories.
We reveal our souls to one another. We discuss our deepest cares
and concerns. Our souls resonate together as we sense and

appreciate all that we have in common, the closeness we enjoy, and how much we have come to care about one another.

Grandma also loved music, including Christmas carols, Stephen Foster melodies, American show tunes from the first half of the century, and especially music from "the old country." There was singing nearly every time the family gathered for holiday celebrations, usually dominated by my Uncle Billy's powerful and melodious baritone voice and my Aunt Gertie's equally powerful alto. Nothing matched the enthusiasm for the German drinking songs, ballads, and polkas. The piano that Mom played when the nine kids were still at home with Grandma was no longer in her home, so they sang there without one. But nearly every child had a piano in his or her own home. And when we gathered, Mom would again play while we all sang. When Mom and Gertie visited my home, Mom played and Gertie sang again as they always had. These German songs are now my soul music. So too are oompah and polka bands, even Lawrence Welk.

Like food, music has an uncanny ability to arouse powerful emotions and connect us to memories of those we love. Though the term usually refers to a variety of rhythm and blues, "soul music" for me is any music that connects us sentimentally with people and places now far away. Traditional music links us with our roots in broader cultures and histories that have shaped us as well as our families and communities. While food seems to nourish our souls indirectly, music often has an immediate effect that passes any thinking process. It feels as if it goes right to our souls, right to where we live, and nourishes us directly. Music of any kind can resonate within us, stir deep emotion, and evoke compelling memories. It permeates or punctuates our daily life. It can accompany quiet moments and intimate conversations. It need not be traditional to touch us.

Soul food or soul music can put us in touch with those we love, whether they are with us or not. We can continue to prepare these foods and listen to this music, allowing it to enrich our home life. We can occasionally make their favorite dishes or select their favorite drinks. We can use their favorite recipes. We can renew, sustain, or find new appreciation for the kind of music they treasured or their favorite composers, performers, or pieces. We can sing or perform the music. We can return to favorite haunts where we ate and drank and enjoyed music with them.

Both food and music have the power to help us heal, to make us feel at home again.

Meeting Them in Familiar Places

When the shell you live in has taken on the savor of your love,
when your dwelling has become a taproot,
then your house is a home.

—*Scott Russell Sanders*

I returned to my parents' home on Cross Street and my hometown many times in the years after Dad died. Mom changed the arrangements she had made at home to care for Dad while he was ill. She sorted through and disposed of most of his clothing and other personal items. She otherwise kept the house very much as it was before he died. Over the years she bought some furniture or carpet when old items wore out and rearranged things in ways that suited her. It seemed very much the same place to me nearly twenty-five years later when she left it for a retirement home.

When I visited, I easily remembered Dad in the various rooms of the house or out in the yard. I saw him napping after a hard day's work, sitting before the television watching the White Sox or Cubs, eating at the kitchen or dining room table, sitting and listening while company chattered away or I played the piano, or joking with my friends. Occasionally, I told my children something about the grandfather they never met when we returned there together or as I remembered incidents in particular places.

I still drive past the site of Wally's Cafe and remember Dad there. The building has changed owners, names, and contents many times, but it still holds memories. I also drive past the site of an earlier home. It was torn down shortly after we moved and replaced by a church parking lot and later an expansion of the church itself. The site still triggers, and the neighborhood still holds, many memories of Dad and life with my parents in the earliest years I can recall. I share them with whoever rides with me.

Mom returned home to the house on Cross Street to live with Grandma. I know it was hard at first, but having Grandma there helped. The real loneliness came several years later when Grandma died. I often wondered what it was like for Mom to live there surrounded by the walls that held the remnants of her husband's and mother's lives. She spoke often of the two of them, and no doubt the place was filled with memories. She found her way back home there. That she still cherished it became clear when she made the painful decision to leave it because it was no longer safe to live there alone.

We can sometimes feel the presence of those we love in the places they lived in and cared about. We feel connected with deceased family members, companions, and friends in places where we felt at home and blended our daily lives with theirs. Their homes and our own, rooms within them, places within those rooms, yards, gardens, and neighborhoods can hold many memories of the special closeness we knew with them. Schools, workplaces, houses of worship, stores and malls, theaters and movie houses, restaurants and coffeehouses, and other favorite gathering places often evoke powerful memories of how our lives were interwoven with theirs. These places echo with greetings and partings, chores and work, schooling, gatherings with family and friends, conversation, shared thoughts and feelings, confidences and secrets, tears and sorrows, laughter and delight, food, music, play and entertainment, and moments of deep connection and intimacy.

The places where we felt at home with those who have died resonate with the love they gave us. In them they provided shelter and protection, physical and emotional security, attention and interest, affirmation and enthusiasm, care and sensitivity, warmth and affection, acceptance and forgiveness, and a sense of belonging. With them there we rooted ourselves and found nurturing life contexts within which we became absorbed in everyday routines, cultivated interests, worked and played side by side, formed life habits and values, developed self-esteem and self-confidence, and shaped our identities and characters. In natural settings, such as gardens, farms, parks, beaches, marshes, hiking trails, forests, and mountains, we replenished ourselves and sensed how we are sustained by earth, water, air, sun, plants and animals, and one another.

Returning home can be an emotionally charged decision. We may choose to stay a while, avoid it temporarily, or leave it behind. When we still share our homes with others, the choice to leave is rarely ours to make alone. Even when painful things happened there, we most often choose to stay. We struggle through our hurt and find ways to feel at home there again.

We can once again make ourselves at home in familiar places much as we did when those we love lived. We can feel we belong there simply because we are so accustomed to their walls and neighborhoods or have lived so well there, as Henry did in the home he shared with Grace for thirty years. In familiar places where we shared life, we can revive connections that still satisfy and sustain us.

We may choose to remodel, redecorate, or rearrange the contents of our homes to accommodate changes in daily life that seem appropriate. But no such changes cancel the life we have lived there or our memories of how we shared it with those we love.

As we continue living in familiar places, unchanged or changed, we can pause occasionally to remember the souls of those who shared their life with us. We can recall the daily lives we knew with them. We can interact with or use things they left behind. We can meditate or pray with them in mind. We can speak with them. We can simply feel close to them.

We can return to places where we were born and raised, where we and those who have died shared life and came to know one another, or where we found soulful connection. We can find many such places in our homes or hometowns. We may sometimes travel far or go to considerable expense when such pilgrimages matter deeply to us. We can remember the places, the lives we led, and those we knew. We can bring others to those places to tell them stories or introduce them to soulful characters who mean so much to us.

Sometimes places become inaccessible to us, for instance, when others now own or occupy them or they have been destroyed. Sometimes returning to them is too difficult or beyond our means. But we can still remember them fondly and return to them indirectly through photographs, videos, or objects that connect us to life within them.

In these and other ways, we learn to live comfortably and securely, to feel at home again within familiar surroundings. We learn to cherish what still nourishes us in those places.

Seeing Them in Others

If you don't believe in ghosts, you've never been to a fam-
ily reunion.

—*Ashleigh Brilliant*

The last Nagel reunion took place one summer day in 1981 at my Aunt Gertie's home in suburban Chicago. We called it the "Nagel" reunion because my Grandma, Mom, and her siblings were Nagels. Grandma had died several years before and her daughter, Clara, nearly twenty years before her. Her eight surviving children were there. Mom and her sisters Christine and Hilde were widowed. Gertie, her fraternal twin Mary, Herm, Billy, and Dick were there with their spouses. A dozen or so of the eighteen in my generation were there, most with spouses and little and growing children of our own. There were somewhere between thirty and forty of us.

It was in many ways like so many of the holiday gatherings that I counted among the most wonderful experiences of my childhood. Though they had more character etched in their features and more white hair, my aunts and uncles were as lively and sometimes challenging and frustrating as ever. My aunts' features only hinted at resemblance to Grandma. My uncles resembled more than ever the grandfather I knew only through photographs. My generation was filled with grown-up versions of the bodies and personalities I remembered, some difficult but most endearing.

The gathering was large and tended to overwhelm, as it always had. I felt as if I wanted to be everywhere at once. We couldn't help recalling and talking about the earlier gatherings, many in Grandma's home. Family soul food was consumed in large quantities, as usual. There was a bit of the old music. But mostly there was joy in seeing one another again.

Clearly, it was still Grandma's family. Yes, it was Grandpa's, too, but none really thought of it that way. In my experience, he has always been a shadowy family figure. He was apparently a difficult man in many respects, few ever talked about him, and fewer still comfortably acknowledged any likeness to him.

I am sure I was not alone as I sensed that Grandma was with us in the warmth, good humor, and laughter we shared. We felt the same welcoming embrace of family, easy acceptance, interest and delight in one another, willingness to overlook shortcomings and set aside differences, and sense of belonging when we went to her home. And there was her great love of children. So many new faces, including my own three, were being introduced to the larger group that day, relatives living and dead.

I sensed her presence, too, in the worry that now and again came to the surface. It is a family resemblance that none are too comfortable about acknowledging. Grandma could worry about anything. She was endearing when she sometimes laughed with others later when she realized how far senseless worry had taken her. Of course, there were other times when her worry drove us to distraction, as it made her controlling and overprotective. But now that we had some distance from those times, we could laugh when someone noticed the family resemblance.

No one ever talked (or for that matter talks) about the pain of missing Grandma. Explicit talk about feelings is not a Nagel inheritance or one of Grandma's legacies. And no one called everyone together to remember or acknowledge Grandma. Yet conversation turned as easily to her as to other subjects.

Many in Mom's generation told stories about growing up in Chicago, life with Grandma, her hardships and trials, and how much *she loved us all. Others in my generation recounted their childhood memories of her as a grandmother. Some told stories of special moments and the wonderful craziness of having her in our lives, even the frequent exasperation. Some no doubt remembered without saying a word. As usual, it was not always easy to find an opening to speak. Some of us stood back from the crowd for a moment and noticed how the rhythms and character of family life were being repeated in my cousins' and my generation. No doubt many joined me in feeling grateful for how the family and the reunion were possible because of her, though none of us said so explicitly.*

I know that family reunions are not for everyone. Many among us go to great lengths to avoid them, and they can be very offputting and painful. But my point is not to persuade anyone to begin planning a reunion. Instead, it is to illustrate one way we can recognize the souls of those who have died in others with whom we survive. We sense connection with them there every bit as much as we do in the things and places they leave behind.

A granddaughter watches her mother prepare for a special family gathering and recognizes her grandmother's attention to detail and care with family treasures. As she strolls through her garden with them, a grandmother observes how her deceased son's children share his curiosity about nature. A bereaved friend thanks others in her circle one day for continuing the once-a-month lunch tradition begun by one who is no longer with them. Over and over, a brother observes how his younger sister has inherited their older sister's uncanny abilities to live fully in the moment and find the best of what her surroundings have to offer. A mother observes her son sitting peacefully beside a stream and sees how reflective and introspective he is, bringing to mind her own father. While visiting his daughter, a widower sees in her his wife's gentle ways with children. A son recognizes his dead father's honesty, concern for justice, and compassion when his brother stands up for someone who has been cheated.

We see how others carry themselves and have become like those who have died in their soulful ways of being in the world. We see how we are the way we are with one another, in part, because they once were with us. When we share our memories of those who have died, we are often reminded of important events and defining moments that made us who we are. We may see resemblances to those who have died in others or in ourselves that we have overlooked. We feel close to those who have died, sensing that we still belong together, in part, because they were once with us.

As I write, some of the third generation in the Nagel family are talking about another reunion. Grandma's children, our parents, aunts, and uncles, are aging, and some are growing fragile. Five of the original nine still live. All but one is widowed. One is remarried. Two of the eighteen cousins have died in recent years, and one has lost a child.

I share the hope that we can gather again before others die. It is by no means a perfect family. And I can understand why, regrettably, some might choose to stay away. But it is my family. I want to see the familiar faces, feel that special family feeling, renew the ties that bind us, delight in the company, and meet some of the many new additions to Grandma's family. And I want to hear the stories of, and renew acquaintance with, the souls of those who are no longer with us.

Finding Our Roots in
Their Life Stories

Tell me whom you love, and I will tell you who you are.

—Anonymous

After Grace died, Henry and his children continued to fill his home with stories of Grace and their life with her. Conversation at Nagel family reunions always included tales and anecdotes about Grandma, rarely about Grandpa. Kathryn gathered stories about Mark and life with him from family and friends and shared them with him before he died. Now she reviews them and adds others of her own in sessions with her children who were too young when Mark died to have clear memories of him. Alex Haley probed his family history and told the world what he found in *Roots*. We often tell stories about those who have died and our lives with them.

Typically, we tell and cherish the stories because they delight or fascinate us. We hold dear their principal characters. We keep their memories alive in and through the stories. We find in them many things that are useful in our practical lives. But we can, and often do, cherish the stories for deeper reasons.

We find our historical roots in the stories we tell of family members, especially our parents and grandparents and others in earlier generations. We find continuity with those who have gone before us. Our lives originate in and emerge from their life histories, histories shaped and colored by cultural and family customs and traditions. Many of these customs and traditions are ways of the soul, ways of making ourselves at home in the world, sharing daily life, and caring for one another.

These historical roots are the most well established of those that sustain and anchor us in the world. They extend through the histories of many generations and this common heritage binds us together. In it we find important aspects of who we are as we take our place within cultural and family histories.

These well-established roots in long-standing custom and tradition are not the only ones we find beneath the surface of the stories we remember about those who have died. We also find newer, personal roots first sent forth and established by our own souls in everyday and intimate life with family and friends. Those roots found fertile ground in their love and nurturing that enabled us to thrive and grow and to become who we are. Their souls may or may not have been animated by well-established customs and traditions. Each generation finds continuity as it passes along some of the customs and traditions it has been given. And each generation finds new connection as it establishes customs and traditions of its own.

Of course, not all of what we find is positive or constructive. As we search the stories of the lives of those who have died for what we can love, we all encounter ambivalence. But we would not be searching if we did not believe that working through the ambivalence would be worth the effort. Some of us readily find an abundance to love and have little difficulty with what disappoints us. Some of us must clear away unfinished business. Some of us must work hard to look past lingering hurt and see the love that is also there. Some of us must struggle to disentangle ourselves from seriously negative ties to find what good, if any, remains to cherish.

What are some of the things worth cherishing? We remember when our lives connected most profoundly with theirs. Our parents gave us the gift of life itself. They raised us in homes where we found shelter, safety, and a sense of belonging. We made homes together and raised families of our own. We experienced many firsts with family and friends. We made lasting contributions to our communities. We marked major life transitions together, celebrating, laughing, taking the fullest delight in life with one another. We wept. We reached out to, helped, and supported one another. We gave of ourselves. We opened ourselves to one another. We sensed that they knew and appreciated our deepest selves, or we theirs. They accepted us unconditionally, even forgave us, or we them. We revealed our love most clearly or gave it most freely.

When we remember such times of deep connection with those who have died, we come home to ourselves. We find the roots of who we are, and always will be, in what we recall. Yes, we are challenged to sort the good from the bad and overcome hurtful or even destructive consequences of the bad. But we must reshape our daily lives and find our ways back home. We must redirect our life stories. And we must do these things with as much autonomy as we can manage. But however we do them, the patterns within our lives and the unfolding of our life stories will always be grounded in the life we have known with those who have died.

Our past life with those we love does not become irrelevant to us because it passes. It does not disappear as if erased by an invisible hand. Though it recedes, its significance lingers. Our cultural, family, and personal history with them is never canceled. Our present life with fellow survivors is continuous with our past life. As Grace taught, and Henry and her family know, we never make a clean break with the past. Rather, we grow through and emerge from it. In the past we became who and what we are today. We are, and always will be, profoundly different for having been loved by and for having loved those who have died.

If we can discover our roots and embrace the good in what we find, they can continue to nourish our souls. The trick, of course, is to find the good.

Touching Our Souls in Mysterious Ways

In quiet moments of reflection she realizes that Mark has no doubt touched and affected her in countless ways that will forever elude her.

—*A widow's story*

There is more to Henry's Grace, my grandmother, Kathryn's Mark, Alex Haley's ancestors, and others whom we love than we will ever know. Earlier I wrote about how, as we live with and remember them, we stand before them as we do before other mysteries in life. They are not like puzzles or problems we can solve or finish. They can always surprise us, show us something more of themselves, challenge or delight us in new ways. We never fully understand or appreciate the complexity of their life stories or the depth of their characters.

We are hardly in a better position to know the souls of those who have died than they were. They were unfathomable when alive and will remain so. We know only aspects of their daily lives and life stories. In everyday life with them, we were ordinarily as unselfconsciously absorbed in things, places, experiences, activities, and interactions with others as they were. Only occasionally did we sense beneath the surface of what we could observe how their souls motivated their everyday expressions, gestures, actions, or habits. We may sometimes have detected how they cared deeply about something in ways they themselves were not aware of, but only rarely. When we saw clearly that they cared about something or someone, it was often far less clear how and why they did. Mostly these depths remained opaque to us.

We know the souls of those who have died best from those rare times when their care and love were most transparent, especially the moments and periods of our deepest personal, family, and community connection with them. As we remember and probe their life stories, we can learn more about them. But because their souls remain mostly hidden from us, as they were from them, we never finish with exploring and interpreting the richness of meaning in their life stories or fathoming the depth of their characters.

Henry's son, William, had had an ambivalent relationship with his mother, Grace, when he was a boy. Almost more than she could handle, she found it hard to be as close with him as she had been with his sisters. Seeing her as a strict teacher, it was difficult for him to accept her as a mother who really cared for him.

When Henry's family gathered and told stories of Grace, William spoke fondly of her kindness when his marriage was not going well but his early experiences still cloud his view of how deeply her soul touched and affected his. Henry tells Grace at night how much of what he sees of her in each of their children. But William does not yet see all that seems obvious to his father.

Henry notes Grace's tenacity in their son. One day he tells William how much he resembles his mother in this respect. William readily concedes, though he had never made the connection, that his mother probably made him as tenacious as he is. Henry observes to Grace that all three of their children care deeply for their own as she did. Without his father's saying anything, William is beginning to recognize how this, too, is one of his mother's legacies, as his appreciation of his mother's love grows.

But William does not yet link his mother with the abilities to read other people, see beneath the surface of what they do, parent as effectively as he does, and give back to his community: things Henry sees in him. Perhaps Henry will one day tell stories that will make these roots of William's character more transparent to him. Or he may say explicitly to William what he has confided to Grace. And William will likely discover connections that now elude him. Perhaps self-reflection will lead him to see them. Or perhaps he will simply continue to be like Grace in many ways that he never recognizes.

Remember Kathryn, Mark, and their two children, Josh and Sarah. Several years after Mark died, and with his blessing in a letter he left her, Kathryn remarried. Kathryn and Jim, a widower himself, were well aware of how different they were because they had both been in good marriages that ended tragically.

Kathryn knows that she is a better parent because she and Mark spent Josh's and Sarah's first years together. And she knows she is more patient, flexible, understanding, tender, and caring because of her life with Mark. She and Jim are both grateful for these legacies, though they speak little of them as they make their own life together.

The longer Kathryn and Jim are together, the more Kathryn notices countless little things she learned in life with Mark that enable her to live intimately with Jim: choosing private nicknames, tuning in to the sensitivities and foibles of a partner, knowing when to confide and when to hold something in reserve that could be needlessly hurtful, finding the laugh buttons, surrendering to the wonders of the moment, balancing give-and-take in managing everyday affairs, and knowing when and how to leave work behind and attend fully to everyday joys and challenges.

In the first months of her new marriage, Kathryn is amazed at how often she sees such connections. She frequently expresses her gratitude in a silent "Thanks, Mark." She then quickly returns to the unfolding intimacy with Jim.

In quiet moments of reflection she realizes that Mark has no doubt touched and affected her in countless ways that will forever elude her. She is a far different person for having known and loved him than she will ever fully comprehend or be able to articulate. Far from distressing her, this brings her great peace. Mark will always be deep within her. But not in any way that will disturb her relationship with Jim. It seems both ironic and wonderful that the ability to give herself fully in her new love is itself, in part, one of Mark's legacies.

Kathryn marvels at how Mark's life will, unseen, touch hers and Jim's in ways that she and he will likely never recognize. She sees no need to discuss such things with Jim in detail, though she may confide some of what she has learned to Josh and Sarah when they are older. It seems enough to her to acknowledge the unseen connections and to give to Jim wholeheartedly. She continues to include a note of thanksgiving for Mark in her evening prayers where she is most grateful for Jim's coming into her life.

When those we love die, we often realize how much we took for granted as we shared our life with them. We may not have paused to acknowledge even the most conspicuous differences they made in our lives. No matter how effectively we may have expressed our appreciation, we commonly believe we did not say enough. We sense that we could not have said it all. Now we can see that taking so much for granted and failing to acknowledge the full extent of our indebtedness to those we love are nearly inevitable because our souls work and touch one another in mysterious ways. Still, we regret not having expressed our gratitude for their legacies. We want to show appreciation even after they have died. We want to acknowledge that their presence in our lives was an irreplaceable gift.

We can express our gratitude directly to those who have died in places where we feel close to them or in prayer. We can voice it in journals, diaries, or other records. We can praise their souls in ceremonies of separation or commemorate them in memorials.

We can devote time in thanksgiving with family members or friends and in our communities. We can tell others how thankful we are for the differences those who have died made in our lives, both those we recognize and those we don't see.

We pay them additional tribute when we pass along to others what we have learned from them. More often than not, we simply show others, just as those we love showed us. We live soulfully in ways they taught us, and, as we do, we touch others' souls in turn.

Learning to Be Soulful

Love is how you stay alive, even after you are gone!
—Morrie Schwartz

Dorothy came to speak with my classes several times during the last years of her life. She was dying of cancer. She told what it was like when the doctor gave her the diagnosis and explained what lay ahead. She told us how the disease ravaged her body. She spoke about the failure of standard treatments and what the experimental treatments were like. She answered the students' questions fully and candidly.

Most memorably, though, she spoke about how life was different for her as she faced her own mortality. Living with illness forced some changes as it undermined her stamina and sometimes shelved her from everyday life. Yet, she insisted she was living some of the best days of her life. Her illness prompted her to reflect on what really mattered in the time she had left to live.

She spoke about how she no longer put off until later what she cared about most. She made sure that every day included living and loving well. She enjoyed her home, the comforts it provided, and the life it held. She made time for her husband. She followed her son's performance career carefully and traveled to see him whenever her *schedule permitted. She enjoyed the company of friends. She walked away from arguments when she could see they were leading nowhere. She realized how much she loved her teaching career and vowed that she would give all that she could to her students as long as her body allowed her to function in the classroom. In the end, she taught to within a few days of her death.*

Each time Dorothy spoke she would come to a point in her presentation when she would walk toward the students and talk from her heart. She said, "You probably think you are very different from me. After all, I am sick and dying. But I am here to tell you that we are not so very different, at least not in the way you may be thinking. I wish I could approach each of you, grab you by the collar, look deeply into your eyes, and make you see that you, too, are dying. We all die. The time for all of us to live is now, not later. The only difference between us may be that I realize how true that is because someone has told me I probably will die before you do. But any one of you could go first. I am doing my best to kiss worry and boredom good-bye and fill my life with what matters most to me. Oh, how I wish that something I say tonight could open your eyes to how important it is for you to do the same, before it's too late."

Dorothy was attempting to awaken the souls of those who listened to her. She wasn't simply conveying information, as teachers so often do. Nor was she telling or showing us how to do anything in particular. Instead, she was speaking about a deeper lesson that she was clearly grateful to have learned. It was a lesson for the soul about how to live the good life. About living fully and richly, not taking life for granted. If we took it to heart, we would be different persons. Our characters would change. I remember my friend Dorothy whenever I pause to reflect on how well I am using the gift of life she cherished so dearly.

Sometimes, like Dorothy, those we love speak to us heart-to-heart before they die about how to thrive in the human condition. Sometimes they casually scatter bits of wisdom and advice in everyday conversation. Sometimes they speak indirectly to us through ethical wills or notes or letters they leave behind. They express their love and concern for us by commending ways of savoring what life offers us. We are told to find satisfaction and fulfillment in the everyday, to care for one another, to cherish and maintain traditions, and to love our families and communities.

In these ways, those we love "talk the talk." But talk alone is rarely compelling. It is more so when, like Dorothy, they also "walk the walk." They gain credibility when we can see how they have used the wisdom they gained in their everyday lives and life stories.

More often we learn how to find the best that life has to offer from how they lived their lives. Typically, they show us without saying anything directly. They likely don't even intend to show us anything. They are simply being at their best. We reconnect with the lessons they have given us when we probe beneath the surface, when we remember and see the depth of soul there was within them.

When we explore the stories of those who have died, we find the patterns of care and love that made them the unique individuals they were and always will be. Soulful ways of caring and loving are among the most precious gifts those who have died have given us. We receive such gifts from everyone we know and love, just as they have received from us and others. We are the individuals we are, in part, because no two of us are touched by the same loved ones in the same ways. Within unique life circumstances, we receive and take to heart different lessons from different people. Sometimes we do so quite self-consciously and deliberately. But often we simply absorb some of the character of those we love without even realizing it.

We have learned far more lessons of the soul from some who have died than from others. A few of us have known great-souled individuals with unusual capacities to love richly and well through virtually all the connections in their lives. Far more commonly, we have known family and friends who have cared and loved well in some areas and in some respects and not so well in others. And we have known and loved a few who have cared and loved well only very rarely.

Part of loving means accepting those we love, flaws and all. Another part of loving them is recognizing and admiring how they have cared and loved well. And part of loving them is appreciating what they have taught us that we choose to imitate in our own lives. We can expand and enrich our love for those who have died as we sort through what we remember, become more aware of the gifts they offered, and embrace the gifts we choose to keep more self-consciously and gratefully.

What are some of the deep lessons of the soul those we love may have given us? A family member or friend may have taught us how to be grateful for and make the best of where we are and what we have. To be flexible and adaptable. To transform a place into a home. To appreciate the shelter, safety, and sense of belonging a home provides. To be resourceful and respect our natural surroundings. To treasure objects and places for the meanings and history they hold. To be open and receptive to what experiences and activities have to offer. To live in the present moment. To be curious and eager to explore. To savor the richness of experiences. To participate wholeheartedly in activities. Or to love what we are doing and do it with care.

A loved one may have taught us how to appreciate and treasure life itself. To appreciate the wonders of, and care deeply about, our bodies, minds, souls, and spirits. To be reflective or introspective. To acknowledge and respect our deepest emotions. To appreciate our own worth and irreplaceability. To develop and maintain self-confidence. To carry ourselves with dignity and self-respect. To stand up for ourselves and be assertive without being aggressive. To be proud without being arrogant. To be humble without being excessively deferential or self-sacrificing.

To recognize and appreciate our limitations and vulnerability. Or to accept and forgive ourselves.

Vaughan was Inez's only child. Her husband, Merle, died when Vaughan was twelve. In his mid-twenties, Vaughan discovered he was infected with HIV, as was his life's partner Robin. It was only a matter of months before Vaughan was dealing with an AIDS infection. Vaughan was active in the AIDS community, and Inez pitched in to do what she could. She was impressed by the love she found there. She was especially moved by her son's deep concern for those who suffered and died abandoned by disapproving families. Vaughan worried, in particular, about what would become of Robin if he were to precede his partner in death.

Inez worked closely with Robin as they attended to Vaughan through the last months, weeks, and days of his dying. They mourned him deeply. Six months later, when Robin became acutely ill and began to die, Inez became his surrogate mother. She offered him what his parents were unable or unwilling to give him. Following in Vaughan's compassionate ways after Robin died, she continued to offer a mother's love in the AIDS community wherever she saw a need.

To be attentive and deeply interested in others. To recognize and treasure the differences that make others the individuals they are. To be open and receptive to the gifts others offer. To be appreciative. To be kind, considerate, and sensitive to vulnerability. To be gentle, comforting, and tender. To be trusting and trustworthy. To be loyal. To be honest and candid. To be discreet and faithful to confidences. To be gracious. To give of ourselves freely and wholeheartedly. To be patient, understanding, and sympathetic. To be accepting and forgiving. To be affectionate. Or to be nurturing. These are soulful ways to connect with one another that loved ones may have shown us.

A loved one may have taught us how to respect, cherish, and thrive within family, community, and cultural traditions. To be tolerant and respect differences in others' wants, needs, and perspectives. To appreciate the value and fragility of harmony, mutual respect, and reciprocity. To be civil and well mannered. To live with integrity. To be truthful, responsible, and dependable. To be dedicated or devoted. To be faithful to promises, commitments, and covenants. To be cooperative. To be peacemakers. To appreciate the worth of negotiation and compromise. To be fair and just. To be empathetic and compassionate. To be responsive to the disadvantaged and most vulnerable among us. Or to be beneficent and charitable.

We may recognize in some of their actions, life patterns, and life stories models of how to be. We may wish to strive to become more like them in some ways. We may even identify things we wish to change in our own life patterns and life stories that reflect the lessons we have learned. We may ask others to help and support us in our efforts. We may help and support others who may wish to emulate those who have died.

These desires should not be confused with idealizing those who have died, with trying to be like them in every respect. Such tendencies are nearly always destructive, whether the person is dead or still alive. And recognizing that we love those who have died despite their imperfections can enable us to forgive ourselves for our own failings. We need to be our own persons even as we choose to follow those who have died. We remain true to ourselves when we acknowledge our own histories. We love and honor those who have died when we make some of the ways of caring and loving they have taught us our own.

When those we love die, we face the profound challenges of going on without them. But, as we have seen, we still retain legacies and deep lessons that enable us to find our way back home, to revive connections, to reclaim meanings. And, as we grieve, we return home to the things that can still nourish us.

But we cannot return to life just as it was before those we love died. Another vital aspect of ourselves moves us in new directions. It works within us as we struggle to transcend our suffering, contend with the unknown, and stretch into the unfamiliar. It enables us to reshape our daily lives, redirect our life stories, and weave new threads into their patterns. It moves us to transform ourselves and become whole in new ways. It revives our faith that life is worth living and breathes new life into our hope for the future. As we grieve we also grapple with spiritual challenges. We now turn to these matters of the spirit.

VI

Life of the Spirit:
Reviving Hope

Loss and Spiritual Pain

And grief still feels like fear. Perhaps, more strictly, like suspense. Or like waiting; just hanging about waiting for something to happen. . . . It doesn't seem worth starting anything. . . . Up till this I always had too little time. Now there is nothing but time. Almost pure time, empty successiveness.

—C. S. Lewis

Early in the movie Shadowlands, *C. S. Lewis speaks with Oxford students about the ideal of courtly love, a love that is pure, perfect, and, above all, unattainable. "The most intense joy lies not in the having, but in the desire." Lewis, author of a scholarly book on this ideal of love in English literature, knows love of a woman only from what he has read. He is a confirmed bachelor in his mid-fifties.*

Later we glimpse Lewis in his public life as a well-known author of popular works on suffering and other spiritual and religious themes, science-fiction novels, and children's books. He concludes a lecture about suffering and wonders aloud about an accident where a bus has killed twenty-four cadets. Could a good God allow such a thing? Does God want us to suffer? He confidently affirms that God "wants us to love and be loved." He intimates that suffering may somehow be a gift from God that helps us to do these things. He is smooth and engaging. But he speaks again as if he has not known suffering personally. His answers to his difficult questions seem too abstract, intellectual, removed.

The movie tells the story of how Lewis learns about love and suffering from firsthand experiences of both. He meets and befriends Joy Gresham, an American novelist and prize-winning poet. His writings had helped her with her conversion to Christianity. She is married to an American writer and has a young son, Douglas, who admires Lewis's children's books. In the course of several meetings Joy meets Lewis's older brother, Warnie, also an Oxford don, and Lewis meets and is kind to Douglas.

From the very beginning, exchanges between Lewis and Joy are lively and high-spirited. Joy asks direct and penetrating questions. She disarms Lewis. Her challenges don't so much sting as intrigue him. She is not out to win points in debate but rather to know better someone she admires. Lewis, in turn, is touched deeply by poetry she shares with him and admires the sensitivity and compassion he sees in it.

They discuss whether writers must draw upon personal experience and how reading may leave us at a safe distance from experience that can hurt us. Joy wonders if Lewis has ever been really hurt. He reveals his sorrow at his mother's death when he was nine. Joy responds with warmth and empathy. On another occasion, Joy reveals her sorrow as her marriage is coming to an end. Lewis asks how he can help. She asks that he be her friend. He says he hopes he is that already.

Joy goes to America to finalize her divorce. When she returns to England to further her career, Lewis agrees to marry her, "only technically." It will be a government wedding to extend citizenship to Joy. The ceremony is brief and perfunctory. No one is to know what they have done. Afterward, they go separate ways.

Some time later, Joy asks Lewis whether he isn't just bursting to share the joke: his friends think them to be unmarried and wicked while they are actually married and up to nothing at all. The joke hadn't even occurred to Lewis. Conversation leads her to see how he has arranged his life so that no one can touch him. He wonders how she can assail a friend with such probing. She makes it clear she *doesn't want to be the kind of friend he seems to have. He says he doesn't understand. She insists he must but that he doesn't like it. Neither does she. She cuts the conversation short and leaves.*

Before long, Lewis telephones Joy at her London apartment. After she falls on the way to answering, they learn that she has cancer. It is far enough advanced that she is not expected to live long. Lewis attends her at the hospital. The doctors avoid telling her directly how bad her condition is. She asks Lewis for honesty. He says they expect her to die. She thanks him. He sighs. She says he seems different, looks at her properly. He says he doesn't want to lose her. She does not want to be lost.

Lewis soon realizes that he loves Joy. He tells her he wants to marry her "before God and the world." She asks if it is to make her an honest woman. He says not. He admits that he is the one who hasn't been honest. They are married in the hospital.

Contrary to all expectations, Joy's cancer enters remission. She and Douglas come to live with Lewis. Joy opens Lewis's heart. To delight in married life. To venture into the English countryside in search of a special place he has known only from a picture that hung in his nursery when he was a boy and still hangs in his office. To savor the miracle of the time they have together. He finds joy and love he has never known before.

The day comes when Joy's remission holds no longer. She returns to the hospital for more treatments. When they have run their course and the illness is not checked, she comes home to die. She doesn't want to leave Lewis. He doesn't want Joy to go.

Finally, one evening Joy admits she is too tired to struggle any more. Lewis replies that she will have to tell him what to do. She says he'll have to let her go. He promises to look after Douglas. He tells her he has never been so happy and that she is "the truest person" he has ever known. They remain in silence together. Joy dies that night.

Lewis's spirit crashes to earth. He tells Warnie that he is afraid of not being able to see Joy again. And that he is afraid that suffering *"is just suffering after all, no purpose, no pattern." Warnie says he does not know what to say to him. Lewis tells him there is nothing to say. He knows that now. "I've just come up against a bit of experience, Warnie. Experience is a brutal teacher. But you learn. My God, you learn."*

A friend who sees how hard he is taking his loss says, "Life must go on." Lewis responds that he doesn't know that it must, but it certainly does. God knows, but does God care?

Warnie insists that Lewis talk to Douglas. Lewis tells the boy how he believed his own mother would get better if he prayed hard enough. But she also died. Douglas agrees that prayer doesn't work that way. Lewis says he loved Douglas's mother very much, perhaps too much. Aware of that, she had asked if it was worth it. They agree it doesn't seem fair. Douglas can't see why she had to get sick, and neither can Lewis. Douglas says he doesn't believe in heaven, and Lewis assures him that that is okay. Douglas would like to see his mother again nevertheless. Lewis agrees. They hold each other and cry.

Like Lewis, we are often profoundly dispirited when those we love die. We feel mired in a place of sadness and anguish with no visible way out. We feel hopeless. We feel life is drained of its meaning. We feel joyless. Where can we find the grace and strength to overcome our anguish and reanimate our capacities for hope, meaning, and joy? Can enduring connection with those who died help us revive our spirits?

We feel abandoned in a world that we fear is chaotic and unfair. We feel deserted by faith when we need it most. We are at a loss as to how we and our families and communities can move ahead into the future without those we love. We fear that joy and laughter are no longer possible. What is to become of us? How are we to overcome what has happened? What is the point of striving? Will we ever be able to move and change?

This anguish is spiritual pain. Like the uprootedness and homesickness we experience in soul pain, spiritual pain resonates deeply within us and reflects some of our most profound fears. We feel soul pain when we realize that we have been wrenched out of what has become familiar and habitual in our everyday lives with those who have died. We are at a loss as to how to return home to and care about what remains the same and still viable in our lives. In contrast, we feel spiritual pain when we are daunted by prospects of going into a new life filled with unknowns and unexplored possibilities. We are at a loss as to how to add new threads and weave new patterns into our lives.

Spiritual pain strikes and lingers in that vital center of our lives that moves us to overcome, to change and grow, and to become. Where we reach for the courage and hope we need to venture into the unknown and embrace the new. Where we search for understanding and perspective on where we and our experiences fit in the ultimate scheme of things. Where we struggle to improve our life circumstances, better ourselves, and come to terms with adversity. Where we reach for the extraordinary exhilaration and joy that life has to offer. Spiritual pain, like soul pain, is some of the worst of losing those we love.

Spirit work is that part of grieving we do as we wrestle with spiritual pain. We struggle to come to terms with what has happened to us. To recover faith that life, death, and suffering are meaningful. To look to the future hopefully. To find joy in living again. Often we draw upon the deepest influences of those who died as we struggle. We mitigate our pain when we find enduring connection with them in our ways of overcoming, searching, becoming, and eventually finding joy in life.

Their Spirits Are with Us

It costs so much to be a full human being. . . .
One has to abandon altogether the search for security,
and reach out to the risk of living with both arms.
One has to embrace the world like a lover.
One has to accept pain as a condition of existence.
One has to court doubt and darkness as the cost of knowing.
One needs a will stubborn in conflict, but apt always
to total acceptance of every consequence of living and dying.

—Morris West

In the letter Joy wrote Lewis to introduce herself, she admires his children's books. And, she adds, "I can't decide whether you'd like to be the child caught in the spell or the magician casting it." Lewis, reading the letter aloud to his brother, says she writes as if she knows him. "I suppose there's something of me in my books, isn't there?" Warnie responds, "I expect it's just the American style. Americans don't understand about inhibition."

When they meet, it is apparent that Joy's is not an inhibited spirit. She is vivacious. She embraces life with enthusiasm. Lewis's spirit, on the other hand, is cautious and reserved. He knows inhibition well. He likes the idea of casting a magic spell, but there is little magic in his own life. When Joy asks him about an annual festival where a boys' choir climbs to the Oxford rooftops to greet the sunrise with song, he says, "I've never gone in for seeing the sights." She asks, "What do you do? Just walk around with your eyes shut?"

Another time, Joy asks whether a picture on his study wall depicts a real place. Lewis says it is called "The Golden Valley," and he believes it is in Herefordshire. When Joy asks whether it is a special place, Lewis says, "It was on my nursery wall when I was a child. I didn't know it was a real place then. I thought it was a view of heaven. I still think I'll come around the bend or over a brow of the hill and there it will be."

Later, Lewis refers again indirectly to the meaning the picture holds for him. He tells a student, "We live in the shadowlands. The sun is always shining somewhere else, around the bend, over the brow of a hill." He has lived in the shadow of his mother's death where joy and happiness are to be found somewhere else.

After they've married "before God" and Joy is in remission, they attend the Oxford sunrise festival. The sun shines gloriously. The boys sing beautifully. Bells ring magnificently. Young people dance energetically. Others dive fully clothed into nearby water. Spirits are high. Joy proclaims, "Sunrise always works." Lewis shares her delight as he imbibes the magic of the moment. His eyes are no longer shut. He sees the world around him with the enthusiasm of a lover.

At this moment, Joy urges Lewis to take her to look for the Golden Valley. It can be the honeymoon they've never had. Not usually spontaneous, Lewis agrees to go. They settle into an English country inn. Lewis orders room service for the first time in his life. They smile broadly. They delight in the escape and the time together.

Next day they ask for a map of the area and locate what they expect is the valley. As they drive in search of it, Lewis wonders why aloud, "It probably won't be the same." But more magic awaits them.

They find a valley remarkably like the picture. They walk together through the open meadow. It begins to rain. They find cover where they can view the valley and listen to the rain. Joy wonders if they should leave. Lewis says, "No, I don't want to be somewhere else anymore. I'm not waiting for anything new to happen. Not looking round the next corner or over the next hill. Here. Now. That's enough." Lewis has found happiness as he understands it. He has emerged from the shadowlands.

In life with Joy, he has emerged from the sheltered, risk-free, in-tellectual life he made for himself at Oxford. He has tapped capacities for deep friendship and love. He has become more open, and more vulnerable.

As conversation in the valley continues, Joy reminds Lewis that the kind of "here and now" happiness he has found and spoken of "is not going to last." Lewis responds, "You shouldn't think about that now. Let's not spoil the time we have together." She insists, "It doesn't spoil it. It makes it real . . . I'm going to die, and I want to be with you then, too. The only way I can do that is if I'm able to talk to you about it now."

Lewis, seeking to reassure her, says, "I'll manage somehow, don't worry about me." Joy presses on, "No. I think it can be better than that. I think it can be better than just managing. What I'm trying to say is that the pain then is part of the happiness now. That's the deal." With our eyes and hearts wide open, she seems to be saying, we can live qualitatively different lives. She kisses him deeply, and they say no more.

The next scenes say it all. We see more of their honeymoon trip and life together while she is in remission. They savor the precious time they have. They cherish one another more deeply as they share it. They live differently in the here and now.

In the concluding scene of the movie, after Joy has died, Lewis is strolling in the golden valley again with Douglas. We hear his voice reflecting over the scene, "Why do we love if losing hurts so much? I have no answers anymore, only the life I've lived. Twice in that life I've been given the choice, as a boy and as a man. The boy chose safety. The man chooses suffering. The pain now is part of the happiness then. That's the deal." Joy is with him still, in the midst of his suffering.

In his journal entries, Lewis ponders his agony. He sees that the worst of it is his intense longing. He desperately clings to all memories of Joy, trying to hold them in mind all at once for fear of losing a single one. But as he clings to them, they begin to lose their distinctness and blur into one another. He fears that he is losing them, that what he still holds of Joy is slipping between his fingers.

But, fortunately, Lewis awakens one morning from an unusually refreshing sleep and feels little of his desperation. Memories of Joy flood his mind and fill his heart. They are so vivid that he notes it is as if it were a visit from Joy herself. He realizes that his longing blocked his ability to remember Joy fully and richly. When the longing subsides, he remembers Joy better. His fear of losing contact with her vanishes.

Later, Lewis comes to liken the period in marriage after one partner dies to the next figure in a dance. Love and loss go together, even as do "the joy then and the pain now." He says none of us wants the agony of grief to be prolonged. What we do want is to live our relationship well and faithfully after loss. The challenge is to learn the next figure of the dance where we can still "be taken out of ourselves" by the one we love though we are separated. If it hurts, so be it. But the less of the hurt the better.

Lewis grasps that the point of the next figure in the dance after loss is to seek as much joy as possible in a continuing relationship. He resolves to return to Joy as often as possible in gladness, even to salute her with a laugh. He writes, "Praise is the mode of love which always has some element of joy in it. . . . Don't we in praise some- how enjoy what we praise, however far we are from it?" As he praises Joy, he finds that the pain now is tempered as aspects of the happiness that was then return.

We remember, as Lewis does, so much of what those we love were like in spirit. We remember how different family members, companions, or friends struggled effectively to come to terms with challenges and overcome adversity in their lives. We recall how they searched for understanding of their place in the greater scheme of things and how their beliefs shaped their lives and their faiths supported them. We recall how they opened them- selves to others, welcomed change, took risks, and aspired to improve themselves and grow. We know something about their fondest hopes and how they pushed themselves to realize their dreams. We recall how they showed us different ways to find joy and happiness in the most extraordinary moments and experiences of their lives. We remember what we glimpsed of the driving forces beneath the surface of their actions. We recall how we respected, admired, appreciated, and were awed by whatever enthusiasm, courage, drive, hope, or faith we saw in them.

We recall the support and encouragement others gave us when we faced challenge and adversity. We remember exploring questions of ultimate meaning and faith. We remember how with some we anticipated, hoped for, and dreamed about the future together. We recall the peak experiences and moments of exhilaration we shared with family members, companions, or friends. We notice how we, as persons, families, and communities, came to be like them in spirit in some ways or were inspired by them in others.

We may or may not believe that spirits can exist without bodies or survive after we die. But we can understand our spirits as the driving forces within us that move us to overcome, search, become and grow, strive, and sometimes rise above the everyday. As such driving forces, our spirits are our souls' companions. Our souls root us in the nourishing soil of the past and in the here and now of everyday life. They enable us to make the best of where we are and to connect with the good in what we already have and have become. In contrast, our spirits reach to the light, seek out and stretch into the new and unfamiliar, and venture into the unknown. They enable us to change and transcend limits in the here and now, in ourselves, and in our perspectives, and to move into the future. They work within us, shaping our dreams, hope, and faith. They motivate us to transform ourselves, families, and communities.

Intimate life with our family members, companions, and friends nourishes our spirits as well as our souls. It enables us to welcome the extraordinary in everyday life and to change and develop as our life stories unfold.

When those we love die, we can feel that their spirits are still with us. We find and reconnect with them in our surroundings. We also reconnect with their spirits as we find traces of them within ourselves. Those who have died have explicitly taught us deep lessons of the spirit. But more often they showed us the way, and we learned by example. Or they encouraged us to find our own ways. We sense how we can use these spiritual lessons as we venture into the next chapters of our lives.

We can revive our spirits by reanimating the spiritual capacities they have instilled in us. We can ask others to support us as we support them. We can tell others how we would like family or community life to be infused in some way with the spirit of those who have died and talk about what we can do together to bring that about. When we do these things, we are sustained by the indelible imprints of their lives on our spirits and those of our families and communities.

As it is with lessons of soul, we don't learn lessons of spirit from all who have died. But a few of us have known great-spirited individuals with unusual capacities who were able to come to terms with adversity, find meaning and a sense of place in the great scheme of things, change and grow in themselves, strive to improve their life circumstances, and rise above the everyday. Far more commonly, we have known family and friends who have taught us valuable spiritual lessons in some areas but not in others. And we have known and loved a few whose spirits failed them more often than not.

Part of loving is accepting the spiritual shortcomings as well as the strengths of those we love. And this remains true in death. We need to resist the impulse to idealize. Loving them with our eyes open is recognizing and admiring how their spirits have served them well when they have. And part of loving them in separation is making some of the ways of the spirit they have taught us our own. This is not to idealize them. We remain true to ourselves when we acknowledge how their inspiration has helped us become who we are. And when we use our own best judgment as we draw upon their inspiration to become what we yet can be.

As we love them by making their spiritual legacies our own, we can experience the power of their spirits to transport and transform us. They can still inspire us in the midst of our suffering.

Resilience

Those who have suffered much become very bitter or very gentle.

—Will Durant

As a toddler, Fredricka was diagnosed with leukemia. Begun early in Freddie's teens, a film called Permission to Die was to deal with how she and her family lived with chronic illness. But soon Freddie is diagnosed with a more aggressive form of leukemia. Likely a result of her treatments, it is expected to end her life.

Freddie is determined to live well as long as her body allows. She has a quick wit and an impish sense of humor. She jokes with her doctors and a counselor. She laughs with and enjoys the company of friends and schoolmates. She struggles to learn the violin and joins the school orchestra. She decorates her room with some of her own creations.

Freddie enjoys a special candor and closeness with her mother. She worries about what will become of her, a widow, when she dies. She is relieved when her mother remarries toward the end of the filming: her mother and older brother will not be left alone.

Freddie uses the uncertainty of her prognosis to ground hope to the very end. Wise beyond her years, she dismisses remarks from peers that she is courageous. She tells her counselor that those who *speak that way could die at any moment. They would be foolish to dwell on that possibility and spoil what life still offers.*

Freddie and a teenaged boy who is also dying of leukemia talk of how difficult it has always been to be perceived as different or special, to be set apart from their peers. They share their fears now that death seems to be drawing closer. They reflect whimsically about reincarnation and agree that they would like to come back as big, fat lazy cats. Anticipating meeting God, he says he would like to ask Him why he died so young and adds that he might try to punch Him if he doesn't like the answer. When asked why she thinks she was afflicted by leukemia, Freddie speculates more seriously that perhaps, in another life, she was scornful of those who were sick.

Freddie knows herself well and participates in treatment decisions. She is keenly aware of the effects of her illness on others and sensitive to their needs. Once, while bleeding internally, she feels a strong urge to "let go." She asks her mother's permission first, and receives it. She passes out but is successfully revived. She later explains that asking permission is "what you do with mothers." She says she "knows when to let go."

Doctors eventually tell Freddie that the treatments are no longer working. She chooses to discontinue them and goes home. The very next day, with her mother at her side, they tell each other of their love and say good-bye. Again with her mother's permission, Freddie "lets go" and dies.

Sixteen-year-old Freddie left a rich legacy for her mother, brother, friends, doctors, and all who come to know her through the film. Her legacy combines richly textured memories of a life well lived until its very end with incomparable lessons about joy in living, coping with vulnerability, hope, wisdom, mutual respect, and most of all love in extreme circumstances.

We are not the first to struggle, like Freddie, with our own mortality or, like Lewis, with the deaths of those we love. Family members, companions, and friends who have died faced these challenges before us. Often, we remember how they themselves came to terms with death and loss. We remember their dying days and how they lived them. We recall how we mourned losses together. We know stories of still other losses in their lives. We recall something of how their experiences shattered their daily lives, disrupted their life stories, and threatened their confidence that life is meaningful. We witnessed some of their physical suffering, helplessness, agony in missing those they loved, soul pain (uprootedness and homesickness), and spiritual pain (hopelessness, feelings of abandonment, and joylessness).

Sometimes, very sadly, we have seen how those we love retreated from the challenges before them. Helplessness overcame some. Others never fully revived their motivation for living. They lost hope. They muddled through what happened to them, managed stubbornly to hang on and survive, but were never as vibrant again. Or worse, they fell into listlessness, resignation, bitterness, or despair. They were and remained deeply dispirited.

Often, however, we remember how family members, companions, or friends found strength within themselves, support from others, and a grace that transcends human understanding, enabling them to face death and loss. They overcame helplessness, found renewed purpose in daily life and hope for the future, and revived their spirits. Some changed and grew through their suffering. They became gentler, more deeply human. Or they embraced life with renewed vigor. Sometimes they spoke directly to us about what enabled them to change and grow in even the most testing circumstances. Or they offered us good advice and counsel when we mourned. More often, we witnessed the resilience of their spirits; we saw how death itself is transforming.

When the time comes for us to die, we can draw inspiration from the resilient spirits of those who have died. We can make use of what they have taught us about how to face, not run away from, our own mortality. To acknowledge and effectively address the challenges it presents. To live our dying days with dignity.

To recognize what matters most to us in the time that remains. To live that time fully and deeply, and even at times joyfully. To find hope short of an unrealistic hope of living forever. To reach out to others who are suffering. To let go of life that no longer nourishes or sustains us. To say good-bye to those who will survive us. To help them to grieve as we anticipate the future when we will be separated. To encourage them to remember us and cherish our legacies. To assure them of our undying love. To help them grasp the meaning of our suffering. To be graceful and grateful. Or to be faithful and hopeful.

We can also draw inspiration from the resilient spirits of those we remember as we grieve their deaths and those of others we love. We can make use of what they have shown us about how to face losses in life. To wrestle with the difficult challenges that separation brings. To avoid the helplessness that derives from our dwelling on what we cannot control: what happens to us when another dies. To overcome that helplessness by focusing instead on what we can control: our responses to what happens to us. To carry and express our pain and anguish. To recognize our own strengths and weaknesses in mourning. To acknowledge when we need the support of others and accept it when it is offered. To distinguish between good and bad advice and counsel. To find value and support in traditional ways of mourning, beliefs, and ceremonies of separation. Or to draw upon faith, religious or not, that life is meaningful and worth living.

When those we love die, it can be very difficult to find motivation for daily living without them. We can draw inspiration from what we have learned from them about how to find our way back home in our physical and social surroundings, and within ourselves. To have the courage to change in response to a reality transformed by our loss. To rebuild our lives and reshape our life patterns. To find joy and laughter again. To revive hope for the future. To redirect our life stories. To find ways of loving those who have died. Or to appreciate how the meanings of their lives transcend death.

We sometimes remember how those we love taught us to see and grasp the possibilities for change and growth in tragic experiences of dying and loss. Not only did they change as they faced death or mourned, they became better for having such difficult experiences.

We can draw inspiration from what they taught us about how to find a confidence we never had before. To face life's most terrible adversities. Or see that what does not overcome us can make us stronger.

We can use what we learned from them about how to grow in self-understanding and self-esteem. Come to know and better appreciate the breadth and depth of our feelings as well as our needs, desires, and capacities for finding meaning in experience. Or value our capacities to love deeply.

We can draw inspiration from them about how to find within ourselves capacities to understand and respond sensitively to others. To listen more effectively to, comfort, and support others who are confronting tragedy. To grow in empathy, compassion, and the capacity to care deeply for and about others. Or to carry these abilities into, and enrich, the full range of our relationships.

Sadly, some we remember realized only too late just how precious our relationships are. We can use what we learned from them about how to identify and appreciate who our true friends are. To cooperate, compromise, and negotiate fairly and appropriately as together we reshape and redirect our family and community lives. To return to life with our fellow survivors with renewed or deepened enthusiasm. To become closer with one another. To be more giving with family and friends, and more appreciative of all they give in return. To build stronger and more lasting ties to one another. Or to delight in and cherish the presence of others while they are still with us.

The resilient spirit within us enables us to face and come to terms with our own mortality and the deaths of others. It motivates us to overcome bitterness, returns us to life with renewed vigor, sustains our hope and faith, enables us to change and grow in the most trying circumstances, and keeps our love alive despite separation. We can love those who died as we draw inspiration from their resilience, first in mourning them and later in facing other losses and our own deaths.

Searching

*Faith means being grasped by a power
that is greater than we are,
a power that shakes us and turns us,
and transforms and heals us.*

—Paul Tillich

My wife, Betty, remembers how her father, who died in 1990, used to lie beneath a tree with his head in his hands or on a root. He would look above, through the leaves, and ponder the open sky. It was as if he were seeking and finding a sense of connection with an encompassing reality. He didn't fully understand it, but he felt embraced by it. Sometimes Betty would join him silently and sense the comforting connection herself.

Betty remembers experiencing that same feeling when she was in church with her maternal grandmother, Nain. From where they sat, they could see a large, round, stained-glass window in the front of the church that depicted Jesus with lambs. Along the aisle next to them was another stained glass image of Jesus with little children. The church was filled with joyful sounds, friends, and fellowship. She felt safe there, not alone with her Nain. She felt as if they and the others were held and supported by something larger, a friendly, benevolent force. She still experiences this comfortable, uplifting, nourishing feeling in some places of worship.

Betty also remembers going with her Nain to visit many of the other churches in her community, including Greek Orthodox,

Catholic, Methodist, Anglican, Baptist, Presbyterian, and Lutheran congregations. They wanted to experience what they were like, to be open to other ways of approaching the great mysteries that religions of the world address. They found that there were many differences in rituals, practices, and beliefs but deep common threads of searching for wisdom and longing for faith.

C. S. Lewis had a brilliant, inquiring mind. He spent a lifetime reflecting on the great mysteries of God, life, death, suffering, and love. When he met the woman who was to become his wife, Joy, he began a spiritual journey. His life with her forced him to move beyond merely thinking intellectually about such mysteries. Each became a living presence in his life that challenged and changed him.

In his journal Lewis tells us how the seemingly solid intellectual foundation of his faith was undermined by Joy's death. He writes, "You never know how much you really believe anything until its truth or falsehood becomes a matter of life and death to you." He no longer searched for a position that he could defend in argument. Instead, he sought understanding and faith that he could live by.

Prayer was part of his searching. At one point in the film Shadowlands, just after Joy's cancer has gone into remission, a clergy friend tells Lewis that his "prayers have been answered." Lewis responds, "I pray because I'm helpless. Need flows out of me waking and sleeping. It doesn't change God. It changes me."

In his early journal entries, it seems to Lewis that God has slammed the door in his face just when he needs him most. He likens God to a vivisectionist, blaming Him for his agony. He reaches for God and senses that there is no response. Later he recognizes that his own desperate longing is the source of his agony. And that is not God's doing, but his own. It has made him like the drowning man who could not be saved because he clung so desperately to his rescuer.

When his desperate longing subsides, Lewis remembers Joy better and feels nearer to her. He also no longer meets the locked door when he turns to God and feels nearer to Him. He sees that God has *given him life, opened his heart to Joy's love, and enabled him to love her even in separation. He praises God, as Joy had, as a means of drawing nearer to Him.*

What is our spiritual place in the greater scheme of things? Is there any way we can feel connected to something greater than ourselves? Do we really belong and are we at home in this world? Is there a way we can ever experience it as a safe, orderly, and trustworthy place? Can there be a point in going on day after day, pursuing purposes, caring, loving, hoping, and aspiring because living is ultimately meaningful and worthwhile? Can we be confident that there is a reason why we have the opportunity to experience and act in this world, even if the reason is elusive? We can take a lifetime in searching for answers to such questions. No matter how settled we may believe our answers are, the deaths of those we love can easily shake our spiritual confidence in them. Their deaths slow us down and bring such questions to the surface with compelling urgency.

The deaths of our loved ones dramatically transform our lives and bring us face-to-face with the great mysteries of life in the human condition. What are we now to make of our being so small and insignificant when compared with the vast expanses of space, time, and history within which we live? How are we to live with the change and impermanence that pervade our lives, that fact that we have little to no control over many of the things that happen to us? How can we accept that we are imperfect, that we fall far short of our highest aspirations? How can we accept that our knowledge is limited, our judgment fallible, and certainty elusive? What are we to make of our being vulnerable to suffering and death?

Finiteness, change, imperfection, uncertainty, and vulnerability are "mysteries" because they challenge us in ways that ordinary problems do not. They are constants in life, too important to ignore and persistently provocative. They present themselves in ever-changing perspectives. They command our attention in some of the most difficult times of our lives. Fresh encounters with them challenge us to modify our previous, tentative understandings and responses to them. We cannot solve them once and for all, answer them definitively, control, manage, or master them. We cannot change them; we can only change in response to them.

We remember how some of those who have died, like Lewis, searched for their own spiritual place and faced the mysteries I have mentioned throughout their lives and especially when those they loved died. They may have talked about or, perhaps more likely, we may have witnessed their spiritual searching. They knew firsthand how life's most trying experiences can humble us, testing and tempering even our firmest convictions. They, too, struggled with disorientation, confusion, and longing for sustaining faith. They searched for the meanings of their own suffering and separation as they experienced the agonies of soul pain and spiritual pain. They sought to understand the grace or good fortune that enabled them to know those they loved, the meanings of the lives of those who died, and love itself. They searched for ways of seeing how death did not cancel the meanings of those lives or of their love for those who lived them. They searched for conviction that would bring them comfort, consolation, and peace.

When we search for our own spiritual place and face life's deepest mysteries, we can take inspiration from the searching spirits of those who died. We can apply what we learned from them and acknowledge the mysteries that surround and pervade the human condition. To face the challenges with courage and hope. To tolerate and respect diverse faiths and convictions that enable different people to come to terms with mystery. To open our minds to the possibilities of alternative responses. To persist in the search. To be faithful, humble, reverent, and devoted when we have found convictions that work for us. To shun dogmatism as dishonest, given the limits of our knowing. To deepen or modify our faiths or spiritual postures when mysteries show us faces we have not seen before.

We can also use what they have taught us about how to seek wisdom and understanding in great religious or philosophical traditions, sacred texts, literature and poetry, or consultation with clergy and other spiritual guides and counselors. To seek or sense the presence of encompassing and benevolent powers through spiritual practices such as worship, ritual, reflection, contemplation, meditation, and prayer. To find spiritual connection within the great scheme of things in such experiences as awe and wonder, humility, grace and good fortune, reverence, fragility and vulnerability, music, beauty, encounters in nature, intimacy, friendship, community, or in places we hold sacred.

The searching spirit within us motivates our efforts to find our spiritual place in the greater scheme of things and to face and respond to the mysteries that pervade the human condition. We can feel deep spiritual connection with those who have died and draw inspiration from them as we return to and deepen a faith that sustains us or as we renew our own searching.

Changing and Growing

*The great metaphors from all spiritual traditions—grace,
liberation, being born again, awakening from illusion—
testify that it is possible to transcend the conditioning of
my past and do a new thing.*

—Sam Keen

Six months before her husband's death, Jacquelyn Mitchard
had a dream. It was a story rich enough to be the subject of a novel.
The next morning she told it to her husband. She had not been a
writer. Yet he predicted that in two years she would be in a different
place. She would be a first-class writer.

On the Today Show, not too long ago, Jacquelyn told her inter-
viewer that she finished her first novel, At the Deep End of the
Ocean, two years to the day after her husband's death. She said she
wanted to show her children that we can expand our dreams, not
contract them, after a tragedy. In part because of her husband's confidence in her, she found ability within herself she did not know was
there.

Antonio and Chris Daniels and their two older sisters were raised by
their mother, Alice, in inner-city Columbus, Ohio. Children in their
part of town seldom escaped from their poor, troubled surroundings.
But Alice was determined that her children would use education as
their way out. She worked during the day, attended school at night,
earned her degree, and became a family counselor to support them.

Chris, the older of the two brothers, was quiet and introspective. Antonio was more outgoing and fun-loving. They loved each other as if they were twins and were inseparable. They played basketball tirelessly and with great passion. They fantasized, as so many do in their circumstances, of one day playing in the NBA against the greatest players on earth. They dreamed of a day when they could pay back their mother for all of her sacrifices. They would buy her a new home and a new car. They would take care of her for a change.

Chris grew to be six feet, ten inches tall. He received a basketball scholarship from the University of Dayton. Antonio, twenty months younger, was smaller. Dayton was not interested in him, but Bowling Green State University was. Both were successful college players. By the time he was a senior, there was serious talk that Chris might be a high NBA draft choice. If so, he would likely receive a contract that would fulfill the brothers' hopes about taking care of their mother. Antonio was playing well, but he did not appear to be the professional prospect his brother was.

Then, in February of his senior year, Chris died suddenly of an irregular heartbeat. The story was covered widely by the national media. Alice hurt terribly. Her son was dead, and she would have to tell Antonio. She knew how much it would hurt him. His brother, best friend, and idol was dead. Antonio collapsed when he heard the news. He wept uncontrollably.

Antonio changed after Chris died. He became more serious. He talked with Chris and vowed that he would make the NBA and take care of his mother for him. He played out his junior year at Bowling Green. He changed his uniform number to 33, Chris's number. He sensed that Chris was with him on the court. Later his mother said that Antonio's choice to fight through the emotions of losing his brother and to keep his dream intact was a sign of his "warrior spirit."

Antonio rededicated himself to the NBA dream he shared with Chris. He spent the summer before his senior year working on his basketball skills and training in the weight room. He changed his body and transformed himself into a different player. He took his play to a new level. He had a magnificent senior year. The most highly touted, major college players at his point guard position did not come close to matching his statistics. He was voted the conference Most Valuable Player by a wide margin.

The NBA scouts took notice. Antonio was chosen the fourth player overall in the NBA draft when the season ended. "We did it, Chris, we did it," he said to himself as he walked to the stage on draft day to be greeted by the NBA commissioner. With his first professional contract, he looked after his mother as Chris would have: he bought her her favorite Columbus home as well as a new car.

Like Jacquelyn and Antonio, we often have stories to tell of how those we love encouraged us to change and grow. Sometimes, like Jacquelyn's husband, they saw potential in us that we barely suspected. Or, like Antonio's brother Chris, their inspiration moved us to transform ourselves and achieve unprecedented excellence. Or, like Antonio's mother Alice, my Dad, and Grandma, they provided everyday support, nurtured us, gave us good educations, and engendered in us a drive to become the best we can be. Or, as Joy did with Lewis, they helped us on an inner journey that transformed our very souls and spirits.

Those we remember taught us to strive, to change and grow in a self-transcending spirit, to become all we can be. When they die, we face daunting challenges of self-transformation. We must reshape the patterns of our daily lives, blending new threads with the old. We must redirect our life stories, venturing into unanticipated chapters where we can never be just as we were before they died. We can revive our own desires to adapt, change, and grow as we embrace what we have learned from them about self-transformation. Recalling stories of how they changed themselves and how they encouraged us can inspire us to continue on our own personal journeys.

We can make use of what they have taught us about how to change and grow as persons. To improve ourselves. To be unafraid of change. To strive to become better no matter what challenges we face. To be grateful for and appreciate our own talents, endowments, and potential. To use them responsibly. To acknowledge our shortcomings. To be resourceful in finding the means, both within and outside ourselves, to overcome them. To be self-motivated and persistent. To value and pursue excellence. To be effectively self-critical about our own progress. To be undaunted by failures and temporary setbacks. To accept and reach out for help and support in our efforts. To grow in our souls, our ways of caring. To grow in our spirits, to become more resilient, faithful, hopeful, compassionate, joyful, enthusiastic, and adventurous. To use wisdom not only to transform ourselves but also to help our families and communities to change and grow.

The self-transcending spirit within us arouses us and motivates our efforts to transform ourselves, to realize our potential, and to face and overcome our shortcomings. When we do, we blossom and become all that we can be. We can love those who died as we draw inspiration from them, as we continue to change and grow.

Striving

Everything that is done in the world is done by hope.
—Martin Luther

Like so many immigrants before him, my Grandpa Nagel came to America in 1914 to escape a coming war and to find and make a better life for himself and his family. Grandma shared his hopes and supported his aspirations. She followed him with their four children and gave birth first to my mother and then to four more in the years that followed.

The Nagel family echoes with stories of how my grandparents struggled to learn a new language and culture. How they made homes in the row houses of Chicago. How they worked hard to make ends meet and feed their growing family. How the changes and struggles took their toll on the relationship between them.

Grandma believed education was a key to success. Her oldest son, Helmut, wanted to continue beyond grammar school into high school. Grandpa blocked his way, thinking he should apprentice as he would have in Germany. Grandma saw that that was not the way in this new country. She stood up to Grandpa, by no means an easy thing to do. She insisted my uncle be allowed to complete high school. She encouraged all her children to do well in school. All but two of the *nine finished high school. One fell just short. One graduate earned a college degree.*

The Great Depression did not diminish Grandma's hopes for better lives for her children. It didn't help that Grandpa stubbornly passed on a very generous offer from the world's leading retailer to market an invention he had patented in the foolish and mistaken expectation that someone else would offer him more. And it didn't help that he left for California for a few years, returned empty-handed, and eventually left for good. The older children found work because of their educations. They pulled together and shared their earnings with Grandma, who kept the household going.

The Nagel children realized much of the American dream. The older ones adapted well to their new environment. In later life, one remained at home, held a good job, and cared for Grandma. The others found good work or married hard-working men. They established homes of their own. They provided better for their children than they had known. They passed on Grandma's legacy of hope through hard work and education. The norm among my cousins is a college or university degree, and several of us have advanced degrees. We, in our turn, have passed along this legacy of hope to our children.

My father, eighteen years older than my mother, was really of an earlier generation. He and his nine brothers and sisters were raised by midwestern tenant farmers around the turn of the century. Because my grandfather Attig died in the 1920s and my grandmother when I was only three, I know very little of their aspirations for their children. It is not a stretch, however, to imagine that they also hoped for better lives for them. They pushed all to stay in school through the eighth grade (the norm for the time). All made it that far. One finished high school and became a teacher. Each one escaped the hardship and poverty their parents knew on the farm.

Dad, like his five brothers, was driven to find more steady, less hazardous, and rewarding work in the city. Still, his and theirs was primarily physical labor and nearly as arduous as farm labor. Life was

better for them, but marginally so. Like my Grandma Nagel, Dad
wanted nothing more than a chance at a better life for his children.
He did all he could to encourage my brother and me to do well in
school and get the education and find the opportunities he never had.
He was so proud of us that it was sometimes embarrassing.

American households echo with similar stories of immigration,
hardship, the Depression, and the like. Some, sadly, resonate with
stories of forced emigration, slavery, prejudice, and persistent dis-
crimination. Alex Haley's *Roots* tells one such story across several
generations. Households around the world resound with comparable tales set within different historical and political contexts.
The stories tell us of an individual, a family, or a community
striving for better lives. They are sometimes stories of ancestors
long dead. More typically, they are stories of our grandparents,
parents, and their siblings. Sometimes they are about our spouses,
companions, or friends, or even our children. The heart of the
stories is determination, courage, and aspiration.

Our loved ones taught our spirits to strive for better lives for
ourselves and those we love. We can revive our own hope as we
catch sight of and draw inspiration from their hopeful spirits.
Recalling the stories of their struggles, we can learn from their
mistakes as well as their successes.

When those we love die, it can be extremely difficult to pick
up where we left off in struggles of our own. Their hopeful spirits
can motivate us in our first hesitant steps and to strive on. We
can draw inspiration from them as we take to heart some of what
they have shown us about how to improve our own life circumstances. To dream and aspire. To envision possibility. To set goals
and plan realistically and practically to achieve them. To be op-
portunistic and entrepreneurial. To be hard-working and determined. To face and overcome obstacles and hardships. To respond to setbacks with renewed effort. To learn from our own
mistakes. Or to endure and persevere courageously.

We can also embrace what we have learned from our loved ones about investing our spirits in our families and communities. They can inspire us to carry on with striving in a compassionate and generous spirit, giving unselfishly to better others' lives. To imagine a brighter future and help others to see the possibilities. To motivate and encourage others to strive for themselves. To unite with others to overcome hardship and adversity, improve living conditions, combat injustice, and realize shared dreams and aspirations. To be disciplined, patient, tireless, devoted, dedicated, and tenacious. To know when to lead and when to follow. To compromise and negotiate when we need to.

We can return to places filled with history, sites of their early lives, homelands, farms, towns, villages, and neighborhoods. The routes of their pilgrimages and migrations. Their homes, schools, workplaces, places of worship, meeting halls, clubs, and associations. Places where they encouraged and supported our own striving. There we can more readily grasp or recall what they had to contend with and can deepen our understanding of the spirit that drove them. We can sense their continuing encouragement and support.

The striving spirit within us arouses us and motivates our efforts to better life circumstances for ourselves and those we love, to face and overcome challenge and seize opportunity. We can love those who died as we draw inspiration from them and continue to live with hope, persistence, and courage.

Joy and Adventure

*All of us have experienced times in our lives that were so
precious and special that if it were possible we would have
had time stand still so we might live that moment forever.*

—*John Aurelio*

Dad worked hard all of his life, on his feet all day, six days
a week. At the end of the day, when he arrived home, he was
exhausted and had little time for physical play with me. I found such
play instead with my older brother, John, and friends. But Dad
recognized that life devoted only to work is joyless. He found most
of his joy in the comfort of a chair in the living room, taking great
delight in following major league baseball. He infected me with that
enthusiasm.

Dad also loved to laugh. Together with Mom, we delighted
in, first, the radio antics of Fibber McGee and Molly, the Great
Gildersleeve, and Amos and Andy and, later, the television comedy
of Red Skelton, George Burns and Gracie Allen, Jack Benny,
Herb Shriner, and George Gobel. I'll never forget how sometimes we laughed until it hurt. I still thrive in that special
agony.

Dad seemed at times to sense that I pushed myself too hard in
school or was a bit too serious. He constantly encouraged me simply
to "have some fun." He was obviously pleased when he saw how

well I took that advice to heart. I share this legacy with my brother. I hear an echo of Dad's words whenever John closes a phone conversation with his familiar watchword, "Live it up." I hear a similar echo as I tell my own children to "be sure to take time to have some fun."

When we feel ready, and no doubt tentatively and in small doses at first, we can begin to temper the seriousness of our life and suffering with joy. Recalling how those who have died opened themselves and affirmed the wonder and magic that everyday life offers can help to rekindle our own enthusiasm for these things. We can revive our own joyful spirits as we embrace what we have learned from them about how to lighten the day for ourselves and others with humor. To break with the rhythms and preoccupations of everyday life and make room for fun again. To be vibrant in the here and now. To find the grace to receive the offerings of the moment. To sense magical opportunity when it arises. To allow silliness to bubble to the surface and find expression. To be spontaneous and playful. To seek out and enjoy interludes of excitement and pleasure. To welcome and delight in surprises. To be once again energetic, cheerful, buoyant, and light-hearted. Even to be transported to the heights of ecstasy and rapture. To be taken out of ourselves through deep emotion and expanding vision. To follow imagination into enchantment. To delight in our own powers to create or perform. To be awed by beauty or commune with nature.

Grandma, too, worked hard throughout her life and set a world's standard for worrying. Still, for all her worry, she simply loved to celebrate. Her children presented her with sons and daughters-in-law and grandchildren in abundance. The occasions for celebration were many, and Grandma was often a glowing presence in the middle of the merry-making. She prepared special dishes, joined in

*the laughter and singing, cried with delight on occasion, and made
the joys of others her own. Soulful as our family gatherings were,
they were often at the same time wonderfully high-spirited.*

We can embrace what we have learned from loved ones by taking time out from everyday life to celebrate in high spirits. Yes,
we will miss them as we mark special occasions such as births,
birthdays, initiations, graduations, weddings, anniversaries, accomplishments, and holidays or gather with family or friends for
parties, reunions, festivals, and feasts. But we can sense that they
are still with us and draw inspiration from them as we allow
ourselves once again to take pleasure in special preparations and
feelings of anticipation. To feel grateful for extraordinary good
fortune. To recognize and honor the joys and accomplishments
of others. To laugh, sing, and dance. To praise generously. To
accept praise and congratulations graciously. To rejoice in shared
blessings. Or lacking special occasion, to take the opportunity to
celebrate life itself, one of its wonders, or the company of
others.

And we can embrace what we have learned from the more
adventurous of our loved ones who were restless and driven to
seek joy in new places, experiences, and activities beyond the
confinements and limitations of their everyday lives. We can follow along similar paths or draw inspiration from them as we take
our bodies, minds, and spirits into uncharted territory in search
of unprecedented satisfaction and fulfillment. Indulge new sights,
sounds, tastes, odors, and sensations to see what is in them. Try
the untried and take risks to open ourselves to new possibilities.
Push ourselves to the limits of our capacities. Taste other ways
of living to find fresh rewards in them. Or adopt alternative
points of view to glimpse otherwise unseen aspects of the world
around us.

The joyful and adventurous spirit pulses within us in those
extraordinary moments, peak experiences, and exquisite activities

that transcend the everyday—in them we feel most vibrantly alive. We can love those who died as we revive this spirit within us and feel our hearts race again as we live joyfully and enthusiastically in ways they have taught us.

Afterword: Grief is a Journey of the Heart

Grief ebbs but grief never ends. Death ends a life but death does not end a relationship. If we allow ourselves to be still and if we take responsibility for our grief, the grief becomes as polished and luminous and mysterious as death itself. When it does, we learn to love anew, not only the one who has died. We learn to love anew those who yet live.

—Julius Lester

When those we love die, we embark on a journey of the heart. We begin in bereavement. The experience of loss deprives us of a living presence, a loved one. Our daily lives are thrown in disarray. Our life stories careen off their expected courses. Our connections with the larger contexts within which we find meaning are strained. We feel devastated and helpless in the face of forces and events we could not control.

We experience heartbreak and miss those we love terribly. We meet their absence everywhere. We long for their return. We feel uprooted and homesick. We feel joyless, hopeless, and as if life is drained of its meaning. We wonder whether we have the heart to live on without them. The courage and motivation to face the challenges of relearning the world we experience. The will to reshape our shattered lives, to redirect our life stories. The faith and hope to sustain us on the journey.

We do not want to stop loving them. We rightly resist those who say we must. We know in our hearts that it matters too much to us and to those who died.

The central challenge as we grieve is learning to love in a new way, to love someone in separation, at least as long as we walk this earth. Nothing is more difficult. Nothing is more important. Nothing is more rewarding.

As we grieve, we seek and find ways of making this transition to lasting love. Ceremonies of separation support and move us. We continue to hold those we love in our hearts, in the vital centers of our lives. We hold them in sadness and loneliness in our emotional core where we miss them and carry our hurt. But at the same time we learn to hold and cherish their legacies in other loving places. We cherish them in memory. We keep them with us in our practical lives. We embrace them in our souls. We hold them in our spirits.

We don't ever entirely finish with grieving because as we grieve and seek lasting love, we are responding to persistent mysteries that pervade our lives. Love and suffering become our lifelong teachers. We are small and insignificant; all of us must die. This becomes more acceptable as we realize that in lasting love we affirm the value of the meaningful differences those we love made. Change and impermanence become more acceptable as we realize that the meanings we embrace, which we shared with those we mourn, continue beyond their physical death. Imperfection becomes more acceptable as we forgive them their shortcomings and sense that they forgive ours. We find consolation in the lasting good of our imperfect love. Not knowing and uncertainty become more acceptable as we find ways of continuing in faith and hope in their absence.

As we grieve and find our ways to lasting love, we also respond to our own suffering. We fulfill our desire to continue loving those who died. We accept their legacies and make them our own. We blend what they have given, and continue to give, into the lives we reshape and redirect. We make ourselves whole again as individuals, families, and communities.

Grieving and lasting love change how we experience the pain and anguish that bereavement brings. We temper our soul pain as we find that they are with us in our souls: We sense their presence as we reconnect with the familiar in our life surroundings and make our way back to feeling at home in our daily lives. We sense their presence within us in our ways of caring about and loving things, places, ourselves, others, and our natural surroundings.

We temper our spirit pain as we find that they are with us in our spirits: We draw inspiration from them as we face the unknown, stretch into the unfamiliar, and give new shape and direction to our lives. We sense their presence within us in our motivations and capacities to soar, better life circumstances for ourselves and others, change and grow, face challenge and adversity, and search for ultimate meaning and consolation.

Though we still miss them, we experience the pain of missing them differently. It is no longer simply a bitterness at deprivation. It becomes a unique pain in separation that we can more easily carry. Yes, we have lost their physical presence. But not all is lost. They have already begun to occupy a different place in our lives. The richness of lasting love consoles us. We miss them even as we cherish their legacies, enjoy the fruition of their lives, and live in gratitude for all they have given and continue to give.

As we grieve and find our ways to lasting love, we respond to two more great mysteries: the lives of those who have died and love itself. Our family members, companions, and friends have compelling presences both before and after they die. We are still drawn to and fascinated by them in separation. Though we draw closer, know them better, and care more deeply about them, we never know them entirely or possess them. As we remember or learn more about them or meet them in the light of new experiences, they reveal new aspects of themselves or challenge us in new ways. Their souls are deeper than we can fathom. Their spirits exceed our reach. Unable, ultimately, to account for the good fortune that brought them into our lives, we are privileged to know and love them. Our appreciation of them can grow indefinitely. Each is and will always be one of a kind and irreplaceable. We cannot change them; we can only continue to change in response to them.

Love itself is something we never finish with, resolve, master, or control. It, too, has a compelling presence in our lives both before and after those we love die. It regularly shows us new faces and demands more of us. Its depth and breadth elude us. It is ours by grace. It arouses wonder and awe. We grow in understanding and appreciation of love's possibilities and rewards indefinitely. Each love is unique and unrepeatable. We cannot change love; we can only continue to change in response to it.

The greater part of this book is about how we can still have and hold those who died in our lives, how we give them places in our hearts. If we are to find the lasting love that is still possible, we need to let go of their physical presence and fervent longing for their return. And we need to address unfinished business with them and disentangle ourselves from negative ties. But, no matter how important those who died and our love for them have been, we did not, nor do we, give our hearts to them alone. We did not, nor do we, receive the good things in life from them alone. We need to let go of any singular, sometimes preoccupying, focus on them and their absence. We need to let go of loving only them to the exclusion of others.

We avoid this kind of trouble in lasting love when we realize that grieving is a journey that brings us to the fullness of life in the flesh and blood, here and now and into the future with those who still survive with us. In this life, we still have our families, friends, and communities. We can and often do welcome and come to love new persons in our lives. And we have room in our hearts for self-love and the many cares that make us unique and separate individuals. It is in the fullness of this life that the legacies of those who have died prove valuable.

We find the good that lasting love offers when we blend cherished memories of those who have died with fresh experiences with those who survive with us. When we remember realistically and resist temptations to idealize or identify excessively. When we value both the legacies that those who have died have given us and all that so many others have given already and still have to offer. And when we use the practical and soulful wisdom of those who died and draw upon their inspiration to enrich the life that we still have to live, including our life with others.

Those who died wanted us to remember and to cherish the good that was in them and our lives with them. And they wanted us to return to, thrive, and prosper in the world where they no longer live, to cherish the life they no longer enjoy. Sometimes they told us this explicitly before they died. Sometimes they told us indirectly in their concern that we not lose ourselves in the process of grieving them.

Some of us have experiences after those we love die that powerfully suggest that they live on, not only in our hearts, but independently. Some of us have encounters so powerful that they are like meetings. Others are visited in dreams or visions. Still others sense in seeming coincidences or in their surroundings that those they love are signaling them. We often experience such encounters as assuring us that they are in good places. That they want us to hold them in our hearts. Or that they want us to live well and continue to love others and ourselves.

Those who died knew that it is truly remarkable to draw breath, a royal thing to be alive. They wanted us to know this in our hearts even in separation from them. We love them when we go on without them by our sides, with lasting love for them in our hearts, and with our hearts open again to the wonders of life on earth.

From my heart to yours, I wish you well on your journey, a journey not only of grief but also love. I hope that this book can be a companion to you as you open your heart to the legacies of those who have died, finding again a lasting love. That your lasting love will temper your sorrow in missing them. That you will thrive again in the world you relearn. That your lasting love will enrich the other parts of your life. That it will continue to make you better for having known those who have died. And that you come once again to sense how it is a privilege to be alive and carry such love within you as you love others and yourself.

It has been a pleasure to share these stories of lasting love with you. I would like to invite you to write me about your own journeys of the heart and the rewards of lasting love you have found. I take great pleasure in meeting people who share their stories when I offer workshops, and I hope one day to meet you on your journey.

Acknowledgments

I have long held that stories of loss and grieving are the heart of the matter and the point of thinking and writing about grieving at all. I owe a great debt of gratitude to all in my classes, workshops, and audiences who have shared their personal stories of grieving with me. Many of the stories I include here are composites of their stories, changed in their details to protect their privacy. Without their candor and generosity, this book would not have been possible. Though they did not always refer explicitly or self-consciously to their desire for lasting love, it was always implicit in what they shared and detectable in their eyes and voices.

I am grateful for the life I share with my own immediate and large extended families and what they have taught me about lasting love. Though they have rarely, if ever, talked explicitly about their feelings of love or grief, members of my families have always talked freely about those who have died and what they remember about them. And their actions and characters clearly embody their legacies. I am grateful for the opportunity to reflect on and learn from life with the Attigs and the Nagels as I wrote this book and to include some stories about them in these pages.

Some of my best friends are grief counselors, therapists, and theorists. I want to thank them for our twenty years of professional affiliation in the Association for Death Education and Counseling and the International Work Group on Death, Dying, and Bereavement (IWG). And for their entrusting me with leadership positions in both organizations. As an applied philosopher, I hold a kind of in-between position in our associations. I am somewhat of an outsider because I have not gone through the same initiation rites of training in any of their clinical or theoretical disciplines. Yet I am grateful for their welcoming me, apparently because of my keen interest in the ideas that shape their understandings of life in the human condition (especially suffering and grieving) and that inform their caregiving practices and because my background in philosophy enables me to bring a fresh and distinctive perspective to bear on those ideas and practices.

Among my colleagues in these associations, I am grateful to Bob Neimeyer, Terrie Rando, Colin Murray Parkes, Steve Fleming, Mal and Dianne McKissock, Rob Stevenson, Judy Stillion, John Stephenson, Janice Nadeau, Bill Worden, Dennis Klass, Phyllis Silverman, Simon Rubin, Ben Wolfe, Sid and Miriam Moss, Ken Doka, and Donna O'Toole for all they have taught me about the pain and anguish of loss, serious obstacles to effective grieving, letting go of troubling aspects of our relationships with those who have died, and the hazards of holding on obsessively or excessively. And for all I have learned from them about helping others to carry the pain, overcome the obstacles, let go when necessary, and avoid the hazards.

I am grateful to many of those I have already mentioned as well as to Jeanne Harper, Chuck Corr, Hannelore Wass, Sally Featherstone, David Meagher, Sandy Bertman, John Morgan, Bob Bendiksen, Edie Stark, Gene Knott, Lu Redmond, Ellen Zinner, and Larry Huston for their warm responses to my earlier writings and presentations on grief and lasting love. And to the many among them who encouraged me to expand and deepen my reflections on lasting love in this book. I am especially grateful to some of those mentioned here and others who have told me how my ideas have helped them in working with those they serve to carry their pain and find lasting love. I hope that what they find here will provide additional support for their fine efforts.

I owe special thanks to three remarkable individuals: First to my one-time funeral director friend Roy Nichols for the many stories he shared with my classes and workshops, what he taught me about helping grieving people to take charge of their own loss experiences and find their own hopeful paths toward renewed wholeness, and his confident assertion that death does not end our relationships with those who have died. Second to my friend and former colleague Don Scherer for his appreciation of the importance of applying the skills of the philosopher in developing understanding of life in the human condition, his own deep understanding and humanity, his enthusiasm for this project, and his careful, patient, and always insightful commentary as the book took shape. And third to Betty Davies, a colleague and friend from IWG who became my wife in 1994, for her patient listening to my thinking out loud and to readings of passages she could as easily have read herself, careful reading of every draft and helpful commentary, abiding enthusiasm for my project, and loving companionship through the highs and lows of the process of completing it.

I am grateful to my agent, Jill Grinberg, for her initial and sustained belief in the central message of the book, guidance in developing the proposal, careful reading and constructive criticism, gentle prodding when my progress slowed, and consummate professionalism with a human face and voice.

Finally, I want to express my gratitude to Joan Bossert, Editorial Director at Oxford, for her enthusiasm for a second book project with me, deep appreciation of the importance of my central theme, gentle ways in calling forth my voice and nurturing the writer within me, skillful guidance in focusing and refining the manuscript, and warm humanity.